Film Architecture:
Set Designs from
Metropolis
to
Blade Runner

Film Architecture:
Set Designs from
Metropolis
to
Blade Runner

Film Architecture: Set Designs from Metropolis to Blade Runner

Edited by
Dietrich Neumann

With essays by
Donald Albrecht,
Anton Kaes,
Dietrich Neumann,
Anthony Vidler, and
Michael Webb

Prestel
Munich · London · New York

This catalogue was first published in conjunction with the exhibition
of the same name held at:
The David Winton Bell Gallery, Brown University, Providence, Rhode Island,
The Academy of Motion Pictures Arts and Sciences Academy Gallery,
Beverly Hills, California, and the Deutsches Architektur-Museum and
Deutsches Filmmuseum, Frankfurt am Main, Germany

Front cover: Set designs and stills from *Metropolis, Asphalt, Mon Oncle,* and *Blade Runner*
Back cover: *Aelita – Queen of Mars*
Frontispiece: Set design for *Metropolis*

Editor: Andrea P. A. Belloli, London
Translated from the German by Almuth Seebohm, Munich
Film synopses and set designers' biographies were written by
Peter Lähn (P. L.)
Thomas de Monchaux (T. d. M.)
Dietrich Neumann (D. N.)

Library of Congress Cataloging-in-Publication Data is available

Calico World reprinted by permission of the publisher from *The Mass Ornament: Weimar
Essays*/Siegfried Kracauer, translated, edited, and with an introduction by Thomas Y. Levin,
Cambridge, Mass.: Harvard University Press © 1995 by the President and Fellows of Harvard
College. Originally published as *Das Ornament der Masse* by Suhrkamp Verlag © 1963.
Bruno Taut, *Artistic Film Program* reprinted by permission of the publisher from *Expressionist
Utopias: paradise, metropolis, architectural fantasy*, edited by Timothy O. Benson, published in
conjunction with an exhibition held at the Los Angeles County Museum of Art,
Oct. 21, 1993 – Jan. 2, 1994; Translation from German by David Britt. Copyright 1993 by
Museum Associates, Los Angeles County Museum of Art. Originally published as
Künstlerisches Filmprogramm, Das hohe Ufer 2 (1920), pp. 86–88.

Prestel Verlag
Mandlstrasse 26, 80802 Munich
Tel.: (89) 38 17 09-0; Fax: (89) 38 17 09-35;
4, Bloomsbury Place, London WC1A 2QA
Tel.: (0171) 3 23 50 04; Fax: (0171) 6 36 80 04;
and 16 West 22nd Street, New York, NY 10010, USA
Tel.: (212) 6 27 81 99; Fax: (212) 6 27 98 66

Prestel books are available worldwide.
Please contact your nearest bookseller or write to one of the above addresses
for information concerning your local distributor.

Designed by Rainald Schwarz, Konturwerk, Munich
Lithography by Krammer, Munich
Typeset by Max Vornehm GmbH, Munich
Printed and bound by Graspo, Zlín

Printed on acid-free paper

ISBN 3-7913-2163-6

Contents

Acknowledgments

Like films and architecture, an exhibition and its catalogue can only be done collaboratively. This project originated from conversations with Diana Johnson, the director of the Bell Gallery at Brown University, Jürgen Keil, the director of the Goethe-Institut in Boston, and Dr. Beeke Sell-Tower, art historian at the Goethe-Institut. All helped tremendously not only with ideas and enthusiasm, but in securing crucial funding for the project, as did Wolfger Pöhlmann of the Goethe-Institut in Munich. In the United States, considerable funds were provided by Brown University and the Rhode Island Committee for the Humanities. In this connection, I would especially like to thank Thomas Roberts.

I am grateful for the organizational help I received from the four venues. Diana Johnson and Richard Benefield of Brown University's Bell Gallery were instrumental in getting the project off the ground and in installing the show for the first time. In Los Angeles, the exhibition was made possible by Ellen Harrington at the Academy of Motion Picture Arts and Sciences in collaboration with the Goethe-Institut in Los Angeles (especially Claudia Volkmar-Clark and Margit V. Kleinman) and with Rodney Punt at the Cultural Affairs Department in L. A. In Frankfurt, the Deutsches Filmmuseum and the Architektur-Museum joined forces to present the exhibition and contributed several drawings from their collections. I would like to thank the director of the Architektur-Museum, Prof. Wilfried Wang, as well as Claudia Dillmann at the Filmmuseum and their teams.

Material for the exhibition and catalogue has come from a large number of collections and individuals who agreed to loan works of art. At the Stiftung Deutsche Kinemathek in Berlin, I would especially like to thank Werner Sudendorf, Peter Mänz, Wolfgang Theis, Peter Latta, Sabine Süß, and Gertrud Schwarzer.

I must also thank Harrison Ellenshaw and Blaine Converse of Buena Vista Studios, Syd Mead, Richard Sylbert, and Michael Webb in Los Angeles, Virgil Mirano, Los Angeles, Victoria Steele and Maya Bartold of the University of Southern California

Special Collections Departments, Leith Adams and Carla Hanawalt at Warner Bros. Archive, and Stuart Ng at the Warner Bros. Archive of the University of Southern California. Mme Sophie Tatischeff, Gérôme Lavelle, and Mme Jacynthe Moreau Lalande in Paris, Bridget Kinally at the British Film Institute in London, Janet Parks, the curator of drawings at the Avery Architectural Library of Columbia University, and Liz Horwitz of the Cooper Hewitt National Museum of Design in New York, Eleanor Mish and Dr. Richard Koszarski at the American Museum of the Moving Image in New York, Silke Krischker, Dr. Barbara Bongartz, and Dr. Gerald Köhler at the Theaterwissenschaftliche Sammlung of Cologne University, and Julius Shulman and Pedro Guerrero.

Thanks also to Bill Rice of Rice Photo in Providence, Peter Riesterer of Kranichphoto Berlin, and Brooke Hammerle and Terry Abbott at Brown University, Barry Salt and Kevin Brownlow in London, Janet Lorenz of the Academy Foundation, Dr. Peter Briggs, curator at the Museum of Art at the University of Arizona in Tucson, Heidrun Klein at the Bildarchiv Preussischer Kulturbesitz in Berlin, Mary Corliss and Terry Giesken at the Museum of Modern Art Film Stills Archive, New York, Anita Kühnel at the Kunstbibliothek Berlin, Dr. Matthias Schirren at the Kunstakademie Berlin, Margo Stipe at the Frank Lloyd Wright Foundation in Taliesin West, Arizona, Marianne de Fleury, director of the Cinémathèque Française Musée du Cinéma in Paris, Jerry Ohlinger, New York, Diane Hellyer and Kathy Landagh at Turner Entertainment, Judy Singer and Julie Heath at Warner Bros., Mary Lippold at Walt Disney Studios, Deborah Cohen at Time Life Syndication, Nancy Lawson Carcione at the Los Angeles County Museum of Art, Janna Robinson at *Architectural Record*, Sabine Bachmann at Warner Home Video, Richard Manning, Brown University, Michael Brown of Brandeis University, and many others who were enormously helpful in many ways.

From Peter Lähn in Frankfurt and Martin Koerber in Berlin I received an enormous amount of very specialized information. Numerous colleagues and friends helped with valuable information and research: Arabella Berkenbilt, Amy O'Reilly, Katrina Walters, Elisabeth Neumann, and Cindy Barton. Donald Albrecht kindly shared his vast knowledge acquired during the preparation of his book *Designing Dreams*, and Michael Webb shared his experiences from presenting his own exhibition, *Hollywood: Legend and Reality*. Don Shay of *Cinefex* magazine, Howard Prouty at the Margaret Herrick Library, Mark Stetson of Stetson Visual Services in Los Angeles, Andrea Kahn at Columbia University, Ralph Eue of Tobis Film in Berlin, Doc Trumbull of the IMAX Corporation, Kathleen James of the University of California at Berkeley, and Jan-Christopher Horak and Klaus Volkmer at the Filmmuseum in Munich all provided additional help and valuable information, as did Lawrence G. Paull, Syd Mead, and Richard Sylbert. I also profited from numerous discussions with my students, among them Scott Gilbert, Sachi Cunningham, Cindy Barton, Sasha Tulchin, Thomas de Monchaux, Karen Popernik, Sarah Rehm Roberts, and many others.

Above all, I am immensely grateful to my editor Andrea Belloli, London, for her patience, wisdom and painstaking work. I would like to thank Diana Johnson, Patricia Huntington, and Martin Koerber, who read large parts of the manuscript and provided extensive editorial advice, and Dr. Almuth Seebohm, David Britt, and Valerie Orlando. I would also like to thank Janice Prifty and Monica Bessette for their unfailing patience and constant support. Brown University's John Rowe Workman Award helped to finance some of my research trips and expenses. My final thanks go to Patricia Huntington, who has helped this project in many ways.

Dietrich Neumann

After Virginia Woolf saw Robert Wiene's film *The Cabinet of Dr. Caligari* in London in 1926, she rapturously described the architecture that the new medium was able to conjure up, a "dream architecture of arches and battlements, of cascades falling and fountains rising, which sometimes visits us in sleep or shapes itself in half-darkened rooms. No fantasy could be too farfetched or insubstantial." In her article "The Movies and Reality," Woolf recognized the competition that the new medium presented to her own metier: "For a moment it seemed as if thought could be conveyed by shape more effectively than by words." This was especially true, she felt, for the depiction of life in the modern metropolis: "We get intimations only in the chaos of the streets, perhaps, when some momentary assembly of color, sound, movement suggests that here is a scene awaiting a new art to be transfixed."[1]

In her analysis, Woolf singled out the two most frequently affirmed insights about potential encounters between film and architecture in the 1920s. The new art of film could depict the intensely exciting experience of life in the modern city, and it could represent the world of dreams, fantasies, and thoughts — "arenas of the soul" — more effectively and provocatively than other media. Woolf's statement, which was echoed by such contemporary writers as Carl Sandburg and Kurt Tucholsky, is typical of the widespread attention that *Caligari* received as part of the process of acceptance of film as a new, independent art form. Writers and architects in particular realized that the medium presented both a challenge to and an affirmation of their own professions.

Caligari's unusual set design lay at the core of its notoriety. The narrative framework had transformed the story about the evil director of an insane asylum who manipulates a sleepwalker into committing murders from a shocking parable about the abuse of power into the deplorable fantasy of a deranged man.[2] Many critics (among them Adolf Loos[3], the famous Viennese architect) wondered whether the film's expressionist spaces were intentionally portrayed as mere insane visions, and whether that might mean that Expressionist art and architecture in general were being disavowed. *Caligari* thus demonstrated how set design could both support a film's narrative and participate stylistically in important contemporary artistic discussions.

Film Architecture: From *Metropolis* to *Blade Runner* presents some of the manifold examples of such a dialogue between film and architecture during the past 75 years. The selection of individual films for this volume intends to elucidate three major roles of film architecture: as a reflection and commentary on contemporary developments, as a testing ground for innovative visions, and as a realm in which a different approach to the art and practice of architecture can be realized. At the same time it intends to demonstrate the compelling visual power and informative quality of the set designers' sketches, paintings and models, which are usually neglected as mere byproducts of the artistic process.

The material presented in both the exhibition and the catalogue takes the intense cinematic debates in Weimar Germany as a starting point, focusing on a number of examples of "Expressionist cinema." Films that responded to the enormous success of *Caligari*, among them *Genuine, Von Morgens bis Mitternachts,* and *Das Wachsfigurenkabinett*, were not simply attempts to profit from the earlier film's success, but represent thoughtful responses to its use of sets as psychologically charged spaces. They were also experiments in exploring the different conditions of stage and cinema. In a development that paralleled the contemporary move in the mid-Twenties from expressionist architectural visions to a "new sobriety" of structure and function, a number of films began to exploit the inherent technical qualities of the medium, such as the increasing facility of the moving camera, superimposition, and montage. In addition, in films such as F.W. Murnau's *Der letzte Mann,* Joe May's *Asphalt,* or Fritz Lang's *Metropolis,* imminent or distant visions of German cities and their architecture are variously represented as busy urban centers with hectic traffic, neon lights, and sober storefronts or as dystopian projections of a future megalopolis. At the same time, *Sunrise*, Murnau's first American film, brought to the United States the imagery of European modern architecture. The set was built on the Fox studio lot in Los Angeles and looked, as a German commentator wrote, "so modern you could freeze, it seems all to be made of stone and steel and glass."[4]

The dystopian image of the city of the future in *Metropolis* sparked immediate responses in the United States and Great Britain, where the films *Just Imagine* and *Things to Come* provided seemingly more positive views of the urban future. Undoubtedly, the climax of attempts to bring modern architecture and its ideology to the screen was reached with *The Fountainhead*, the 1948 adaptation of Ayn Rand's novel inspired by the life of Frank Lloyd Wright. A general disenchantment with the results of the Modern Movement that began in the 1950s and '60s was reflected in, and even anticipated by, the French director Jacques Tati's brilliant cinematic and architectural comedies *Mon Oncle* and *Playtime*. The next decades brought fears of urban decay, the growing threat of pollution and potentially destructive class differences, all of which are mirrored in Ridley Scott's *Blade Runner*, in which the Los Angeles of 2019 makes specific visual and architectural reference back to Lang's *Metropolis*. In *Batman*, the future Gotham City is presented as a brutalist, modernistic nightmare. *Dick Tracy*, finally, provides a nostalgic alternative by creating the style of an imaginary pre-modernistic New York.

From the very beginning, encounters between film and architecture have been unavoidable. They included the much-lamented use of arbitrarily selected or previously employed sets, compelling portraits of the speed and excitement of city life, propaganda documentaries of modern architecture, and painstakingly accurate historical reconstructions, as well as Hollywood's characteristic studio styles of the 1930s and '40s. Perhaps the most fascinating cases — and the ones for which the term *film architecture* seems most fitting — are those in which architecture is created for a particular movie and exists only for and through film, but nevertheless reflects and contributes to contemporary architectural debates. On such occasions, the mass-medium of film can play an important role in the reception, criticism and dissemination of architectural ideas.

The hope that film could adopt such a role, is as old as the discussion of the medium itself. The American writer Vachel Lindsay, who in 1915 published one of the very first books on film theory, *The Art of the Moving Picture*, claimed in a chapter entitled "Architecture in Motion" that "the architects, above all, are the men to advance work in the ultra-creative photoplay."[5] Their importance was not just for the filming of historical dramas but also for the representations of the architecture of the future. Lindsay explained that, as a result of such films, America would become a kind of testing ground for new architectural ideas, "a permanent World's Fair … if courageous architects have the campaign in hand."

The potential relationships between film and architecture may never have been more passionately discussed than during the era of silent film in the Weimar Republic. As evidenced by the sheer number of texts on the subject, architect's expectations for the new medium could hardly have been higher. Some even hoped for a "rebirth of architecture" through the collective experience of space made possible by the lens of the camera.[6] Indeed, it is within the discussion of film that emerging discussions about space in architecture found a first fruitful forum, several years before the concept of the centrality of spatial experience was adopted as a primary tenet of the theory of the Modern Movement. The absence of technical and financial constraints of the "real world" also seemed to promise an ideal domain for a different approach to the art and practice of architecture. Only in film would the designer be able to create a total environment for a particular figure, a *Gesamtkunstwerk* in its purest sense. Not only might a designer be required to invent cities, individual buildings, and spaces but also to provide them with a history, with patterns and traces of use, in order to connect them to the film's narrative and endow them with meaning. "The set in order to be a good set, must act. Whether realistic, expressionistic, modern, or historical, it must play its role … The set must present the character before he appears, must indicate his social position, his tastes, his habits, his lifestyle, his personality."[7] wrote the French architect and set designer Robert Mallet-Stevens in 1929. Film thus also provided the only realm in which one of the central dogmas of architectural modernism could be readily fulfilled, the notion that form and function are logically and inextricably connected.[8] As Hugo Häring noted in 1924, "Space in film only needs to be unique, singular, designed for one event only, one instance of joyful bliss, one moment of horror."[9] Freed from the constraints of actual construction, Expressionist film architecture could aspire to the ideals of the other arts, to the expression of essential feelings in architectural form.

Many of the questions discussed in the early decades of the new medium are still valid today. Interviews and shorter statements have for the most part replaced the articles and manifestos typical of the 1920s. When Anton Furst, the production designer of *Batman*, claimed to have created "an integral reality of its own," or when Richard Sylbert, production designer for the film *Dick Tracy*, muses about the support that his sets can provide for actors and the storyline, their approaches and concerns echo the enthusiastic and thoughtful statements of the 1920s.

In the plentiful literature on the history of film, the function of set design (especially in the depiction of urban visions) has received little attention. For a long time, it was the "most distinguished and least acknowledged" of the different crafts in film.[10] Luis Buñuel wrote in 1927 that a film, "like a cathedral, should remain anonymous, because people of all classes, artists in most different fields, have worked hard to erect this most massive structure, all the industries, all kinds of technicians, masses of extras, actors, set and costume designers."[11] Despite many similar statements, film analysis has traditionally emphasized the role of the director and the actors, as exemplified in the long-lived "auteur" theory. Buñuel's comparison hints at the fact that architecture also comes about collaboratively, and here too historiography has traditionally privileged the role of the architect over that of other participants or contributing factors in the building process.

Another reason for the long neglect of the subject of film architecture is the fact that too often set design is only noticed in a "collective state of distraction," as Walter Benjamin characterized encounters with both film and architecture.[12] Expansive sets, whose construction might have taken months and cost millions, often show up on screen for mere minutes or even seconds, and the spectator might indeed be distracted by the plot at this very moment. Closer examination of sets requires a certain disrespect for the technical conditions of the medium, which characteristically determine and limit the time and space for its contemplation. We have to stop the film, so to speak, in order to study frame enlargements or stills or rewind the film to see a specific scene several times. In this particular situation, sketches, drawings, blueprints, and models gain even more importance than they might possess for actual built architecture. In fact, often they are the only key to a fuller picture of the ephemeral existence of architecture in film.

In recent years, a renewed interest in set design, and especially in film architecture, has become apparent. Indeed, the increasing number of publications, exhibitions, and conferences on the subject of film and architecture is large enough to indicate the emergence of an entire new field of study, crossing the boundaries between two leading art forms of the twentieth century.[13] The fantastic or visionary designs of unrealized projects by architects have long been recognized as important contributions to the history of architecture. Architectural set designs deserve to occupy a similar position.

After seeing *Metropolis* in Madrid in 1927, Luis Buñuel's critique culminated in a passionate plea for strong ties between film and architecture: "Now and forever the architect is going to replace the set designer. The movies will be the faithful translator of the architect's boldest dreams." Buñuel's prophecy did not entirely come true. Architects have not replaced set designers (to some critics, recent architectural developments seem to suggest rather the opposite). But film has indeed — on numerous occasions — faithfully translated the boldest dreams (and the worst nightmares) of architecture.

Dietrich Neumann

Notes

[1] Virginia Woolf, "The Movies and Reality" (1926), reprint in Harry M. Geduld, ed., *Authors on Film* (Bloomington and London: Indiana University Press, 1972), pp. 86–81.
[2] Uli Jung and Walter Schatzberg, "Ein Drehbuch gegen die CALIGARI-Legenden," in *Das Cabinet des Dr. Caligari: Drehbuch von Carl Mayer und Hans Janowitz* (Hamburg: Edition Text+Kritik, 1995), pp. 89–108.
[3] Adolf Loos, "L'Inhumaine, Histoire féerique," *Neue Freie Presse* (Vienna), 29 July 1924.
[4] Arnold Höllriegel, "Hollywood sucht den 'europäischen' Film," *Berliner Tageblatt*, no. 589, 19 December 1926.
[5] Vachel Lindsay, *The Art of the Moving Picture* (1915), in Dennis Camp, *The Prose of Vachel Lindsay* (Peoria: Spoon River Poetry Press, 1988), vol. 1, pp. 211–337.
[6] Heinrich de Fries, "Raumgestaltung im Film," *Wasmuths Monatshefte für Baukunst*, nos. 1–2 (1920–21), pp. 63–82.
[7] Robert Mallet-Stevens, "Le Décor moderne au cinéma" (1929), quoted in Jean-François Pinchon, *Rob. Mallet-Stevens: Architecture, Furniture, Interior Design* (Cambridge, MA: MIT Press, 1990), p. 92.
[8] See also Juan Antonio Ramirez, "Ten Lessons (or Commandments) about Architecture in the Cinema," *Design Book Review*, no. 24 (Spring 1992), pp. 9–12.
[9] Hugo Häring, "Filmbauen," *Der Neubau: Halbmonatsschrift für Baukunst* 6 (10 June 1924), pp. 117–18.
[10] Mary Corliss and Carlos Clarens, "Designed for Film: The Hollywood Art Director", *Film Comment* 14, no. 3 (May–June 1978).
[11] Luis Buñuel, "Metropolis" (1927), in *Metropolis, un film de Fritz Lang* (Paris: Cinémathèque Française, 1985), p. 15.
[12] Walter Benjamin, "The Work of Art in the Age of Mechanical Reproduction" (1934–35), in Hannah Arendt, ed., *Illuminations: Walter Benjamin Essays and Reflections* (New York: Schocken, 1968), pp. 217–51.
[13] Apart from classics such as Léon Barsacq, *Le Décor de film: 1895–1969* (Paris: Henri Veyrier, 1970); Lotte Eisner, *The Haunted Screen* (Berkeley: University of California Press, 1973); and Mary Corliss and Carlos Clarens, *Designed for Film*, exh. cat. (New York: Museum of Modern Art, 1978), among the most notable recent publications are: Juan Antonio Ramirez, *La Arquitectura en el cine: Hollywood, La Edad de oro* (Madrid: Hermann Blume, 1986); Donald Albrecht, *Designing Dreams: Modern Architecture in the Movies* (London and New York: Thames and Hudson, 1987); Helmut Weihsmann, *Gebaute Illusionen: Architektur im Film* (Vienna: Promedia, 1988); Robert S. Sennett. *Setting the Scene:* The Great Hollywood Art Directors (New York Harry N. Abrams, 1994); and Helmut Weihsmann *Cinetecture: Film, Architektur, Moderne* (Vienna: PVS Verleger, 1995). In the past few years, a number of magazines have produced special editions about the topic, for example: *Cinema and Architecture, Iris* 12 (1991); *Cinemarchitecture, Design Book Review*, no. 24 (Spring 1992); *Ausstattung, Cinema* no. 40 (1994); Maggie Toy, ed., *Architecture & Film, Architectural Design Profile* 112 (1994); *Architecture decor et cinema, CinémAction* 75, no. 2 (1995).

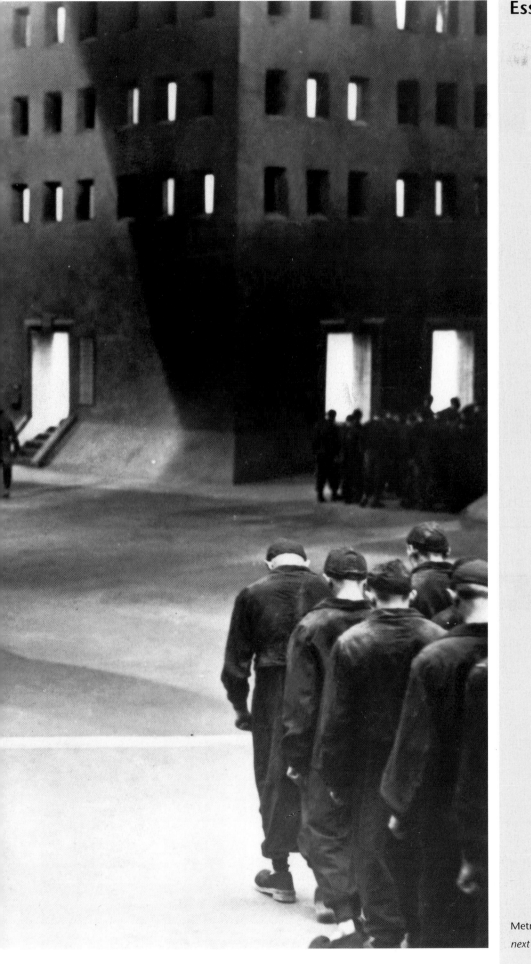

Essays

Metropolis, The Workers' Underground City.
next page: Der Golem, The Ghetto on Fire.

In this essay, I want to examine that aspect of film which has acted, from the beginning of this century, as a sort of laboratory for the exploration of the built world — of, that is, architecture and the city. The examples of such experimentation are well known and include the entire roster of filmic genres: science fiction, adventure, *film noir*, action films, documentaries. Film, indeed, has even been seen to anticipate the built forms of architecture and the city: we have only to think of the commonplace icons of Expressionist utopias to find examples, from *Das Cabinet des Dr. Caligari* (fig. 1) to *Metropolis*, that apparently succeeded, where architecture failed, in building the future in the present. The installation of a recent exhibition in Los Angeles by the Viennese architectural firm Coop Himmelblau even suggested a moment of contemporary closure, when at last architecture might have been seen to have caught up with the imaginary space of film. In recent years, other designers, searching for ways to represent movement and temporal succession in architecture, have similarly turned to the images forged by the Constructivist and Expressionist avantgardes, images themselves deeply marked by the impact of the new filmic techniques. From the literal evocations of Bernard Tschumi in his *Manhattan Transcripts* (1980) and projects for the urban park La Villette in Paris to more theoretical and critical work on the relations of space to visual representation in the projects of Elizabeth Diller and Ricardo Scofidio, the complex question of film's architectural role is again on the agenda. In their new incarnation, such neo-constructivist, Dadaist, and expressionist images seem to reframe many earlier questions about the proper place for images of space and time in architecture, questions that resonate for the contemporary critique of the "image" and the "spectacle" in architecture and society.

And yet the simple alignment of architecture and film, as the following discussion will confirm, has always posed difficulties, both theoretically and in practice. On the one hand, it is obvious that film — the modernist medium par excellence — has been the site of envy and even of imitation for those more static arts concerned to produce effects or techniques of movement and space-time interpenetration. Painting, from Duchamp's *Nude Descending the Staircase*; literature, from Virginia Woolf's *Mrs. Dalloway*; poetry, from Marinetti's *paroles en liberté*; architecture, from Sant' Elia to Le Corbusier — all have sought to reproduce movement and the collapse of time in space, and montage, or its equivalent, has been a preoccupation in all the arts since its appearance, in primitive form, with rapid-sequence photography. On the other hand, it is equally true that modernism's roots in the Enlightenment insured that film, as well as all the other arts, were bound, in the manner of Gotthold Ephraim Lessing, to draw precise theoretical boundaries around the centers of their conceptually different practices — practices understood as distinct precisely because of their distinct media, each one, like Lessing's own poetry and painting, more or less appropriate to the representation of time *or* space. Thus, despite the aspirations of avant-garde groups — from Dada to Esprit Nouveau — to syncretism and synaesthesia, the relations of the arts still could not be conceived without their particular essences being defined. As if the arts were so many nations, romantically rooted in soil and race, each with characteristics of its own to be asserted before any treaties might be negotiated. Of all the arts, however, it is architecture that has had the most privileged and difficult relationship with film. An obvious role model for spatial experimentation, film has also been criticized for its deleterious effects on the architectural image.

When in 1933, Le Corbusier called for film aesthetics that embodied the "spirit of truth," he was only asserting what many architects in the '20s and, more recently, in the '80s saw to be the mutually informative, but properly separate realms of architecture and film. While admitting that "everything is Architecture" in its architectonic dimensions of proportion and order, Le Corbusier nevertheless insisted on the specificity of film, which "from now on is positioning itself on its own terrain . . . becoming a form of art in and of itself, a kind of genre, just as painting, sculpture, literature, music, and theater are genres."[2] In the present context, debates as to the nature of "architecture in film," "filmic architecture," or filmic theory in archit-

Anthony Vidler

The Explosion of Space: Architecture and the Filmic Imaginary

I am kino-eye. I am a builder. I have placed you, whom I've created today, in an extraordinary room which did not exist until just now when I also created it. In this room there are twelve walls shot by me in various parts of the world. In bringing together shots of walls and details, I've managed to arrange them in an order that is pleasing and to construct with intervals, correctly, a film-phrase which is the room.
Dziga Vertov, 1923[1]

Fig. 1: Das Cabinet des Dr. Caligari *(Robert Wiene; Germany, 1919)*.

ectural theory are interesting less as a guide to the writing of some new *Laocoön* that would rigidly redraw the boundaries of the technological arts than they are to the establishment of possibilities of interpretation for projects that increasingly seem caught in the hallucinatory realm of a filmic or screened imaginary — somewhere, that is, in the problematic realm of hyperspace.

Cineplastics

The obvious role of architecture in the construction of sets (and the eager participation of architects themselves in this enterprise), and the equally obvious ability of film to "construct" its own architecture in light and shade, scale and movement, allowed from the outset for a mutual intersection of these two "spatial arts." Certainly, many modernist filmmakers had little doubt regarding the cinema's architectonic properties. From George Méliès's careful description of the proper spatial organization of a studio in 1907 to Eric Rohmer's reassertion of film as "the spatial art" some 40 years later, the architectural metaphor, if not its material reality, was deemed essential to the filmic imagination.[3] Equally, architects such as Hans Poelzig (who together with his wife, the sculptor Marlene Poelzig, sketched and modeled the sets for Paul Wegener's *Der Golem, wie er in die Welt kam* [fig. 2] and Andrei Andreiev (who designed the sets for Robert Wiene's *Raskolnikoff* [1923]) had no hesitation in collaborating with filmmakers in the same way as they had previously served theater producers.[4]

As the architect Robert Mallet-Stevens observed in 1925: "It is undeniable that the cinema has a marked influence on modern architecture; in turn, modern architecture brings its artistic side to the cinema. Modern architecture does not only serve the cinematographic set (*décor*), but imprints its stamp on the staging (*mise–en–scène*), it breaks out of its frame; architecture 'plays.'"[5] Of course, for filmmakers (like Sergei Eisenstein) originally trained as architects, the filmic art offered the potential to develop a new architecture of time and space unfettered by the material constraints of gravity and daily life.

Out of this intersection of the two arts a theoretical apparatus was developed that at once saw architecture as the fundamental site of film practice, the indispensable real and ideal matrix of the filmic imaginary, and at the same time posited film as the modernist art of space par excellence — a vision of the fusion of space and time. The potential of film to explore this new realm, seen as the basis of modernist architectural aesthetics by Siegfried Giedion, was recognized early on. Abel Gance, writing in 1912, was already hoping for a new "sixth art" that would provide "that admirable synthesis of the movement of space and time."[6] But it was the art historian Elie Faure, influenced by Fernand Léger, who first coined a term for the cinematic aesthetic that brought together the two dimensions: "cineplastics." "The cinema," he wrote in 1922, "is first of all plastic. It represents, in some way, an architecture in movement which should be in constant accord, in dynamically pursued equilibrium, with the setting and the landscapes within which it rises and falls."[7] In Faure's terms, "plastic" art was that which "expresse[d] form at rest and in movement," a mode common to the arts of sculpture, bas-relief, drawing, painting, fresco, and especially dance, but that perhaps achieved its highest expression in the cinema.[8] For, as Faure put it, "the cinema incorporates time with space. Even better, time, in this way, really becomes a dimension of space."[9] By means of the cinema, Faure claimed, time became a veritable instrument of space, "unrolling under our eyes its successive volumes ceaselessly returned to us in dimensions that allow us to grasp their extent in surface and depth."[10] The "hitherto unknown plastic pleasures" thereby discovered would, finally, have the effect of creating a new kind of architectural space, akin to that imaginary space "within the walls of the brain":

> The notion of duration entering as a constitutive element into the notion of space, we will easily imagine an art of cineplastics blossoming which would be no more than an ideal architecture where the "cine-mimic" will . . . disappear, because only a great artist could build edifices that constitute themselves, collapse, and reconstitute themselves again ceaselessly by imperceptible passages of

Fig. 2: Der Golem, wie er in die Welt kam *(Paul Wegener; Germany, 1920).*

tones and modeling which will themselves be architecture at every instant, without our being able to grasp the thousandth part of a second in which the transition takes place. [11]

Such an art would, Faure predicted, propel the world into a new stage of civilization, one in which architecture would be the principle form of expression based on the appearance of mobile industrial constructions, ships, trains, cars, and airplanes together with their stable ports and harbors. Cinema would then operate, he concluded, as a kind of privileged "spiritual ornament" to this machine civilization, as "the most useful social play for the development of confidence, harmony, and cohesion in the masses." [12]

Spaces of Horror

Critics of the first generation of German Expressionist films had already experienced such a "cineplastic" revolution in practice. The spate of immediate postwar productions in 1919 and 1920, including Wegener's *Golem*, Karl-Heinz Martin's *Von Morgens bis Mitternachts* (fig. 3), and, of course, Robert Wiene's *Caligari*, demonstrated that, in the words of the German art critic and *New York Times* correspondent Hermann G. Scheffauer, a new "stereoscopic universe" was in the making. In a brilliant analysis published at the end of 1920, Scheffauer hailed the end of the "crude phantasmagoria" of earlier films and the birth of a new space:

> Space — hitherto considered and treated as something dead and static, a mere inert screen or frame, often of no more significance than the painted balustrade-background at the village photographer's — has been smitten into life, into movement and conscious expression. A fourth dimension has begun to evolve out of this photographic cosmos. [13]

Thus, film began to extend what Scheffauer called "the sixth sense of man, his feeling for space or room — his *Raumgefühl*," in such a way as to transform reality itself. No longer an inert background, architecture now participated in the very emotions of film. The surroundings no longer surrounded, but entered the experience as presence: "The frown of a

tower, the scowl of a sinister alley, the pride and serenity of a white peak, the hypnotic draught of a straight road vanishing to point — these exert their influences and express their natures; their essences flow over the scene and blend with the action." [14] The "scenic architect" of films such as *Caligari* had the ability to dominate "furniture, room, house, street, city, landscape, universe!" The "fourth dimension" of time extended space into depth, "the plastic [was] amalgamated with the painted, bulk and form with the simulacra of bulk and form, false perspective and violent foreshadowing were introduced, real light and shadow combat[ted] or reinforce[d] painted shadow and light. Einstein's invasion of the law of gravity [was] made visible in the treatment of walls and supports." [15]

Scheffauer provided a veritable phenomenology of the spaces of *Caligari*, all constructed out of walls that were at once solid and transparent, fissured and veiled, camouflaged and endlessly disappearing, and all presented in a forced and distorted perspective that pressed space both backwards and forwards, finally overwhelming the spectator's own space, incorporating it into the vortex of the whole movie (figs. 4, 5, 6). In his description of the film's environments, Scheffauer anticipated all the later commonplaces of expressionist criticism from Siegfried Kracauer to Rudolf Kurtz:

> A corridor in an office building: Wall veering outward from the floor, traversed by sharply defined parallel strips, emphasizing the perspective and broken violently by pyramidal openings, streaming with light, marking the doors; the shadows between them vibrating as dark cones of contrast, the further end of the murky corridor, giving vast distance. In the foreground a section of wall violently tilted over the heads of the audience, as it were. The floor cryptically painted with errant lines of direction, the floor in front of the doors shows cross lines, indicating a going to and fro, in and out. The impression is one of formal coldness, of bureaucratic regularity, of semi-public traffic.
> A street at night: Yawning blackness in the background — empty, starless, abstract space, against it a square, lopsided lantern hung between lurching walls. Doors and windows constructed or painted in wrenched perspective. Dark segments on the

Fig. 3: Von Morgens bis Mitternachts *(Karl-Heinz Martin; Germany, 1922).*

Fig. 4, 5: Das Cabinet des Dr. Caligari.

Fig. 6: Das Cabinet des Dr. Caligari, Courtyard of the Insane Asylum.

pavement accentuate diminishing effect. The slinking of a brutal figure pressed against the walls and evil spots and shadings on the pavement give a sinister expression to the street. Adroit diagonals lead and rivet the eye.

An attic: It speaks of sordidness, want and crime. The whole composition a vivid intersection of cones of light and dark, of roof-lines, shafts of light and slanting walls. A projection of white and black patterns on the floor, the whole geometrically felt, cubistically conceived. This attic is out of time, but in space. The roof chimneys of another world arise and scowl through the splintered window-pane.

A room; or rather a room that has precipitated itself in cavern-like lines, in inverted hollows of frozen waves. Here space becomes cloistral and encompasses the human — a man reads at a desk. A triangular window glares and permits the living day a voice in this composition.

A prison-cell: A criminal, ironed to a huge chain attached to an immense trapezoidal "ball." The posture of the prisoner sitting on his folded legs is almost Buddha-like. Here space turns upon itself, encloses and focuses a human destiny. A small window high up and crazily barred, is like an eye. The walls, sloping like a tent's to an invisible point, are blazoned with black and white wedge-shaped rays. These blend when they reach the floor and unite in a kind of huge cross, in the center of which the prisoner sits, scowling, unshaven. The tragedy of the repression of the human in space — in trinity of space, fate and man.

A white and spectral bridge yawning and rushing out of the foreground: It is an erratic, irregular causeway, such as blond ghouls might have built. It climbs and struggles upward almost out of the picture. In the middle distance it rises into a hump and reveals arches staggering over nothingness. The perspective pierces into vacuity. This bridge is the scene of a wild pursuit. . .

Several aspects of the market place of a small town . . . the town cries out its will through its mouth, this market place. [16]

Caligari, then, produced an entirely new space, one that was both all-embracing and all-absorbing in depth and movement.[17] But the filmic medium allowed the exploration of other kinds of space than the totalizing plasticity modeled by Walter Röhrig, Walter Reimann, and Hermann Warm for Wiene's film. Schef-

fauer identified the "flat space" of Martin's *Von Morgens bis Mitternachts,* designed by Robert Neppach, which — rather than being artificially constructed in the round like *Caligari* — was suggested in black, white, and gray as "a background, vague, inchoate, nebulous."[18] Above and around this inactive space that made the universe into a flat plane, there was only "primeval darkness"; all perspective was rendered in contrasts of white planes against blackness. There was also the "geometrical space" found in Reimann's film fantasy *Algol;* here, "the forms are broken up expressionistically, but space acts and speaks geometrically, in great vistas, in grandiose architectural culminations. Space or room is divided into formal diapers, patterns, squares, spots, and circles, of cube imposed upon cube, of apartment opening into apartment."[19] Finally, there was what Scheffauer termed "sculptural" or "solid" space, such as that modeled by the Poelzigs for Wegener's *Golem*:

> Professor Poelzig conceives of space in plastic terms, in solid concretions congealing under the artist's hand to expressive and organic forms. He works, therefore, in the solid masses of the sculptor and not with the planes of the painter. Under his caressing hands a weird but spontaneous internal architecture, shell-like, cavernous, somber, has been evolved in simple, flowing lines, instinct with the bizarre spirit of the tale. . . The gray soul of medieval Prague has been molded into these eccentric and errant crypts. . . Poelzig seeks to give an eerie and grotesque suggestiveness to the flights of houses and streets that are to furnish the external setting of this film-play. The will of this master-architect animating facades into faces, insists that these houses are to speak in jargon — and gesticulate! [20]

Pan-Geometries

In assimilating filmic space with the theoretical types of *Raum* adumbrated in German philosophy and psychology since Theodor Vischer, and in proposing the relativity of spatial forms in the face of continuous optical movement in a way that reminds us of the historical relativity of optical forms demonstrated by Alois Riegl, Scheffauer seems also to have been anticipating the more scholarly account of perspectival history developed between 1923 and 1925 by Erwin Panofsky. Panofsky's essay "Perspective as Symbolic Form" set out to show that the various perspective systems developed from Roman times to the present were not simply "incorrect" instances of representing reality, but were instead endowed with distinct symbolic meanings of their own, as powerful and as open to reading as iconographical types and genres. Panofsky even took note of the modernist will to break with the conventions of perspective, seeing it as yet another stage of perspective vision. He cited the Expressionist resistance to perspective as the last remnant of the will to capture "real, three-dimensional space," as well as El Lissitzky's desire to overcome the bounds of finite space:

> Older perspective is supposed to have "limited space, made it finite, closed it off," conceived of space "according to Euclidian geometry as rigid three-dimensionality," and it is these very bonds which the most recent art has attempted to break. Either it has in a sense exploded the entire space by "dispersing the center of vision" ("Futurism"), or it has sought no longer to represent depth intervals "extensively" by means of foreshortenings, but rather, in accord with the most modern insights of psychology, only to create an illusion "intensively" by playing color surfaces off against each other, each differently placed, differently shaded, and only in this way furnished with different spatial values (Mondrian and in particular Malevich's "Suprematism.") The author believes he can suggest a third solution: the conquest of "imaginary space" by means of mechanically motivated bodies, which by this very movement, by their rotation or oscillation, produce precise figures (for example, a rotating stick produces an apparent circle, or in another position, an apparent cylinder, and so forth.) In this way, in the opinion of El Lissitzky, art is elevated to the stand-point of a non-Euclidian pan-geometry (whereas in fact the space of those "imaginary" rotating bodies is no less "Euclidian" than any other empirical space.) [21]

Despite Panofsky's skepticism, it was, of course, just such a "pan-geometric" space that architecture hoped to construct through abstraction and technologically induced movement. Architects from Lissitzky to Bruno Taut were to experiment with this new "pan-geometry," as if — in Ernst Bloch's words — it would enable them finally "to depict empirically an imaginary space."[22] For Bloch, the underlying Euclidian nature of all space offered the potential for architecture to approach "pan-geometry" in reality; basing his argument on Panofsky's essay, he commended the Expressionists for having generated rotating and turning bodies that produced "stereometric figures . . . which at least have nothing in common with the perspective visual space (*Sehraum*)." Out of this procedure emerged "an architecture of the abstract, which wants to be quasi–meta–cubic."[23] For Bloch, this potential allowed modern architecture to achieve its own "symbolic allusions," even if these were founded on the "so-called Euclidian pan-geometry" criticized by Panofsky.[24] In this illusion, the architects were encouraged by cinematographers, who, at least in the '20s, and led by Fritz Lang and F.W. Murnau, accepted the practical rulings of the Universum Film A.G., or Ufa, whose proscription against exterior filming supported the extraordinary experimentation in set design of the Weimar period.

Psycho-Spaces

But the attempt to construct these imaginary new worlds was, as Panofsky noted, not simply formalistic and decorative; its premise was from the outset psychological, based on what Rudolf Kurtz defined as the "simple law of psychological aesthetics that when we feel our way into certain forms exact psychic correspondences are set up."[25] Hugo Münsterberg, in his 1916 work *Film: A Psychological Study*, had already set out the terms of the equation film = psychological form.[26] For Münsterberg, film differed from drama by its appeal to the "inner movements of the mind":

> To be sure, the events in the photoplay happen in the real space with its depth. But the spectator feels that they are not presented in the three dimensions of the outer world, that they are flat pictures which only the mind molds into plastic things. Again the events are seen in continuous movement; and yet the pictures break up the movement into a rapid succession of instantaneous impressions . . . the photoplay tells us the human study by overcoming the

Fig. 7: Von Morgens bis Mitternachts *(Karl-Heinz Martin; Germany, 1922).*

Fig. 8: Algol *(H. K. Werckmeister; Germany, 1920).*

forms of the outer world, namely space, time, and causality, and by adjusting the events to the forms of the inner world, namely, attention, memory, imagination, and emotion.[27]

Only two years later, in one of his first critical essays, Louis Aragon was to note this property of film to focus attention and reformulate the real into the imaginary, the ability to fuse the physical and the mental, later to become a Surrealist obsession. Seemingly anticipating the mental states of André Breton's *Nadja* or of his own *Paysan de Paris*, but revealed in film, Aragon meditated on "the door of a bar that swings and on the window the capital letters of unreadable and marvelous words, or the vertiginous, thousand-eye facade of the thirty-story house."[28] The possibility of disclosing the inner "menacing or enigmatic meanings" of everyday objects by simple close-up techniques and camera angles, light, shade, and space established, for Aragon, the poetic potential of the art: "To endow with a poetic value that which does not possess it, to willfully restrict the field of vision so as to intensify expression: these are two properties that help make cinematic decor the adequate setting of modern beauty."[29] To accomplish this, however, film had no need of an artificially constructed "décor" that simulated the foreshortening of perspective or the phobic characteristics of space; the framings and movements of the camera itself would serve to construct reality far more freely. In his 1934 essay "Style and Medium in the Motion Pictures," Panofsky himself argued against any attempt to subject the world to "aesthetic prestylization, as in the expressionist settings of *The Cabinet of Dr. Caligari*," an exercise he characterized as "no more than an exciting experiment." "To prestylize reality prior to tackling it amounts to dodging the problem," he concluded. "The problem is to manipulate and shoot unstylized reality in such a way that the result has style."[30]

The Lure of the Street

In such terms as these, from the mid-'20s on, critics increasingly denounced what they saw as the purely decorative and staged characteristics of Expressionist film in favor of a more direct confrontation with the "real." If, as Panofsky asserted, "the unique and specific possibilities of film" could be "defined as *dynamization of space* and, accordingly, *spatialization of time*," then it was the lens of the camera, and not any distorted set, that inculcated a sense of motion in the static spectator and thence a mobilization of space itself: "Not only do bodies move in space, but space itself does, approaching, receding, turning, dissolving and recrystallizing as it appears through the controlled locomotion and focusing of the camera and through the cutting and editing of the various shots."[31] And this led to the inevitable conclusion that the proper medium of the movies was not the idealization of reality, as in the other arts, but "physical reality as such."[32] Marcel Carné's frustrated question "When Will the Cinema Go Down into the Street," calling for an end to artifice and the studio set and a confrontation of the "real" as opposed to the "constructed" Paris, was only one of a number of increasingly critical attacks on the architectural set in the early '30s.[33]

Among the most rigorous of the new realists, Siegfried Kracauer, himself a former architect, was consistent in his arguments against the "decorative" and artificial and in favor of the critical vision of the real which film allowed. From his first experience of film as a pre-World War I child to his last theoretical work on the medium, published in 1960, Kracauer found the street to be both site and vehicle for his social criticism. Recalling the first film he had seen as a boy, entitled, significantly enough, *Film as the Discoverer of the Marvels of Everyday Life*, Kracauer remembered being thrilled by the sight of "an ordinary suburban street, filled with lights and shadows which transfigured it. Several trees stood about, and there was in the foreground a puddle reflecting invisible house facades and a piece of sky. Then a breeze moved the shadows, and the facades with the sky below began to waver. The trembling upper world in the dirty puddle — this image has never left me."[34]

For Kracauer, film was first and foremost a material — not a purely formal — aesthetics that was essentially suited to the recording of the fleeting, the temporally transient, the momentary — that is, the modern — and that possessed a quality that made "the street" in all its manifestations an especially favored subject. If the snapshot stressed the random and the fortuitous, then its natural development in the motion picture camera was "partial to the least permanent components of our environment," rendering "the street in the broadest sense of the word" the place for chance encounters and social observation.[35] But for this to work as a truly critical method of observation and recording, the street would first have to be offered up as an "unstaged reality"; what Kracauer considered film's "declared preference for nature in the raw" was easily defeated by artificiality and "staginess," whether the staged "drawing brought to life" (*Caligari*) or the more filmic staging of montage, panning, and camera movement. Lang's *Metropolis* was an instance in which "a film of unsurpassable staginess" was partially redeemed by the way in which crowds were treated "and rendered through a combination of long shots and close shots which provide exactly the kind of random impressions we would receive were we to witness this spectacle in reality."[36] Yet for Kracauer, the impact of the crowd images was obviated by the architectural settings, which remained entirely stylized and imaginary. A similar case was represented by Walter Ruttmann's *Berlin, die Sinfonie der Großstadt* (Berlin, Symphony of a Great City; 1927) (fig. 9), in which — in a Vertov-like manipulation of shot and montage — the director tried to capture "simultaneous phenomena which, owing to certain analogies and contrasts between them, form comprehensible patterns . . . he cuts from human legs walking in the street to the legs of a cow and juxtaposes the luscious dishes in a deluxe restaurant with the appalling food of the very poor" (fig. 6).[37] Such formalism, however, tended to concentrate attention not on things themselves and their meaning, but on their formal characteristics. As Kracauer noted with respect to the capturing of the city's movement in rhythmic shots, "tempo is also a formal conception if it is not defined with reference to the qualities of the objects through which it materializes."[38]

For Kracauer, the street, properly recorded, offered a virtually inexhaustible subject for the comprehension of modernity; its special characteristics fostered not only the chance and the random, but, more importantly, the necessary distance, if not alienation, of the observer for whom the camera eye was a precise surrogate. If in the photographs of contemporaries of Eugène Atget (fig. 10) one might detect a certain melancholy, this was because the photographic medium, intersecting with the street as subject, fostered a kind of self-estrangement allowing for a closer identification with the objects being observed: "The dejected individual is likely to lose himself in the incidental configurations of his environment, absorbing them with a disinterested intensity no longer determined by his previous preferences. His is a kind of receptivity which resembles that of Proust's photographer cast in the role of a stranger."[39] Hence, for Kracauer and his friend Walter Benjamin, the close identification of the photographer with the flaneur, and the potential of *flânerie* and its techniques to furnish models for the modernist filmmaker: "The melancholy character is seen strolling about aimlessly: as he proceeds, his changing surroundings take shape in the form of numerous juxtaposed shots of house facades, neon lights, stray passers-by, and the like. It is inevitable that the audience should trace their seemingly unmotivated emergence to his dejection and the alienation in its wake."[40] In this respect, what Kracauer saw as Eisenstein's "identification of life with the street" took on new meaning as the flaneur-photographer moved to capture the flow of fleeting impressions, what Kracauer's teacher Georg Simmel had characterized as "snapshots of reality." "When history is made in the streets, the streets tend to move onto the screen," Kracauer himself concluded.

Filming the City

Other critics were more optimistic about the potential of filmic techniques to render a version of reality that might otherwise go unrecorded, or better, to re-construe reality in such a way that it might be critically

Fig. 10: Unknown photographer, Paris, passage des panoramas, *ca. 1900.*

Anthony Vidler

Fig. 11: Lithograph by Benoist, Nantes, Pedestrian arcade.

apprehended. Thus, Benjamin's celebrated eulogy of the film as liberation of perception in "The Work of Art in the Age of Mechanical Reproduction" was a first step in the constitution of the filmic as *the* modern critical aesthetic:

> By close-ups of the things around us, by focusing on hidden details of familiar objects, by exploring commonplace milieus under the ingenious guidance of the camera, the film, on the one hand, extends our comprehension of the necessities which rule our lives; on the other hand, it manages to assure us of an immense and unexpected field of action. Our taverns and our metropolitan streets, our offices and furnished rooms, our railroad stations and our factories appeared to have us locked up hopelessly. Then came the film and burst this prison world asunder by the dynamite of the tenth of a second, so that now, in the midst of its far flung ruins and debris, we calmly and adventurously go traveling. With the close-up, space expands; with slow motion, movement is extended . . . an unconsciously penetrated space is substituted for a space consciously explored by man. . . The camera introduces us to unconscious optics as does psychoanalysis to unconscious impulses.[41]

Unconscious optics, the filmic unconscious, was, for Benjamin, itself a kind of analysis, the closest aesthetic equivalent to Freud's *Psychopathology of Everyday Life* (1901) in its ability to focus and deepen perception.

In this characteristic, film obviously outdistanced architecture. Benjamin's remark that "architecture has always represented the prototype of a work of art the reception of which is consummated by the collectivity in a state of distraction" was made in this very context: the assertion of the "shock effect" of the film as that which allows the public, no longer distracted, to be once more put in the position of the critic. Thus, the only way to render architecture critical again was to wrest it out of its uncritically observed context, its distracted state, and offer it to a now attentive public — that is, to make a film of the building.

Or of the city. In an evocative remark inserted apparently at random among the unwieldy collection of citations and aphorisms that make up the unfinished "Passagen-Werk," Benjamin opened the possibility of

yet another way of reading his unfinished work: "Could one not shoot a passionate film of the city plan of Paris? Of the development of its different forms [*Gestalten*] in temporal succession? Of the condensation of a century-long movement of streets, boulevards, passages, squares, in the space of half an hour? And what else does the flaneur do?"[42] In this context, might not the endless quotations and aphoristic observations of the "Passagen-Werk," carefully written out on hundreds of index cards, each one letter-, number-, and color-coded to cross-reference it to all the rest, be construed as so many camera shots ready to be montaged into the epic film *Paris, Capital of the Nineteenth Century*, a prehistory of modernity, finally realized by modernity's own special form of mechanical reproduction?

While obviously no "film" of this kind was ever made, an attempt to answer the hypothetical question "What would Benjamin's film of Paris have looked like?" would clarify what we might call Benjamin's "filmic imaginary." Such an imaginary, overt in the "Passagen-Werk" and his contemporary essay "The Work of Art in the Age of Mechanical Reproduction" and covert in many earlier writings from those on German Baroque allegory to those on historical form, might, in turn, reveal important aspects of the theoretical problems inherent in the filmic representation of the metropolis. For in the light of Benjamin's theories of the political and social powers of mechanical reproduction as outlined in his "Conversations with Berthold Brecht," it is clear from the outset that any project for a film of Paris would in no way have resembled other urban films of the interwar period, whether idealist, expressionist, or realist. Rather, it would have involved Benjamin in an act of theoretical elaboration, which, based on previous film theory and criticism, would have constructed new kinds of optical relations between the camera and the city, film and architecture. These would no doubt have been based on the complex notion of "the optical unconscious," an intercalation of Freud and Riegl, which appears in Benjamin's writings on photography and film from the late '20s and early '30s.

On one level, Benjamin's fragmentary remark is easily decipherable. What he had in mind was evidently an image of the combined results of the flaneur's peripatetic vision montaged onto the history of the nineteenth century and put in motion by the movie camera. No longer would the implied movement of Bergsonian mental processes or the turns of allegorical text have to make do as pale imitations of metropolitan movement; now the real movement of the film would, finally, merge technique and content as a proof, so to speak, of the manifest destiny of modernity. In this sense, Benjamin's metaphor of a Parisian film remains just that: a figure of modernist technique as the fullest expression of modernist thought, as well as the explanation of its origins.

It is certainly not too difficult to imagine the figure of Benjamin's flaneur, Vertov-like, carrying his camera as a third eye, framing and shooting the rapidly moving pictures of modern life. The etchings of Jacques Callot, the thumbnail sketches of Saint-Aubin, the "tableaux" of Sebastien Mercier, the rapid renderings of Constantin Guys, the prose poems of Baudelaire, the snapshots of Atget, are all readily transposed into the vocabulary of film, which then literally mimics the fleeting impressions of everyday life in the metropolis in its very techniques of representation. Indeed, almost every characteristic Benjamin associated with the flaneur might be associated with the film director with little or no distortion. An eye for detail, for the neglected and the chance; a penchant for joining reality and reverie; a distanced vision, set apart from that distracted and unselfconscious existence of the crowd; a fondness for the marginal and the forgotten: these are traits of flaneur and filmmaker alike. Both share affinities with the detective and the peddler, the rag-picker and the vagabond; both aesthetisize the roles and materials with which they work. Equally, the typical habitats of the flaneur lend themselves to filmic representation: the *banlieu,* the margins, the zones and outskirts of the city; deserted streets and squares at night; crowded boulevards, phantasmagoric passages, arcades, and department stores — the spatial apparatus, that is, of the consumer metropolis.

On another level, however, if we take Benjamin's image literally rather than metaphorically, a number of puzzling questions emerge. A film of Paris is certainly conceivable, but what would a film of "the *plan* of Paris" look like? And if one were to succeed in filming this plan, how then might it depict the development of the city's "forms" — its boulevards, streets, squares, and passages — at the same time "condensing" a century of their history into half an hour? How might such a film, if realized, be "passionate?" If, as Benjamin intimated, the model of the film director was to be found in the figure of the flaneur, how might this figure translate his essentially nineteenth-century habits of walking and seeing into cinematographic terms? It seems that, step by step, within the very movement of Benjamin's own metaphor, the ostensible unity of his image is systematically undermined, as if the result of making a film of the plan of Paris were to replicate the very fragmentation of modernity the metropolis posed, the flaneur saw, and the film had concretized. Benjamin's image thus emerges as a complex rebus of method and form. Its very self-enclosed elegance, beginning with the film and ending with the flaneur as director (a perfect example of a romantic fragment turning in on itself according to the rules of the German philosopher Schelling), seems consciously structured to provoke its own unraveling. It is as if Benjamin inserted his cinematographic conundrum into the formless accumulation of the "Passagen-Werk's" citations and aphorisms to provoke, in its deciphering, a self-conscious ambiguity about the implied structure of his text and, at the same time, a speculation on the theory of film which he never wrote.

It was not simply that the flaneur and the filmmaker shared spaces and gazes; for Benjamin, these characteristics were transferred, as in analysis, to the spaces themselves, which became, so to speak, vagabonds in their own right. He spoke of the phenomenon of the "*colportage* or peddling of space" as the fundamental experience of the flaneur, in which a kind of Bergsonian process allowed "the simultaneous perception of everything that potentially is happening in this single space. The space directs winks at the flaneur."[43] Thus, the flaneur as rag-picker and peddlar participates in his surroundings, even as they cooperate

Fig. 12: Lithograph by Benoist, Nantes, upper arcade.

Fig. 13: Giovanni Battista Piranesi, le Carceri. *Eleventh plate, 1760.*

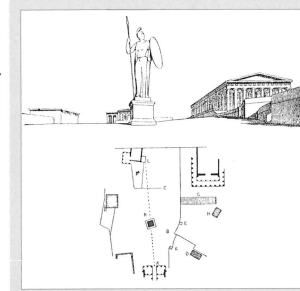

Fig. 14: Auguste Choisy's analysis of the Acropolis (from his *Histoire de l'architecture* of 1899) as used by Le Corbusier in his *Vers une architecture* (1923).

Fig. 15: Giovanni Battista Piranesi, *Seventh plate from* I Carceri, *1760.*

with him in his unofficial archaeology of spatial settings. And, to paraphrase Benjamin, "what else does the film-maker do" for a viewer now opened up "in his susceptibility to the transient real-life phenomena that crowd the screen?"[44]

Architectural Montage

Here, we are returned to Eisenstein's "street," reminded, in Benjamin's desire to have shot a "passionate" film, of Eisenstein's own long analyses of the notion of filmic "ecstasy," the simultaneous cause and effect of movement in the movie. The "ecstatic" for Eisenstein was, in fact, the fundamental shared characteristic of architecture and film. Even as architectural styles had, one by one, "exploded" into each other by a kind of inevitable historical process, so the filmmaker might force the shot to decompose and recompose in successive explosions. Thus, the

> principles of the Gothic . . . seem to explode the balance of the Romanesque style. And, within the Gothic itself, we could trace the stirring picture of movement of its lancet world from the first almost indistinct steps toward the ardent model of the mature and post mature, "flamboyant" late Gothic. We could, like [the art historian Heinrich] Wölfflin, contrast the Renaissance and Baroque and interpret the excited spirit of the second, winding like a spiral, as an ecstatically bursting temperament of a new epoch, exploding preceding forms of art in the enthusiasms for a new quality, responding to a new phase of a single historical process.[45]

But Eisenstein went further. In an essay on two Piranesi engravings for the early and late states of the *Carceri* series, he compared architectural composition itself to cinematic montage, an implicit "flux of form" which holds within itself the potential to explode into successive states (fig. 15).[46] Building on his experience as architect and setdesigner, Eisenstein developed a comprehensive theory of what he called "space constructions" that found new meaning in the romantic formulation of architecture as "frozen music":

> At the basis of the composition of its ensemble, at the basis of the harmony of its conglomerating masses,

in the establishment of the melody of the future overflow of its forms, and in the execution of its rhythmic parts, giving harmony to the relief of its ensemble, lies that same "dance" that is also at the basis of the creation of music, painting, and cinematic montage.[47]

For Eisenstein, a kind of relentless vertigo was set up by the play of architectural forms in space, a vertigo that is easily assimilable to Thomas De Quincey's celebrated account of Coleridge's reaction to Piranesi's *Carceri* or, better, to Gogol's reading of the Gothic as a style of endless movement and internal explosions.[48]

And if Eisenstein was able to "force" — to use Manfredo Tafuri's term — these *representations* of architectural space to "explode" into the successive stages of their "montage" decomposition and re-composition, as if they were so many "shots," then it was because, for Eisenstein, architecture itself embodied the principles of montage; indeed, its special characteristics of a spatial art experienced in time render it the predecessor of film in more than simple analogy.

In his article "Montage and Architecture," written in the late '30s as part of his uncompleted work on montage, Eisenstein set out this position, contrasting two "paths" of the spatial eye: the cinematic, in which a spectator follows an imaginary line among a series of objects, through sight as well as in the mind — "diverse positions passing in front of an immobile spectator" — and the architectural, in which "the spectator move[s] through a series of carefully disposed phenomena which he observe[s] in order with his visual sense."[49] In this transition from real to imaginary movement, architecture is film's predecessor. Where painting "remained incapable of fixing the total representation of an object in its full multi-dimensionality," and "only the film camera had solved the problem of doing this on a flat surface," "its undoubted ancestor in this capability [was] . . . architecture."[50]

Here, Eisenstein, former architect and an admitted "great adherent of the architectural aesthetics of Le Corbusier," turned to an example of the architectural "path" which precisely parallels that studied by Le Corbusier himself in *Vers une architecture* (1923) to exemplify the "promenade architecturale": the successive perspective views of the movement of an imaginary spectator on the Acropolis constructed by Auguste Choisy to demonstrate the "successive tableaux" and "picturesque" composition of the site.[51] Eisenstein cited Choisy's analysis at length with little commentary, asking his reader simply "to look at it with the eye of a filmmaker": "[I]t is hard to imagine a montage sequence for an architectural ensemble more subtly composed, shot by shot, than the one which our legs create by walking among the buildings of the Acropolis."[52] For Eisenstein, the Acropolis was the answer to Victor Hugo's assertion of the cathedral as a book in stone: "the perfect example of one of the most ancient films."[53] Eisenstein found in the carefully sequenced perspectives presented by Choisy the combination of a "film shot effect," producing an obvious new impression from each new, emerging shot, and a "montage effect," in which the effect was gained from the sequential juxtaposition of shots. The Russian filmmaker speculated on the desirable temporal duration of each picture, discovering the possibility that there was a distinct relationship between the pace of the spectator's movement and the rhythm of the buildings themselves, a temporal solemnity being provoked by the distance between buildings.

Le Corbusier, who was apparently less faithful in his reproduction of Choisy's sequence, concentrated on the second perspective, shown together with the plan of the visual axis of entry from the Propylea to the former statue of Athena (fig. 14).[54] For the architect, this demonstrated the flexibility of Greek "axial" planning as opposed to the rigidity of the academic Beaux–Arts: "[F]alse right angles have furnished rich views and a subtle effect; the asymmetrical masses of the buildings create an intense rhythm. The spectacle is massive, elastic, nervous, overwhelming in its sharpness, dominating."[55] The plan of the mobile and changing ground levels of the Acropolis was only apparently "disordered." There was an inner equilibrium when the entire site was viewed from afar.

In this common reliance on Choisy, we might be tempted to see the final conjunction of architectural and filmic modernism; the rhythmic dance of Le Corbusier's spectator (modeled no doubt on the movements of Jacques Dalcroze) anticipating the movement of Eisenstein's shots and montages (fig. 16). For both analysts, the apparently inert site and its strangely placed buildings were almost literally exploded into life, at once physical and mental. For both, the rereading of a canonical monument provided the key to a "true" and natural modernist aesthetic.

And yet, as both writers ceaselessly reiterated, such correspondences were, when taken too literally, false to the internal laws of the two media, architecture and film. If Le Corbusier agreed that "everything is Architecture," he also called for film to concentrate on its own laws; Eisenstein, similarly, abandoned a career as an architect and stage designer precisely because the film offered a new and different stage of representational technique for modernity. For Le Corbusier, architecture was a setting for the athletic and physical life of the new man, its objects and settings the activators of mental and spiritual activity through vision; for Eisenstein, architecture remained only a *potential* film, a necessary stage in aesthetic evolution, but already surpassed.

Both would have agreed with Robert Mallet-Stevens, who was troubled by the invasion of the decorative into filmic architecture, by the potential to create "imaginary" forms that illustrated rather than provided settings for human emotions. Mallet-Stevens warned against the tendency to view architecture as a photogenic aid to film, thereby creating a "foreseen" dynamic that in real space would be provided by the human figure: "[T]he ornament, the arabesque, is the mobile personage who creates them."[56] Rather than expressionist buildings imitating their cinematic counterparts, he called for a radical simplification of architecture which would, in this way, offer itself up naturally to filmic action, always preserving the distance between the real and the imaginary: "Real life is entirely different, the house is made to live, it should first respond to our needs."[57] Properly handled, however, architecture and film might be entirely complementary. Mallet-Stevens cited a screenplay by Ricciotto Canudo that would perhaps realize this ideal:

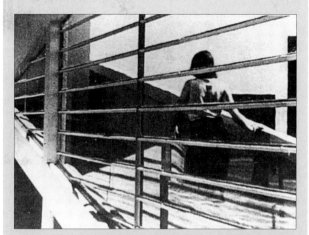

Fig. 16: L'Architecture d'aujourd'hui *(Pierre Chenal; France, 1929):* Villa Savoye, Poissy by Le Corbusier, 1929.

Fig. 17: L'Inhumaine *(France, 1924).*

Fig. 18: Florian Köpp and Michael Willadt, Imagination Machine IMT2PO *(1992):* Virtual Spaces Created in a Computer.

It concerned the representation of a solitary woman, frighteningly alone in life, surrounded by the void, and nothingness. The decor: composed of inarticulate lines, immovable, repeated, without ornament: no window, no door, no furniture in the "field" and at the center of these rigid parallels a woman who advanced slowly. Sub-titles become useless, architecture situates the person and defines her better than any text.[58]

In this vision of a cinematic architecture that would through its own laws of perspective return to the essential characteristics of building, Mallet-Stevens echoed Le Corbusier and anticipated Eisenstein. He also, in his depiction of a decor framed as the very image of isolation, agoraphobic or claustrophobic, answered those in Germany who were attempting to "express" in spatial distortion what a simple manipulation of the camera in space might accomplish.

Such arguments between two possibilities of filmic architecture have hardly ceased with the gradual demise of cinema and the rise of its own "natural" successors, video and, more recently, digital hyperspatial imaging. That their influence on architecture might be as disturbing as those observed by Le Corbusier and Mallet-Stevens is at least possible to hazard, as buildings and their spatial sequences are designed more as illustrations of implied movement or, worse, as literal fabrications of the computer's eye view. It is certainly possible to develop an all-too-easy critique of contemporary attempts to construct "virtual reality" as simply replicating the perspectival forms of previous "reality representations." But there is one consideration that makes the contemporary question entirely different from that of the '20s or the '40s, or even from that of Lessing's 1750s: the fact that the technologies and means of representation have changed once again, this time bringing architecture and film closer than ever before. Where in the '20s and after, film and architecture were, in a fundamental sense, entirely different media utilizing their respective technologies, the one to simulate space, the other to build it, now, by contrast, the increasing digitalization of our world has rendered them if not the same, at least coterminous.

And in this condition, we are no longer, or not for long, talking about "virtual reality," but rather about "virtual space" — in the sense of William Gibson's *Virtual Light* (1993). Virtual space (and not hyperspace, or cyberspace, those confections of the '70s and '80s) would be that space that is neither flat nor deep; neither surveyed nor unsurveyed; neither changing nor unchanging (fig. 18). It would be, and perhaps be for the first time, a space that was entirely indifferent to any differences among bodies, things, and positions. Constituted of endless strings, represented on apparently flat screens, it would exist without us and would not expect us to exist. Here, the dynamic interplay of subject and object, object and space, assayed by modernism would give way to an endless *mise-en-abyme*, where not even the myth of interactivity could dispel the unease of a wall that looked back — but not at you. Jeremy Bentham would not be at home in this space, nor would Mike Davis, who relies on Bentham's model of surveillance, nor even would Gibson himself, to whom we must attribute its first imagining. Rather, no one is or could be at home here, where the old-fashioned cowboy hacker, the mutant, the cyborg, and the postmodernist, posthumanist subject are simply revealed as themselves mutations of the old, well-worn subject of Cartesian origin. If for Georg Lukács, the post-technological world of modernism was one of transcendental homelessness, then the world of digital encoding does not even afford this vagabond-like identity, where, for example, the space of the everyday and the space of DNA are merged and morphed with diabolical effect. Physico-spatial metaphors like nets and highways fail in the face of such totalizing absorption, leaving us with only a screen imaginary, or perhaps a screen nostalgia, that we may believe for an instant positions us in front of it, subjects in front of a screen, and not, as is more probably the case, it in front of us.

Notes

This essay is based on an article published under the same title in *Assemblage* 21 (1993), pp. 45–59.

[1] Dziga Vertov, *Kino-Eye: The Writings of Dziga Vertov*, ed. and with introduction by Annette Michelson, trans. Kevin O'Brien (Berkeley and

Los Angeles: University of California Press, 1984), p. 17.
[2] Le Corbusier, "Esprit de vérité" (1933), trans. in Richard Abel, *French Film Theory and Criticism: A History/Anthology*, (Princeton: Princeton University Press, 1988), vol. 2, pp. 111–13.
[3] George Méliès, "Les Vues cinématographiques" (1907), in Marcel L'Herbier, *L'Intelligence du cinématographe* (Paris: Editions Corea, 1946), pp. 179–87; Eric Rohmer, "Cinema, The Art of Space" (1948), in Eric Rohmer, *The Taste for Beauty*, trans. Carol Volk (Cambridge: Cambridge University Press, 1989), pp. 19–29.
[4] The best discussion of the architectural contribution to set design in the context of the Expressionist '20s, is still Lotte H. Eisner, *L'Ecran démoniaque* (Paris: Eric Losfeld, 1965).
[5] Robert Mallet–Stevens, "Le Cinéma et les arts: L'Architecture" (1925), in L'Herbier (note 3), p. 288.
[6] Abel Gance, "Qu'est-ce que le cinématographe? Un Sixième Art" (1912), in L'Herbier (note 3), p. 92.
[7] Elie Faure, "De la cinéplastique" (1922), in L'Herbier (note 3), p. 268. The English translations in this paragraph are my own.
[8] Ibid., p. 268.
[9, 10] Ibid., p. 275.
[11] Ibid., p. 276.
[12] Ibid., p. 278.
[13] Herman G. Scheffauer, "The Vivifying of Space" (1920), in Lewis Jacobs, ed., *Introduction to the Art of the Movies* (New York: Noonday Press, 1960), pp. 76–85. The essay appeared in Scheffauer's collection of essays, *The New Vision in the German Arts* (New York: B.W. Huebsch, 1924). As Dietrich Neumann has noted, Scheffauer was considerably indebted to Heinrich de Fries, who published an article entitled "Raumgestaltung im Film" in *Wasmuths Monatshefte für Baukunst*, nos. 1–2 (1920–21), pp. 63–75, even to the extent of repeating de Fries's mistakes as well as paraphrasing entire passages (see pp. 133–34).
[14] Ibid., p.78.   [15] Ibid., p.79.   [16] Ibid., pp. 79–81.
[17] Scheffauer's analysis was echoed by the art critic Rudolf Kurtz:
Perpendicular lines tense towards the diagonal, houses exhibit crooked, angular outlines, planes shift in rhomboidal fashion, the lines of force of normal architecture, expressed in perpendiculars and horizontals, are transmogrified into a chaos of broken forms. . . A movement begins, leaves its natural course, is intercepted by another, led on, distorted again, and broken. All this is steeped in a magic play of light, unchaining brightness and blackness, building up, dividing, emphasizing, destroying [Rudolf Kurtz, *Expressionismus und Film* (1926), as cited in Siegbert Solomon Prawer, *Caligari's Children: The Film as Tale of Terror* (New York: Da Capo Press: 1988), p. 189].
[18] Ibid., p. 82.   [19] Ibid., p. 83.   [20] Ibid., p. 84.
[21] Erwin Panofsky, *Perspective as Symbolic Form*, trans. Christopher S. Wood (New York: Zone Books, 1991), p. 70. Panofsky's essay "Die Perspektive als 'symbolische Form'" was first published in *Vorträge der Bibliothek Warburg 1924–1925* (Leipzig and Berlin: B.G. Teubner, 1927), pp. 258–330.
[22] Ernst Bloch, "Die Bebauung des Hohlraums" (1959), in Jack Zipes and Frank Mecklenburg, trans., *The Utopian Function of Art and Literature: Selected Essays* (Cambridge, MA.: MIT Press, 1988), p. 196.
[23] Ibid.
[24] Bloch referred directly to Panofsky's essay (ibid., p. 96).
[25] Kurtz, cited in Prawer (note 17), p. 189.
[26] Hugo Münsterberg, *Film: A Psychological Study* (1916), (reprint New York: Dover Publications, 1969). For a general study of his theory, see Donald L. Fredericksen, *The Aesthetic of Isolation in Film Theory: Hugo Münsterberg* (New York: Arno Press, 1977).
[27] Münsterberg, cited in Gerald Mast and Marshall Cohen, eds., *Film Theory and Criticism: Introductory Readings*, 3rd ed. (New York: Oxford University Press, 1985), p. 332.
[28] Louis Aragon, "Du décor" (1918), trans. in Abel (note 2), vol. 1, p. 165.
[29] Ibid., p. 166.
[30] Erwin Panofsky, "Style and Medium in the Motion Pictures" (1934), in Mast and Cohen, eds. (note 27), p. 232.
[31] Ibid., p. 218.
[32] Ibid., p. 232.
[33] Marcel Carné, "Quand le cinéma descendra-t-il dans la rue?" (1933), trans. in Abel (note 2), vol. 2, pp. 127–29. Carné himself, however, continued to rely on sets built in the studio, meticulously imitating the real streets of Paris.
[34] Siegfried Kracauer, *Theory of Film: The Redemption of Physical Reality* (London: Oxford University Press, 1960), p. xi.
[35] Ibid., p. 52. Kracauer elaborated:
The affinity of film for haphazard contingencies is most strikingly demonstrated by its unwavering susceptibility to the "street" — a term designed to cover not only the street, particularly the city street, in the literal sense, but also its various extensions, such as railway stations, dance and assembly halls, bars, hotel lobbies, airports,etc. . . . Within the present context the street, which has already been characterized as a center of fleeting impressions, is of interest as a region where the accidental prevails over the providential, and happenings in the nature of unexpected incidents are all but the rule . . . there have been only a few cinematic films that would not include glimpses of a street, not to mention the many films in which some street figures among the protagonists [p. 62].
[36] Ibid., p. 62.
[37] Ibid., p. 65.
[38] Ibid., p. 207.
[39, 40] Ibid., p. 17.
[41] Walter Benjamin, "The Work of Art in the Age of Mechanical Reproduction" (1935), trans. in Mast and Cohen, eds. (note 2), pp. 689–90.
[42] Walter Benjamin, "Das Passagen–Werk," vol. V, 1 of *Gesammelte Schriften* (Frankfurt am Main: Suhrkamp, 1982), p. 135.
[43] Ibid., p. 527.
[44] Siegfried Kracauer, *Theory of Film: The Redemption of Physical Reality* (London: Oxford University Press, 1960), p. 170.
[45] Sergei Eisenstein, *Nonindifferent Nature*, trans. Herbert Marshall (Cambridge: Cambridge University Press, 1987), p. 122.
[46] Ibid., pp. 123–54. For a discussion of Eisenstein's filmic interpretation of Piranesi in the context of the European avant-garde, see Manfredo Tafuri, *The Sphere and the Labyrinth* (Cambridge, MA: MIT Press, 1990), pp. 55–64.
[47] Eisenstein (note 45), p. 140.
[48] See Eisenstein (note 45), pp.159–65, an analysis of Gogol's "On the Architecture of Our Time" (1831) along the same lines as his discussion of Piranesi.
[49] Sergei Eisenstein, "Montage and Architecture," in *Towards a Theory of Montage*, ed. Michael Glenny and Richard Taylor, trans. Michael Glenny, vol. 2 of *Selected Works* (London: BFI Publishing, 1991), p. 59.
[50] Ibid., p. 60.
[51] Auguste Choisy, *Histoire de l'architecture* (Paris: E. Rouveyre, 1899), vol. 1, p. 413.
[52] Eisenstein (note 49), p. 60.
[53] Ibid.
[54] Le Corbusier, *Vers une architecture* (Paris: G. Cres, 1923), p. 31.
[55] Ibid.
[56] Mallet-Stevens (note 5), p. 289.
[57] Ibid., p. 290.
[58] Ibid., p. 288.

Fig. 19: Metropolis *(Fritz Lang; Germany, 1926).*

Fig. 20: Metropolis *(Fritz Lang; Germany, 1926).*

Anton Kaes

Sites of Desire:
The Weimar Street Film

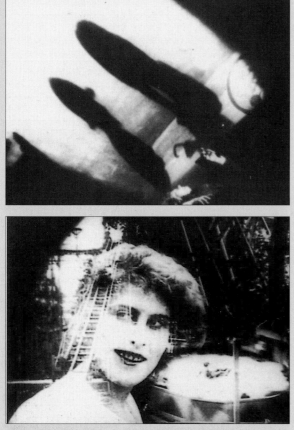

Fig. 1, 2: Die Straße *(Karl Grune; Germany, 1923). Frame enlargements by Barry Salt, London.*

Fig. 3: Umberto Boccioni, The Street Invades the Home, *1911. Oil on canvas, 100 x 100 cm. Sprengel Museum, Hannover.*

An interior space. A middle-aged man, looking drawn and tired, lies on the sofa in a crammed living room, while his dour wife prepares dinner in the kitchen. The man stares vacantly at the ceiling. Suddenly, streetlights go on outside his window, projecting moving shadows into his room (fig. 1). He watches the light effects, which resemble the flicker of a projector. In a mock shadow play, pedestrians rush by; a flaneur addresses a woman and follows her deliriously; passing vehicles refract the light into a myriad of luminous rays. Transfixed and aroused by the spectacle, the man sits up, visibly yearning for the bustling life behind the shadows. He looks out the window, down onto the street. Another space — urban and kinetic — opens up. A close-up of his face registers his captivated gaze. In a film–within–the–film insert, demarcated as a private hallucination, the film shows us what he sees: cars and trains in wild motion, thrill seekers enjoying themselves on fairground rides, a circus clown making faces, an organ grinder. The final image, held longer than all of the other shots, is of a smiling young woman who seems to beckon to him with her eyes (fig. 2). Compressed within a frame, these vignettes of city life overlap each other, thereby producing, in the manner of a cubist painting, multiple perspectives, simultaneity, and dizzying dynamics. The window itself becomes the screen (doubling the actual screen) as we see the man watch the spectacle from his own home. The private realm has proven not to be safe from the rapacious life of the street; the two contrasting spheres — street and home, exterior and interior, public and private — exist here in one frame, reminding us of Umberto Boccioni's famous Futurist painting *The Street Invades the Home* (fig. 3). In an urban environment, the street's presence is tangible; it even defines the relationship between two people. As his wife calls the man to dinner, she finds him standing at the window, lost in his voyeuristic gaze, longing for the street. She walks over, looks out the window herself, and sees — nothing: the camera shows only distant traffic. Gripped by a sudden impulse, the man grabs his hat and umbrella, runs out the door and down the stairs and plunges into the street. The camera

cuts away from him to an endless procession of vehicles and pedestrians streaming by; he has become no more than a particle swept along in the maelstrom of a busy metropolitan street at nightfall.

Thus begins the film *Die Straße*, directed by Karl Grune and first shown in Berlin in November 1923. Following the narrative trajectory of *Von Morgens bis Mitternachts*, the widely acclaimed play by Georg Kaiser, written in 1912 and staged in 1917 (fig. 4),[1] *Die Straße* dramatizes the transformation of a meek office clerk into a feverish seeker of ecstasy. Fleeing from domestic dullness into the street, both Kaiser's and Grune's antiheroes are driven by the promise of excitement, of adventure, risk, and self-transcendence. Their Nietzschean goal is a vitalistic, Dionysian life that would transform their regulated and repressed existence. But their searches end in despair. Kaiser's nameless protagonist kills himself in a grandiose finale with Christian overtones ("Ecce homo," he intones before he dies), while the similarly anonymous character of Grune's film returns to his home, shamed and penitent, after a night that sees him alternately exhilarated, bewildered, frenzied, and forlorn. His wife silently serves him the warmed-up soup he had not eaten the night before. The adventure is over; the experience of the street, with its passion and danger, seems nothing more than the product of an overwrought imagination. The street: was it a dream, a vision, a movie?

The film's contradictory reactions to urban experience encapsulates the whole range of emotions associated with the big city throughout modern history, running the gamut from idolization to condemnation, from intoxication and elation to feelings of anxiety and apocalypse. *Die Straße* embodies all these attitudes, ultimately emphasizing the negative view that resonates with the historical moment in which the film appeared. Its premiere on 29 November 1923 occurred in a month of unprecedented political and social turmoil in Germany. On 9 November 1923, Hitler and his followers had marched through the streets of Munich intending to overthrow the government (the putsch and the "national revolution" were stopped within hours). On 16 November, the wildly galloping inflation had finally come to a halt (the Rentenmark was being introduced after the exchange rate had come to exceed four thousand billion marks to the dollar). Unrest and separatist activities continued in the occupied Rhineland, and communist–inspired revolts in Saxonia and Hamburg at the end of October had cost several lives. Assassinations of political figures in broad daylight occurred frequently between 1919 and 1923, as did large and violent demonstrations, protest marches, and street fights — altogether an apocalyptic scenario of a civil war raging within Germany that left the citizens confused, fearful, agitated. In 1923, the streets of Berlin were a dangerous place.

Grune's film *Die Straße* makes no explicit reference to political events, but implicitly takes part in the denigration of the public sphere. It depicts the street as a perilous site, rife with vice and crime, doubly harmful because of its seductive allure. The film is about the politics (and the price) of desire. Blinded by his hunger for life, the protagonist enters the street as a phantasmagorical space in which appearances deceive and imagination runs wild. Women are prostitutes; men are gamblers, cheats, and murderers; the street itself is a cesspool of decadence. Burning with desire, he covetously stares at a streetwalker, but all of a sudden her smiling head turns into a skull. His hallucination, made possible by superimposition, evokes a Baroque image that associates sexuality with *vanitas* and the transitoriness of worldly life. Further, this link between prostitution and death points to the fear of venereal disease, widespread among the numerous streetwalkers following World War I. (It is estimated that there were a hundred thousand prostitutes in Berlin in the mid-'20s.) Within the film's narrative, the image serves as an early warning sign of the existential danger that inheres in the nexus of city, night, and woman. In particular, the association made between the allure of the city and the fatal attraction of the prostitute is a classical trope dating back to the nineteenth century. The film splits woman into two irreconcilable halves: the woman in the street, who blends characteristics of the New Woman and the old femme fatale, and the woman in the house, who is portrayed as motherly, devoted, nurturing.[2]

The architects of Grune's film designed the street as a psychological, visionary space in which even inanimate objects are imbued with a life of their own. An advertising sign for an optometrist is transformed into a huge pair of blinking eyes that seem to follow our hapless adventurer (fig. 5). Connoting both the inner disposition of the protagonist (he is "all eyes") and the watchful function of the all-seeing camera, this hallucinatory, surreal image of things endowed with eyes also stands in for the film audience's gaze. Once again, the experience of walking the streets is linked to the experience of watching a film. The promise of new sights and unexpected wonders drives flaneurs and movie-goers alike. Cinema had become a form of compensation, the site of a possible, fuller reality that could not be had in a life dominated by bureaucracy and instrumental reason. Excess, ecstasy, and transgression were the early cinema's goals. Seduction, adultery, gambling, madness, murder, and mayhem were its motifs. And the metropolis was its setting. "Film is currently the vital power station of the big city dweller," wrote Gerhart Pohl in 1927.

> Cinema, the mass theater of the twentieth century, offers more than relaxation after work, more than inexpensive attractions. In film, four million people seek to fulfill their desire for relief from an empty and hectic existence, the desire to experience other countries which their meager wages make impossible, the desire to make love to women they would ordinarily never even meet, and to experience joys and troubles that are foreign to them. [3]

The artificiality of the studio sets only enhanced the magic of the street as a site of wonder and adventure. In the case of *Die Straße*, the production company actually relished the confusion between the make-believe world of the studio and the reality of the city. Their advertising brochure contained a brief essay, "Nachtaufnahme," in which Eugen Klöpfer, the film's "hero," vividly described the preparations for the filming of a night scene:

> Attention! Action! The play begins. . . And becomes reality. Forgotten are the gawking onlookers behind the barbed wire fence, forgotten is the lit

Fig. 4: Von Morgens bis Mitternachts *(Karl-Heinz Martin; Germany, 1922).*

Fig. 5: Die Straße.

Fig. 6: Ludwig Meidner, Ich und die Stadt, 1913. Oil on canvas, 60 x 50 cm. Private collection.

Fig. 7: Ludwig Meidner, Wannsee Bahnhof, 1913. Black ink on wove paper, 46.4 x 59.9 cm. Los Angeles County Museum of Art, The Robert Gore Rifkind Center for German Expressionist Studies.

dock of the Steglitz town hall tower, forgotten is Berlin's dark silhouette . . . or the annoying apparatus of the set. Only the radiant facade-city, with its surging human masses, its wildly circling illuminated signs, its hammering cars and ringing cyclists, lives.

I myself am no longer me. Instead, I am a medium who staggers hypnotized through the unchained chaos of the street. Limbered up and goaded on by the diverse desires for dance and frenzy and play and love. A person full of longing for unknown, shrill, enticing, smiling objects and people . . . until the light of the floodlights is put out and the nocturnal apparition fades before the reality of the starry night.[4]

The borders between the real and the simulated Berlin had become porous. The sheer technical accomplishment of having a wide avenue built in the studio with shop windows, cafés, bars, a dancing hall, and a police station attracted much attention when the film was produced. Reviewers marveled at the lifelike size of the sets and the powerful illusion they created. The set was a completely controlled, artificial environment that could be modulated and lighted to produce different moods: the shimmering nocturnal street, the dimly lit hallways and dark interiors, the windswept gray and empty street in the early morning.[5]

The design of the fake city, with its painted surfaces and subtly distorted dimensions, was the work of Ludwig Meidner, the well–known Expressionist painter of cityscapes and street scenes (figs. 6, 7).[6] His work for Die Straße represents his first and only involvement with film architecture (figs. 5, 12), but the film's project completely dovetailed with his own ambivalent fascination with the city. "The time has come at last," he had already written in 1914, "to start painting our real homeland, the big city which we all love so much."[7] Echoing the Futurist celebration of the modern, fast-paced metropolis, Meidner extolled the big city street as a metaphor for the new urban experience that required a different aesthetic:

A street is composed not of tonal values, but is a bombardment of whizzing rows of windows, of screeching lights between vehicles of all kinds and a thousand jumping spheres, scraps of human beings, advertising

signs, and shapeless colors. Painting in the open air is all wrong. We can't record instantaneously all the accidental and disorganized aspects of our motif and still make a picture out of it. We must organize, courageously and deliberately, the optical impressions we have absorbed in the great world outside, organize them into compositions. It is emphatically not a question of filling an area with decorative and ornamental designs à la Kandinsky or Matisse. It is a question of life in all its fullness: space, light and dark, heaviness and lightness, and the movement of things — in short, of a deeper insight into reality.[8]

Meidner criticized what he termed the vagueness and fuzziness of Impressionist pointillism and demanded instead sharp contours, heavy contrasts, diagonal lines of force, and, above all, explosive energy and intensity.

As the painter's subject matter was no longer nature but the industrial landscape constructed by engineers — "tumultuous streets, the elegance of iron suspension bridges, the gasometers . . . the rolling telephone wires and the harlequinade of the advertisement pillars"[9] — Meidner's own compositions came to display an aggressive and nonorganic, "constructed," cubo-futurist look. In contrast to his enthusiastic manifestoes, his series of Apocalyptic Landscapes (1912–13) emphasizes the dark and menacing side of the modern city and its threat to the individual. One of his numerous self portraits, I and the City (1913) shows an anguished face surrounded by a cataclysmic clutter of tumbling houses and disintegrating chimneys, steeples, and telegraph posts (fig. 6). A sense of anxiety and foreboding not found in the work of the Futurist and Cubist painters who influenced him dominates most of Meidner's street scenes. But he was not alone in presenting the metropolitan street in Germany as the locus of alienation and disharmony. George Grosz's numerous depictions of utter chaos in the streets, Ernst Ludwig Kirchner's paintings of streetwalkers in Berlin, and the attempts by such poets as Jakob van Hoddis (Meidner's close friend) or Alfred Lichtenstein to approximate in their verses the proliferation, incongruity, and simultaneity of visual impressions in the metropolis all come to mind.[10]

By the 1920s, Berlin had become the imaginary center of urban culture, drawing artists, intellectuals, tourists, migrants, and immigrants into its orbit like a magnet. The city had grown from one million inhabitants in 1877 to two million in 1905 and, after swallowing up the outlying areas, to nearly four million in 1920. Not surprisingly, a city of this size inspired paeans and tirades; it engendered feelings of exaltation and repulsion and led to euphoria and depression. The city became the primordial site of modernity to which painters, poets, and filmmakers returned obsessively. Encapsulating both the beauty and the ugliness, the exuberance and the gridlock, of urban life, Berlin always posed a challenge to representation. Its proliferation of signs, its chaotic diversity, and its kineticism pushed practitioners in various media to explore their limits.

The lack of language in silent film, which matches the weak ego boundaries characteristic of the city–dweller, increased the importance of the characters' surroundings. Architecture plays a major role in the silent street film, establishing the milieu that determines the fate of the characters. Buildings in silent films tend to engulf their struggling protagonists; the mise-en-scène often becomes the enemy. As Gilles Deleuze has stated.

> The non-organic life of things, a frightful life, which is oblivious to the wisdom and limits of the organism, is the first principle of Expressionism, valid for the whole of Nature, that is, for the unconscious spirit, lost in darkness, light which has become opaque, *lumen opacatum*. From this point of view natural substances and artificial creations, candelabras and trees, turbine and sun are no longer any different. A wall which is alive is dreadful; but utensils, furniture, houses and their roofs also lean, crowd around, lie in wait, or pounce. Shadows of houses pursue the man running along the street.[11]

Deleuze's comments are particularly apt for the filmic representation of the modern metropolitan street, in which everything becomes semioticized precisely because there is no other way to express inner thoughts, memories, desires, and anxieties than in exteriorized form through signs. Where nobody speaks, everything speaks.

"The street is not an arbitrary site," averred a reviewer of Grune's film in 1924;

> it is the most characteristic site of the pictorial vision of film today . . . it affords a vision solely focused on the exterior — and not the nuanced, less antithetical view which is basically characteristic of the interior view. Film demands movement from antithesis to antithesis: in its structure (crass juxtaposition of contrasting scenes), in its lighting (showing either glaring night or day but never dawn or dusk), as well as in its psychology (emphasizing absolute characters). What is missing everywhere are the *sfumato*, the scale, the transitions.[12]

It seems that silent film's inevitable and innate focus on the external traits of the visible world — sets, gestures, movement — brought film, once again, into a structural affinity with the experience of the street characterized by its chance encounters of strangers (whose intentions have to be "read" from outward signs), its focus on silent glances or stares, and its lack of any depth or psychological subtlety. On a perceptual level, then, there is not much difference between experiencing the street (which implies "reading" the exteriors of buildings and people) and watching a silent movie (whose lack of dialogue directs attention onto surfaces such as faces and sets). This may be another sign of the symbiotic, even synergetic relationship between cinema and the urban experience.

As in the case of the film's spectator, the urban flaneur loses himself for the moment — an experience Siegfried Kracauer called "Straßenrausch" (an intoxication with the street).[13] In his review of *Die Straße*, Kracauer wrote:

> The individuals of the big city streets have no sense of transcendence, they are only outer appearance, like the street itself, where so much is going on without anything really happening. The swirl of the characters resembles the whirl of atoms: they do not meet, but rather bump up against each other, they drift apart without separating. Instead of living connected with things, they sink down to the level of inanimate objects: of automobiles, walls, neon lights, irrespective of time, flashing on and off. . . Love is copulation,

Fig. 8: Berlin, Friedrichstraße, *at the turn of the century.*

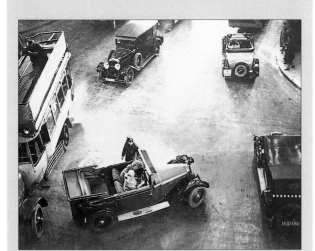

Fig. 9: Asphalt *(Joe May; Germany, 1929).*

Fig. 10: Hintertreppe *(Leopold Jessner; Germany, 1921).*

murder is accident, and tragedy never occurs. A wordless and soulless coexistence of directed automobiles and undirected desires. . .[14]

Kracauer's perceptive analysis of the commodification and instrumental rationality pervading modern city life suggests a way in which the urban landscape had radically reshaped the relationship of the subject to his surroundings. This revolutionary shift in the status of the subject explains, I believe, the obsessive fascination of artists with representing the city and the metropolitan street.

One of the last silent films, Joe May's melodrama *Asphalt*, exhibits the characteristic nexus of the street film: forbidden sexuality, criminality, and guilt in the milieu of a hectic and sensually excited metropolis (fig. 9). A young policeman falls in love with a young jewel thief and, because of her, falls under suspicion of having murdered her former lover. Out of a sense of duty, his own father, a senior constable, is forced to arrest him. But the woman, who herself has fallen in love with the policeman, testifies that he acted in self-defense. The pulp fiction material, signaled by the subtitle *The Policeman and Diamond Else*, was elevated by high production values with no expense spared. As with other street films, even the outdoor shots are highly stylized, a completely controlled "realism." Not only interiors but also streets and cityscapes were built in the studio. In *Asphalt*, the large traffic artery, the primary site in the film, measured a record four hundred meters in length and contained display windows (local shops were asked to show their wares for advertising purposes.) The studio street was lit with thousands of light bulbs in order to achieve the effect of a metropolitan street. The film's architect, Erich Kettelhut, described how the street was constructed "as the pedestrian sees it: sometimes swifter, then quieter again, gliding past the moving and the stationary, here and there, glancing forwards and to the side, upwards or into windows. It was necessary to provide the camera and its operator the most movement possible."[15] Achieving the desired realistic as well as deeply symbolic effect proved a particularly difficult task for the studio. Erich Pommer, the film's producer, elaborated further:

This film was created from the visual possibilities of the milieu and its effects upon the life of individuals. . . This street is no longer merely environment, no longer background. Fate appears, and the path of an individual is altered, naturally, simply, and nevertheless incomprehensibly. A scene springs to life, its emissions alter a person's life. The street becomes then a symbol of human life — an unending conjoining of fates.[16]

In this manner, the street appears as the existential site of modernity, in which the individual is both the object of, and unwitting participant in, a series of incomprehensible and uncontrollable processes. The dynamization of the setting in the street film is only a symptom of how the urban landscape had radically reshaped the relationship of the subject to his or her surroundings. In this genre, the street is emblematic of the metropolis, a central theme of literary modernism from Rilke's *Malte Laurids Brigge* (1910) to Döblin's *Berlin Alexanderplatz* (1929), from Georg Heym's poem "Gott der Stadt" (1911) to Brecht's poetry collection entitled *Aus dem Lesebuch für Stadtbewohner* (1930). Like the literature about the big city, the *Straßenfilm* (street film) bears witness to Germany's tormented experience of modernity.

The street film, the filmic subgenre inaugurated by *Die Straße*, was seen at the time in opposition to the *Kammerspielfilm* (chamber play film), named after the intimate *Kammerspiel*, which Max Reinhardt had developed at the turn of the century for the staging of intimate, psychologically complex melodramas. Lupu Pick and Carl Mayer's *Scherben* (Shards; 1921), Leopold Jessner's *Hintertreppe* (Backstairs; 1921) and Lupu Pick's *Sylvester* (1923) explored psychic spaces, emphasizing subtle gestures and silences that spoke volumes. These films unfolded their melodramatic plots (keeping to the Aristotelian unity of space and time) in domestic narratives articulated in claustrophobic sets consisting of bedroom, kitchen, and stairs (fig. 10). An occasional glimpse of the dark and gray outside provided no relief to the unremitting gloom of the private sphere with all its repressed and pent-up emotions that inexorably led to murder or suicide (fig. 11). These films present the criminal act as an escape from the unbearably monotonous life in which the protagonists find themselves. Similar to the style of Naturalism in theater, the working-class or lower middle-class characters are shown essentially to be creatures without the ability to articulate themselves; their lack of speech and rational thought finds refuge in compulsive gestures and instinctual behaviors. Silent film, with its emphasis on gesture and facial expression and through the use of close-ups and extreme light/dark contrasts, was the perfect medium for communicating unspoken and inexpressible pathos. F.W. Murnau's *Der letzte Mann*, not unlike *Die Straße*, contrasts both settings: the static, narrow, and repressive one of the home (the realm of old, haggard housewives) and the mobile, cosmopolitan, and adventurous site of the street, with its elegant hotel, glistening surfaces, and flirtatious young women (fig. 12). Again, as in *Die Straße,* the glorious life of the big city is shown as deceptive. The experience of the street as an alluring, but ultimately ruinous site is replayed in many other films of the period: Georg Wilhelm Pabst's *Die freudlose Gasse* (Joyless Street; 1925), Bruno Rahn's *Dirnentragödie* (The Tragedy of a Prostitute; 1927), Pabst's *Tagebuch einer Verlorenen* (Diary of a Lost Girl; 1927), and *Die Büchse der Pandora* (Pandora's Box; 1929). Murnau's *Sunrise*, made for Fox in Hollywood in 1927, also reflects the basic grammar of the Weimar street film. Moral tales of urban living, these films work through escape fantasies only to reject them — a structure that is similar to the movie experience itself: after exposing ourselves to transgression and the dark side of human nature, we return from the alternative dream space into the reality of daily life.

The street film also lent a visual grammar to crime stories that took place in public spaces: streets, stations, squares, towers, and derelict buildings that loomed over or closed in on the protagonists as they tried to escape their fate — in vain. The urban melodrama such as Fritz Lang's *Metropolis* and the entire genre of American *film noir* partake of this tradition. It is no accident that in the 1940s and '50s, many of the German exiles to Hollywood reinvented the traditional American gangster film in the image of the Weimar street film.

The term *film noir* was invented by French film critics after World War II who were in love with such movies because of their angst-ridden look and their existential message. Directors like Lang, Billy Wilder, and Robert Siodmak were known to make full use of visionary studio architecture and controlled lighting. Their emphasis on milieu, mood, and atmosphere (in contrast to Hollywood's usual emphasis on action and editing) produced a visual style that is still associated with a cinema in which the individual is up against larger forces. It is architecture's contribution to cinema to translate these deeply felt forces into lasting images.

Notes

[1] There is also a 1920 film version of Kaiser's *Von Morgens bis Mitternachts*, directed by Karl-Heinz Martin, who was known for his innovative staging of Expressionist plays, and with Ernst Deutsch as the protagonist (see pp. 72, 73). The film was apparently shown only once in Germany to a small audience (in Munich's Regina Lichtspiele in 1922); after a copy was found in Japan, it premiered in Germany in 1963. The sets consisted of black walls painted with white lines and abstract shapes. See *Von Morgens bis Mitternachts* (Munich: Filmmuseum München, 1993).
[2] Katharina Sykora elaborates further on the gender issues involved here in her essay "'Die Hure Babylon' und die 'Mädchen mit dem eiligen Gang': Zum Verhältnis 'Weiblichkeit und Metropole' im Straßenfilm der Zwanziger Jahre," in Katharina Sykora *et al.*, eds., *Die Neue Frau: Herausforderung für die Bildmedien der Zwanziger Jahre* (Marburg: Jonas Verlag, 1993), pp. 119–40. On the city/woman nexus, see also Elizabeth Wilson, *The Sphinx in the City: Urban Life, the Control of Disorder, and Women* (London: Virago Press, 1991); Elizabeth Grosz, "Bodies — Cities," in Beatriz Colomina, ed., *Sexuality and Space* (Princeton: Princeton Architectural Press, 1992), pp. 241–54.
[3] Gerhart Pohl, "Deutsche Kulturchronik," *Neue Bücherschau* (January 1927).
[4] Eugen Klöpfer, "Nachtaufnahme," in *Die Straße* 6 (brochure) (Berlin: Hansa-Film-Verleih, 1923), p.17. All translations in this essay are my own.
[5] On the status of "film cities," see Siegfried Kracauer's essay of 1926, "Kalikowelt," in *Ornament der Masse* (Frankfurt am Main: Suhrkamp, 1963), pp. 271–78 (see also pp. 144–45 of the present volume); Alfred Polgar, 'Im romantischen Gelände," *Berliner Tageblatt*, 6 March 1928; Karl Prümm, "Empfindsame Reisen in die Filmstadt," in Wolfgang Jacobsen, ed., *Babelsberg: Ein Filmstudio 1912–1992* (Berlin: Argon, 1992), pp. 117–34; Dr. Ernst Ulitzsch, "Die nächtliche Straße," *Der Kinematograph* 18, no. 894 (6 April 1924), pp. 7–8.
[6] On Meidner, see Thomas Grochowiak, *Ludwig Meidner* (Recklinghausen: Aurel Bongers, 1966); Carol S. Eliel, *The Apocalyptic Landscapes of Ludwig Meidner* (Munich: Prestel, 1989); Charles W. Haxthausen, "Images of Berlin in the Art of the Secession and Expressionism," in *Art in Berlin 1815–1989*, exh. cat. (Atlanta: High Museum of Art, 1989), pp. 61–82.
[7] Ludwig Meidner, "An Introduction to Painting Big Cities" (1914), in *Ludwig Meidner: An*

Fig. 11: Sylvester *(Lupu Pick; Germany, 1923).*

Fig. 12: Die Straße *(Karl Grune; Germany 1923).*

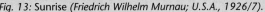

Fig. 13: Sunrise *(Friedrich Wilhelm Murnau; U.S.A., 1926/7).*

Expressionist Master, exh. cat. (Ann Arbor: University of Michigan Museum of Art, 1978), p. 30.
[8] Ibid.
[9] Ibid., p.31.
[10] See also *Stadtbilder: Berlin in der Malerei vom 17. Jahrhundert bis zur Gegenwart,* exh. cat. (Berlin Museum, 1987); Anthony Sutcliffe, ed., *Metropolis 1890–1940* (Chicago and London: University of Chicago Press, 1984); Charles W. Haxthausen and Heidrun Suhr, eds., *Berlin: Culture and Metropolis* (Minneapolis and Oxford: University of Minnesota Press, 1990); Peter-Klaus Schuster, ed., *George Grosz: Berlin-New York,* exh. cat. (Berlin: Nationalgalerie, 1994); Frank Whitford, "The City in Painting," in Edward Timms and David Kelley, eds., *Unreal City: Urban Experience in Modern European Literature and Art* (New York: St. Martins Press, 1985), pp. 45–64.
[11] Gilles Deleuze, *Cinema 1: The Movement–Image,* trans. Hugh Tomlinson and Barbara Habberjam (Minneapolis: University of Minnesota Press, 1986), p. 51.

[12] W.H., "Nächtliche Großstadtstraße im Film," *Film–Kurier,* no. 7 (8 January 1924).
[13] See Siegfried Kracauer, "Erinnerung an eine Pariser Straße," in *Straßen in Berlin und Anderswo* (Berlin: Arsenal, 1987), p. 7. On Kracauer's and other Weimar intellectuals' fascination with the street and the city, see Eckhardt Köhn, *Straßenrausch: Flânerie und kleine Form: Versuch zur Literaturgeschichte des Flâneurs bis 1933* (Berlin: Arsenal, 1989); Michael Bienert, *Die eingebildete Metropole: Berlin im Feuilleton der Weimarer Republik* (Stuttgart: Metzler, 1992).
[14] rac [Siegfried Kracauer], "Die Straße," *Frankfurter Zeitung,* 3 February 1924.
[15] Erich Kettelhut, "Asphalt," *Reichsfilmblatt,* 9 March 1929.
[16] Erich Pommer, "Kritische Filmschau," *Deutsche Filmzeitung,* 12 April 1929.

Shortly before Christmas 1924, the evening strollers on Berlin's "entertainment mile," Kurfürstendamm, were treated to an extraordinary spectacle. The entire facade of Berlin's largest movie theater, the Ufa Palast, had been tranformed into an enormous billboard, advertising the newest film by the acclaimed director Friedrich Wilhelm Murnau. As a prominent critic noticed excitedly, "The entire front ha[d] been rebuilt as a perspectival view of skyscrapers."[1] The film thus advertised, *Der letzte Mann*, was, in the following months, to become world-famous — not for its skyscrapers, but for its daringly innovative cinematographic style. Indeed, one has to look very carefully to see any skyscrapers in Murnau's film at all, even though contemporary reports tell us that he and his two set designers, Robert Herlth and Walter Röhrig, had gone to great expense to build sets offering an illusion of 30-story high-rises in the center of their city. These buildings did not purport to present a Berlin of the future — after all, everything else, the cars and elevated trains, kept their contemporary look. Instead, they served as icons of the metropolis in general, presented as a fast-paced, heartless place.

Oversized billboards had become the latest fashion in the German film industry, which was in the process of adopting American standards, in Berlin alone adding about 20 movie theaters, each with over a thousand seats, to its stock of about 380 theaters between 1924 and 1929.[2] Bringing images from the screen into the street, these enormous advertisements narrowed the gap between film and reality and merged, for an instant, film and architecture.

The fact that skyscrapers had been chosen to represent Murnau's brilliant melodrama — and the fact that they had been used in the film at all — reveals the contemporary fascination with a building type that stood at the center of widespread debates about the future of German cities. Whereas the period's architectural and urbanistic debates are remembered today primarily for their focus on the Bauhaus and the "new sobriety" of modern architecture, they were, in fact, much more complex, harboring a wealth of different, often well-argued positions on the urban questions of the time, such as city vs. country living, industrialisation vs. agrarianism, Americanism vs. medievalism.

A number of films, it seems, reflected these debates. Four years before Murnau's *Der letzte Mann*, Hans Werckmeister's *Algol* not only warned of the pernicious powers of machines but also juxtaposed the image of a skyscraper city as the location of vice and despair with that of a small town as the site of freedom and happiness. In *Aelita — Queen of Mars*, a Russian production conceived under the influence of the German discussions, the affluent ruling class on Mars lives under a dictatorship in a city with towering skyscrapers and gargantuan viaducts, and an army of slaves is kept in underground caverns to operate the power stations. The image of a futuristic city represents a repressed feudal society. In January 1927, these films were joined by *Metropolis*, one of the most startling and remarkable productions of its time, also, of course, advertised by oversized skyscraper billboards. "Thea von Harbou [the author of the script] was not only sensitive to all the undercurrents of the time, but indiscriminately passed on whatever happened to haunt her imagination. *Metropolis* was rich in subterranean content that, like contraband, had crossed the borders of consciousness without being questioned,"[3] wrote Siegfried Kracauer. Indeed, the film's success rested on the fact that it dealt with a large number of (not only urban) issues that had been widely discussed in recent years and were familiar to a broad audience. *Metropolis* addressed problems of the urban poor and social unrest, generational conflicts, vices and virtues of technology, and contemporary doubts about the redeeming power of religions. As has frequently been pointed out, many of these themes had been the leitmotiv of recent publications, films, and theater productions.[4] These literary sources not only established a number of topics that found their way into the melting pot of *Metropolis*; their public performance also created visual paradigms of compelling power. For example, in 1922, Max Reinhardt's Schauspielhaus, which Hans Poelzig had just turned into a gargantuan, magically illuminated cave, provided the compelling frame for Ernst Toller's *Machinenstürmer* (Machine Stormers; 1919) under the direction of Karl-Heinz Martin. The

Dietrich Neumann

Before and after *Metropolis*: Film and Architecture in Search of the Modern City

Fig. 1: *Decoration of the Ufa Palast am Zoo, Berlin, for the premiere of* Der letzte Mann, *23 December 1924.*

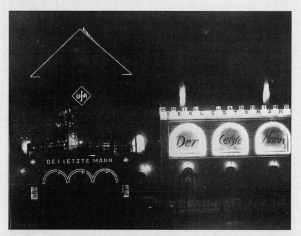

Fig. 2: Algol *(H.K. Werckmeister; Germany, 1920):* Robert Herne's Office. *Frame enlargement by Gerhard Ullmann, Munich.*

Fig. 3: *Unknown artist, Photomontage for theater decoration for the premiere of* Metropolis, *1926. British Film Institute, London.*

Fig. 4: Fritz Lang, Broadway, New York, 1924.

Fig. 5: Metropolis: Night in Metropolis.

Fig. 6: Metropolis: Maria in the Catacombs.

Fig. 7: Metropolis: Joh Fredersen's Office.

sets, created by John Heartfield, were celebrated by contemporary critics such as the prominent Max Osborn as showing the "grandiose truth of everyday life."[5] In these sets, we find direct inspiration for the climax of *Metropolis*: a view of the gigantic machine about to be destroyed by Luddite workers.[6]

But *Metropolis*, as the film's title indicates, was predominantly concerned with the city itself. Fritz Lang, who later often admitted that he had been more interested in the visual imagery of the film than in its social content, recalled how his original idea had been based on his fascination with the skyscrapers of New York which he saw for the first time in 1924 on a promotional tour for his medieval epic, *Die Nibelungen*:[7]

> The view of New York by night is a beacon of beauty strong enough to be the centerpiece of a film. . . There are flashes of red and blue and gleaming white, screaming green . . . streets full of moving, turning, spiraling lights, and high above the cars and elevated trains, skyscrapers appear in blue and gold, white and purple, and still higher above there are advertisements surpassing the stars with their light.[8]

Lang's enthusiastic descriptions of this phenomenon are still palpable in von Harbou's screenplay of *Metropolis* as

> a restless roaring sea with a surf of light. In the flashes and waves, the Niagara Falls of light, in the colour-play of revolving towers of light and brilliance *Metropolis* seems to have become transparent. The houses, dissected into cones and cubes by the moving scythes of the search-lights, gleamed, towering up, hovering, light flowing down their flanks like rain. The streets licked up the shining radiance, themselves shining, and the things gliding upon them, an incessant stream, threw cones of light before them.[9]

Lang tried to capture the overwhelming impression of the multitude of lights on Broadway and their constant movement with his photographic camera by exposing the film twice (fig. 4).[10] And, no doubt, his photographs directly informed the cinematography in the night-views of *Metropolis* (fig. 5).

Although partially adapting Lang's enthusiasm for this "beacon of beauty," von Harbou gave complexity, depth, and a sense of mystery to his vision. When Freder discovers the dark side of his city, he confronts his father, the almighty ruler: "[Y]our great glorious, dreadful city of Metropolis roars out, proclaiming that she is hungry for fresh human marrow and human brain and then the living food rolls on, like a stream, into the machine-rooms, which are like temples, and that, just used, is thrown up."[11]

One is instantly reminded of Oswald Spengler's anti-urban notion of the city as a man-eating monster, which he had formulated in 1918 in his first drafts for *Decline of the West*: "Now the giant city sucks the country dry, insatiably and incessantly demanding and devouring fresh streams of men till it wearies and dies in the midst of an almost uninhabited waste of country."[12] Von Harbou developed this image into a complex and compelling metaphor for the city as a being, whose individual but interdependent spaces — the skyscrapers, machine halls, and catacombs — fulfilled a body's functions as its heart, hands, and mind. The creators of the city of Metropolis, mainly Lang, von Harbou, and the three designers Erich Kettelhut, Otto Hunte, and Karl Vollbrecht, went to great lengths to devise a variety of memorable urban spaces that are all part of a complex three-dimensional entity. There are several spatial layers underground: the ancient catacombs, gigantic caves with quarters for the workmen, and the halls with the mighty machines. Above ground are the towering buildings and many layers of traffic, overshadowed by the sublime "New Tower of Babel" in the center. Somewhere in this city are a Gothic cathedral, a sports stadium, a nightclub, and pleasure gardens for the *jeunesse dorée*. Emphasis is clearly placed on vertical connections between these different parts. Staircases, steeply inclined tunnels, and especially elevators play a central role in the film.

Von Harbou adopted visions of subterranean spaces, often used as metaphorical realms of the oppressed, which had been popular in late nineteenth-century science fiction.[13] Prominent among novels with such a theme were H. G. Wells's *Time Machine* (1895) and *When the Sleeper Awakes* (1897). In the only contemporary critique of *Metropolis*'s urban vision, it was in fact Wells who sharply criticized this vertical organization of a city.[14] Wells recognized "decaying fragments" of his own *When the Sleeper Awakes,* which described the London of the future as a monstrous skyscraper fortress with dark underground factories and the apartments of the privileged in the higher, lighter regions. Having apparently never been happy with this novel, which he termed "one of the most ambitious and least satisfactory of my works,"[15] he had long been convinced that such a vision was outdated,[16] arguing that the development of the real estate market would lead to the location of industry and housing for the poor in suburbs instead of underneath the city: "This vertical social stratification is stale old stuff. So far from being a hundred years hence, *Metropolis* in its forms and shapes is already as a possibility a third of a century out of date."[17] Wells suggested that if Lang had talked to some contemporary architects, his vision would have been more accurate.

Such accusations were not entirely fair. Wells had gotten tangled up between his two envisioned roles as prophet and novelist, a predicament from which *Things to Come*, his own film about the urban future made 10 years later, would also suffer. Of course, Lang and von Harbou had *not* intended to produce a realistic projection of urban development or even an ideal city, because such a utopia would have provided an unlikely background for a dramatic battle between good and evil. And given Lang's interest in the architectural profession, we can assume that he was familiar with the highly publicized visions of contemporary architects, such as Antonio Sant' Elia's *Città futurista* of 1914 (fig. 9), the glass cathedrals and garden cities of Germany's Expressionist architects (fig. 11), Le Corbusier's *Plan voisin* of 1922, Hugh Ferriss's visions of a future New York (1922–29) (p. 114, fig. 2), or contemporary visualizations in American popular magazines (fig. 10). Instead of attempting to accurately predict the future or design a pleasant utopia, as architects would usually do, *Metropolis* illustrated very real *contemporary* fears and ambiguous attitudes about cities.

Of course, many Germans shared Lang's naive enthusiasm for the skyline of New York and regarded sky-

scrapers as a fascinating icon of modernity, whether used as toys and in advertising or as the subject of lighthearted American film comedies such as Harold Lloyd's *Safety Last*, which had had great success in Germany in 1923 as *Ausgerechnet Wolkenkratzer* (Especially Skyscrapers). Among architects, town planners, and politians, however, there had been heated discussions and bitter fights about urban questions that mirrored widespread doubts about this building form. The debate about skyscrapers often served as a platform for the anti-Americanism of conservative architects, planners, and journalists. Innumerable statements accused American skyscrapers of depriving their neighbors of light and air and of being the most vulgar symbols of rampant capitalism, of being, as Cornelius Gurlitt, a prominent art historian, put it, "the worst invention of mankind."[18] Even the liberal Siegfried Kracauer called them "towering monsters, owing their existence to the unlimited greed of beastly capitalism, assembled in the most chaotic and senseless fashion, clad in a luxurious fake architecture, which is far from appropriate for its profane purpose."[19] On the other hand, Kracauer and many others seemed determined that Germany should build skyscrapers nevertheless, as long as they were different from the American examples. In the eyes of many, a "Germanization of the skyscraper"[20] offered the chance to create, on a higher cultural level, a valid alternative to this American invention, revealing for the first time "the true inner meaning of the skyscraper."[21] The German high-rise building, such critics claimed, would be less historicist than the American skyscraper, and, as a result of highly restricted and socially responsible city planning, there would be only one huge building at the center of each city, a modern version of the medieval cathedral. To a large degree, these skyscraper projects owed their attraction to their apparent symbolic and political potential. Many conservatives believed that the erection of such buildings could "prove visibly that the Germans are not a dying populace, but able to work and able to build new paths to a new ascent."[22] The lost war and the enormous reparation payments of the Versailles treaty led to a desperate nationalism and the idea that a

Fig. 8: Metropolis.

Fig. 9 (left): Antonio Sant' Elia, Electric Power Station, 1914.
Fig. 10 (right): A vision of New York in the future from Scientific American, 1913.

Fig. 11: Hans Scharoun, Volkshausgedanke, 1919. Watercolor, 47.6 x 36 cm. Akademie der Künste, Berlin.

Fig. 12: Friedrich Wilhelm Murnau, New York City's Skyline from the Brooklyn Bridge, 1926. Enlargement from 3-D photograph by Heinrich Gräfenstein.

Fig. 13: Metropolis: The Workers' Underground City.

Fig. 14: Walter Gropius, Monument for the March Dead in Weimar, 1920–22. Reinforced concrete.

monumental symbolic gesture could demonstrate the emergence of an unvanquished German will after the war, offering reconciliation with the lost spirituality of the Middle Ages.

Thousands of such projects were designed and published, among them compelling examples like the Messe Tower in Leipzig and Otto Kohtz's Reichshaus am Königsplatz in Berlin (p. 102, figs. 14, 16). Young, liberal, avant-garde architects rejected such monumental attempts at single buildings in the centers of cities and tried their hands at skyscraper designs made out of glass or in heterogeneous forms that reacted to local conditions (p. 102, fig. 15). For anyone familiar with architectural debates in the Weimar Republic, the central view onto the skyscrapers in *Metropolis* combined an exaggerated version of the dark streets of American cities with the notion of a central tower that had played such an important part in recent discussions and that represented the most conservative contemporary approach to skyscraper design and town planning in Germany. The most striking antithesis to the looming tower above is the workers' living quarters underground. In the central square is a monument with a huge gong that calls them to work, a symbol of repression (fig. 13). Significantly, the base for this gong was modeled on Walter Gropius's dynamic monument for striking miners who had been shot dead in Weimar during riots in 1921 (fig. 14). Right-wing politicians had heavily critized Gropius for this monument. Thus, in both levels of Metropolis — underground and above ground — one finds references to contemporary debates on monumental architecture and the architecture of monuments. Meanwhile, the only references to Expressionist architecture in Germany are to be found in places of vice, such as the Yoshiwara Nightclub and the pleasure gardens frequented by sons of the elite, thereby successfully labeling such architecture as decadent. It is no coincidence that Yoshiwara, the name of Tokyo's amusement quater, was chosen; von Harbou's novel contains numerous openly racist allusions to Asians and their nefarious dealings with gambling, crime, and prostitution. In contrast, the old Gothic Cathedral, where the final reconciliation takes place, clearly identifies the city as

German, or at least Northern European.

The experience of the city itself in *Metropolis* is one of fear, danger, and oppression, of loneliness and unsuccessful struggle. In her novel, Thea von Harbou had offered a preferable counterpart to urban life, very much in accordance with contemporary discussions: When Freder's new friend Josaphat is kidnapped from the city by airplane, he kills the pilot and parachutes into an idyllic landscape where he is nursed by a kind country woman before returning to the city to join Freder in his fight.

Two years after Lang's visit in 1926, his colleague Murnau went to the United States to produce *Sunrise* and also eagerly documented street scenes in New York and Los Angeles. Interestingly, just as Lang had attempted to capture the multitude of impressions on Broadway by exposing images twice, Murnau used a 3-D camera to record the particular depth of urban spatial experience.[23] He photographed the view through the suspension cables of the Brooklyn Bridge onto Manhattan's skyline, or a pedestrian's view into the depths of the street-canyons of New York (figs. 12, 15). Murnau's photographs show all the characteristics of the then popular, commercially available three-dimensional photographs, especially their particular emphasis on depth of field.[24] *Sunrise* in particular profitted from this emphasis on space, the city being displayed and conquered horizontally and through a carefully orchestrated ride on a trolleycar from the green suburbs through the industrialized outskirts into the heart of the city, toward the impressive vista of the central square. What Murnau created here was the opposite of what Lang and von Harbou had attempted; the vertical layering of Metropolis was juxtaposed with a carefully demonstrated horizontal organization. Whereas Lang's *Metropolis* had brought glimpses and impressions of the American city to Europe, Murnau imported the vision of a modern European city into an American film, thus creating the first examples of the European brand of modern architecture in the United States. For both men, photographs of New York City played a crucial role in the form-finding process.

Murnau made the city-country conflict a central theme in his film, picking it up again in *City Girl* (1931; originally called *Our Daily Bread*, it was eventually finished by the studio without his supervision.) According to Murnau, the later film was "about the estrangement of the modern city dwellers and their ignorance about Nature's sources of sustenance."[25] In *City Girl*, a young peasant, Lem, goes to the city, meets Kate, a waitress in a diner, marries her, and takes her home. She is met with utter distrust by Lem's father, but eventually wins him over. The city itself is not shown, but is evoked most prominently by postcards of skyscrapers which Lem buys to send home, by the small diner in a crowded street, and by Kate's bare room close to an elevated railroad, where she nurtures a sickly little plant on her windowsill. An illuminated billboard across the street advertises tours to the countryside with an image of a couple in a rowboat — Murnau's ironic reference to the key scene in *Sunrise*.

It was Lang's *Metropolis* that had an almost immediate impact on urbanistic visions in other films and in popular culture, where the debate about monumentality and the role of the skyscraper continued. The first response was the British film *High Treason* (Maurice Elvey, 1929), which presented London in the near future, with some modest high-rise buildings with helicopter pads reflecting the British reluctance to experiment at all with high-rise buildings during the 1920s (fig. 16). The American science fiction comedy *Just Imagine* followed in 1930. This film's gigantic set of a future city reflected Hugh Ferriss's recently published drawings for a "Metropolis of Tomorrow," featured high-rise buildings spaciously located on a grid extending endlessly, and was intended as a bright, sophisticated, and entertaining response to Lang's dark masterpiece. Many years later, in films such as *Blade Runner* and *Batman*, the influence of *Metropolis* was still apparent.

Gargantuan billboards above theater entrances continued to be a preferred means of advertising movies throughout the 1920s. For *Asphalt*, the hugely successful urban drama of 1928, the facade of Berlin's Ufa Palast am Zoo carried a billboard on which illuminated office buildings with blinking advertisements formed the backdrop for an array of cutout cars and double-decker buses that were mechanically kept in con-

stant motion (p. 111, fig. 7). The often-described vision of the contemporary city as a whirlpool of light, speed, and rushing traffic — in itself somewhat utopian[26] — was presented here to be seen from precisely the streets it claimed to represent, adding to the effect. In the same year, Lang and von Harbou's next film was released, *Woman in the Moon*. It did not deal with urban issues at all, but with space travel. Von Harbou had, once again, instinctively chosen a topic of widespread interest, Germany's "rocket craze."[27] Skyscrapers, however, still acted as an icon of modernity capable of catching the attention of the public strolling on the Kurfürstendamm. For the premiere of *Woman in the Moon*, Rudi Feld, head designer at Ufa, turned the entire facade of the Ufa Palast into a dark blue depiction of space, studded with hundreds of small lightbulbs, showing the moon on the left and a three-dimensionally modeled globe on the right (figs. 17, 18). On the surface of this miniature earth, an excited commentator saw "an excellently built skyscraper city, whose buildings are lit up from inside; this city, however, is built as a crater, so that a shining rocket can shoot out of it and later return into it."[28]

The skyscrapers on such billboards and the ones on film sets remained, apart from a few minor examples, practically the only ones that could be built during the 1920s in Germany. Seeing an oversized image of Greta Garbo, Adolf Behne, the shrewd chronicler of urban life in Weimar, argued that one should not underestimate the evocative power of such advertisements: "The street, a giant collective, creates a new type of human being. . . Since antiquity there have not been such images of gods and goddesses."[29] Architecture had begun to act in the movies; skyscrapers had risen to the status of film stars.

Fig. 15: Friedrich Wilhelm Murnau, Downtown New York City, 1926. Enlargement from 3-D photograph by Heinrich Gräfenstein.

Fig. 16: High Treason (Maurice Elvey; England, 1929).

Fig. 17: Rudi Feld, Decoration of the Ufa Palast am Zoo, Berlin, for the premiere of Frau im Mond, 1929.

Dietrich Neumann

Fig. 18: Detail of figure 17.

Notes

[1] Willy Haas, "Der letzte Mann," *Film–Kurier* (24 December 1924).

[2] Uta Berg-Ganschow and Wolfgang Jacobsen, "Kino-Marginalien," in Uta Berg-Ganschow and Wolfgang Jacobsen, eds., *Film . . . Stadt . . . Kino . . . Berlin* (Berlin: Argon, 1987).

[3] Siegfried Kracauer, *From Caligari to Hitler: A Psychological History of the German Film* 1947 (Princeton: Princeton University Press, 1974), p. 150.

[4] Anton Kaes, "Metropolis: City, Cinema, Modernity," in Timothy Benson, ed., *Expressionist Utopias*, exh. cat. (Los Angeles County Museum of Art, 1993), pp. 146–65. Kaes mentions, among others, Georg Kaiser's plays *The Coral* and *Gas*, or Karel Chapek's play *R.U.R.* (1924); the films *Algol* and *Aelita* were also influenced by Kaiser's play and in turn contributed to the visual imagery of *Metropolis*.

[5] Max Osborn, *Die Maschinenstürmer*, in *Berliner Morgenpost*, 13 July 1922.

[6] An American critic, Hermann George Scheffauer, described it enthusiastically to his audience at home: "The last picture is one of the most grandiose ever built up on the modern stage. It is the birth, the apotheosis of the Mechanistic Age. . . It has ponderous upright boilers, a walking-beam, a tremendous red flywheel, ladders and galleries for the engineer, a substructure of brick, and furnace doors red and roaring with flame" (Hermann George Scheffauer, "The Machine Stormers," in H.G. Scheffauer, *New Vision in the German Arts* [New York: B.W. Huebsch, 1924], pp. 224–53).

[7] "German Director Tells of Visit to Hollywood," *New York Times*, 11 November 1924.

[8] Fritz Lang, "Was ich in Amerika sah: Neuyork — Los Angeles" (1924), quoted in Fred Gehler and Ulrich Kasten, *Fritz Lang: Die Stimme von Metropolis* (Berlin: Henschel Verlag, 1990), p. 9.

[9] Thea von Harbou, *Metropolis* (1927), reprint (Boston: Gregg Press, 1975), p. 37.

[10] Erich Mendelsohn, *Amerika: Bilderbuch eines Architekten* (1926), reprint with commentary by Herbert Molderings (Wiesbaden: Vieweg Verlag, 1991), pp. 44, 90. One of the photographs taken in preparation for the filming of *Metropolis* was given by Lang to his friend the architect Erich Mendelsohn, who included it in this photographic essay about American architecture. The inclusion of a film director's photograph in this book was especially fitting, since the volume represents an attempt to apply cinematographic principles to a photographic report. As El Lissitzky wrote in 1927: "Turning the pages of this book is as captivating as a dramatic movie" (idem, p. 90)

[11] Von Harbou (note 9), p. 37.

[12] Oswald Spengler, *The Decline of the West* (London: George Allen and Unwin, 1926), p. 102.

[13] Rosalind Williams, *Notes on the Underground* (Cambridge, MA: MIT Press, 1992), pp. 121–75.

[14] Herbert George Wells, "Mr. Wells Reviews a Current Film," *New York Times Magazine*, 17 April 1927, pp. 4, 22.

[15] J.R. Hammond, *An H.G. Wells Companion: A Guide to the Novels, Romances and Short Stories* (London: Macmillan, 1979), p. 94.

[16] Ibid., p. 95.

[17] Wells (note 14), p. 4.

[18] Cornelius Gurlitt, "Stadt der Zukunft," *Bauwelt* 5, no. 21 (1914), p. 21.

[19] Siegfried Kracauer, "Turmhäuser," *Frankfurter Zeitung*, 2 March 1921, p. 1.

[20] Rainer Stommer, "Germanisierung des Wolkenkratzers: Die Hochhausdebatte in Deutschland bis 1921," *Kritische Berichte* 3 (1982), pp. 36–54.

[21] Martin Mächler, "Zum Problem des Wolkenkratzers," *Wasmuths Monatshefte für Baukunst* 5 (1920-21), p. 260.

[22] Bruno Möhring, "Über die Vorzüge der Turmhäuser," Stadtbaukunst alter und neuer Zeit 1 (1920), p. 353.

[23] Two hundred of Murnau's stereoscopic photographs have recently been rediscovered. See Ursula von Keitz, "Die sichtbare Stadt," in *Kino*Movie*Cinema: 100 Jahre Film*, exh. cat. (Berlin: Martin Gropius Bau, 1995) pp. 44–48.

[24] 3–D cameras had been available since the turn of the century. Taken with a heavier, special camera with two lenses, the photographs could only be viewed three dimensionally through a viewing apparatus. The photographic prints were developed directly from the film and glued onto cardboards 9 by 18 centimeters in size to fit the standard viewing device.

[25] Murnau, quoted in Lotte Eisner, *Murnau* (Berkeley: University of California Press, 1973), p. 197.

[26] Compare Siegfried Kracauer's sarcastic review of the famous documentary *Berlin, Die Sinfonie der Großstadt*: "[L]uckily all this senseless commotion is not Berlin itself, but just the result of confused ideas, which some writers' brains have cooked up about a metropolitan city according to their senses" ("Wir schaffens," *Frankfurter Zeitung*, 17 November 1927).

[27] Michael J. Neufeld, "Weimar Culture and Futuristic Spaceflight Fad in Germany, 1923–1933," *Technology and Culture* 31 (1990), pp. 725-52. Thea von Harbou had originally planned to have *Metropolis* end with the flight of Fredersen and Maria in a rocket out of the city. See Reinhold Keiner, *Thea von Harbou und der deutsche Film bis 1933* (Hildesheim: Olms, 1984), p. 103.

[28] Quoted in Michael Esser, "Der Alltag der Arbeiter," in *Kino*Movie*Cinema* (note 23), pp. 57–62.

[29] Adolf Behne, "Kunstaustellung Berlin," *Das neue Berlin*, no. 8 (1929), pp. 150–52.

What a difference a half-century makes. Fifty years ago, New York was America's favorite celluloid city, an El Dorado of capitalism where ruthless ambition was rewarded with a future of economic and social transformation. Now, however, as depicted in a spate of recent popular films, not only is New York no longer the dramatis personae in America's future; it has become a cartoon of its former self. From delirium to decay to nostalgia for a mythical past in the face of an impossible future, this cinematic empire has gone the way of the world's greatest civilizations.

Delirious New York

"New York," wrote newspaper columnist Walter Winchell in 1954, "is a glorious monument to the 20th century."[2] Writing from the vantage point of one of New York's most glamorous decades, Winchell described a place that had produced some of the century's most avant-garde literature, theater, art, and architecture. Film, however, was the medium that represented the city most persuasively to the general public. Popular filmmakers took the chaos of the city — social trends, historical facts, tabloid reports of dockside crimes, hype about the latest skyscrapers, gossip about society nightclubbers — and gave it the coherent shape of fiction, providing vast audiences with new frames in which to perceive New York's reality. King Vidor's *The Crowd* (1928) stood out as one of the most compelling portraits of New York in the late '20s. Its skyline served as an icon of hope for the arriving protagonist; a gigantic skyscraper (shot in an amazing trick sequence), with vast offices inside, stood for the sabering indifference of the masses.

Part fiction, part fact, celluloid New York was further amplified by filmmakers' geographical distance from the real New York. Fritz Lang's *Metropolis*, for example, was a futurist projection of an awesome, but soulless technocracy. Inspired by Lang's first glimpse of New York's skyline, the film was actually designed and made at the Ufa studios outside Berlin. Hollywood created its first great portraits of New York in the late 1920s, when movie studios three thousand miles from the real New

York fashioned an imaginary city on darkened sound stages. Fox Film's 1930 release of *Just Imagine*, a musical-comedy version of *Metropolis*, presented the flip side of Lang's chilling urban vision, a multilevel, setback-moderne city of commerce with a skyline in the shape of ever-rising stock charts (fig. 1).[3]

For the millions of Americans suffering because of the Depression, this movie-made Manhattan offered a place in which to ascend upward and onward. Indeed, the modern city — and its busy hotels, shops, and office buildings — provided the place for people of different backgrounds and classes to intersect and interact and be transformed in the process. Joan Crawford rose from shop girl to tycoon's mistress in its department stores.[4] Fred Astaire and Ginger Rogers danced in its nightclubs far above the city's bread lines. And Greta Garbo floated through its glass-enclosed penthouses overlooking unlimited vistas of shimmering skyscrapers. In fact, movie-made skyscrapers, such as the ones in *Child of Manhattan* (Edward Buzzelli; 1933) or those in Busby Berkeley's famous ballet scene in *42nd Street* (Lloyd Bacon; 1933) were the only ones being built at this time, sustaining the public's hope for the future of the city and, by extension, for themselves (figs. 2, 3).

Naked New York

The 1940s and '50s brought with them a new New York aesthetic. Jolted by the harsh reality of World War II, the powerful immediacy of wartime documentaries, and the artistic prestige of postwar Italian neo-realist cinema, many of Hollywood's leading filmmakers fled the stylized confines of sound stages and shot on real locations in New York. Such films as *The Naked City* (Jules Dassin; 1948), *On the Waterfront* (Elia Kazan; 1954), and *The Sweet Smell of Success* (Alexander Maekedrick; 1957) focused on the city's vital, gritty presence (figs. 4, 5). These films extolled an earthy New York whose Weegee-esque underside proved to be as compelling an image for moviegoers as the effervescent high life depicted in celluloid skyscrapers (figs. 2, 3). Signaling this evolution in New York's cinematic image, 1940s and '50s movies took place on the streets, on

Donald Albrecht

New York, Olde York: The Rise and Fall of a Celluloid City[1]

Fig. 1: Just Imagine *(David Butler; U.S.A., 1930).*

Fig. 2: Child of Manhattan *(Edward Buzzelli; U.S.A., 1933).*

Fig. 3: 42nd Street *(Lloyd Bacon; U.S.A., 1933).*

Donald Albrecht

Fig. 4: Naked City *(Jules Dassin; U.S.A., 1948). The Museum of Modern Art, Film Stills Archive, New York.*

Fig. 5: On the Waterfront *(Elia Kazan; U.S.A., 1954).*

Fig. 6, 7: *Richard Sylbert, Conceptual sketch for* Dick Tracy *(Warren Beatty; 1990):* Roof of the Club Ritz *(above),* The Shack outside the City *(below). Charcoal and ink on heavy tracing paper, approx. 25 cm x 30 cm.*

the docks, in lacquered black cars. Increasingly graphic cinematography captured the city's own stark contrasts.

Released in 1961, Blake Edwards's *Breakfast at Tiffany's* was a hard-edged fairy tale that blended the impulse toward realism with a stylized sense of glamour.[5] The film expressed the last gasp of high-style New York, before fashion's "youthquake" made elegance obsolete. The Cinderella character of Holly Golightly — played by Audrey Hepburn — embodied the city's ability to turn a country bumpkin into a cosmopolitan sophisticate. Her easy chic of black Givenchy dresses lured a generation to New York.

Breakfast at Tiffany's also straddled the fault line between a fondly remembered New York and one we would rather forget. Its New York was poised between a city confident in its postwar role as the world's cultural and financial capital and one on the brink of bankruptcy. Still, author John Cheever's New York, a city "filled with a river light,"[6] was about to descend into the dark and alienating locus of Kitty Genovese's murder.[7]

Nihilistic New York

As post-Winchell New York declined in the 1960s and '70s, a decidedly unglamorous city appeared on screen. Such films as *Midnight Cowboy* (John Schlesinger; 1969) and *Taxi Driver* (Martin Scorsese; 1976) blended real-life stories of urban alienation, bankruptcy, and poverty into the city's ever-evolving movie persona, creating another mythic New York: a cesspool of graffiti-filled subways and crime-ridden streets.[8] Far from the energized crowds of earlier cinematic New York, Martin Scorsese's taxi driver spent his days and nights alone in his cab and in single-occupancy flop houses, his sole attempts at social interaction occurring in porn theaters. In *Escape from New York* (John Carpenter; 1981), the Manhattan of the near future was a maximum-security prison. Inhabited and controlled by criminal gangs, this was a city of abandoned skyscrapers, garbage-strewn streets, and anarchy. By the late 1960s, the future was offering the specter of decay for a once-proud city.

Retro New York

Nostalgia was a keynote of the mid-1970s. The humiliating end of the Vietnam War, the oil crisis, the Bicentennial — all made Americans yearn for clear victory, economic plenty, and the country's lost innocence. Films about New York produced at this time were also suffused with nostalgia — less nostalgia for an earlier city, however, than nostalgia for an earlier city depicted in the movies.

Film, of course, has an exceptional capacity to capture the palpable details of a particular moment's clothes, hairstyles, mannerisms, and gestures. That's what makes the cinema such a powerful source of nostalgia, especially for a new crop of '70s directors raised on classic Hollywood movies. Woody Allen and Martin Scorsese created some of the first of the retro–New York movies, reviving their childhood memories of the on– and offscreen city. Allen's *Manhattan* (1978), mostly filmed on location in New York, featured vintage black–and-white cinematography and a score with music by George Gershwin, while Scorsese's 1977 *New York, New York* was shot on lavish, stylized sets built on sound stages in Hollywood.[9] Both set the neurotic entanglements of contemporary New Yorkers against the romantic certainties of old Hollywood.[10]

Allen and Scorsese's bittersweet evocations of a bygone New York were far more personal and ambiguous than a series of later retro movies which includes *Batman*, *Dick Tracy*, and *The Hudsucker Proxy* (Ethan and Allen Cohen; 1994). In these films, the retro theme was reduced to a simplistic mind-set. New York was no longer a visionary city of complex forces, but a cartoon in which caricatures of good and evil did battle, and good always won.

Batman opens with a sinister, but romantic image of Manhattan skyscrapers, nostalgically recalling the real view that inspired *Metropolis*. However, while the New York of *Metropolis* was a dynamic, futuristic construction of the era's most progressive trends in architecture and design, *Batman*'s New York — named Gotham City — is a decaying post-Industrial Revolution city without a future. Anton Furst's sets offer viewers a pastiche of visual quotations from turn-of-the-century designers, ranging from illustrators such as Gustave Doré to architects Otto Wagner, Louis Sullivan, and Antonio Gaudí, who dreamed of the industrially sublime city. In *Batman*, buildings appear "like hell erupted through the pavement and kept on growing," according to director Tim Burton.[11] Under these immense buildings — cantilevering outward and bridging up and over the city — there is no sunlight, only muted grays, inky blacks, steam, and fog. Furst's late nineteenth-century version of the city of the future becomes almost Piranesian in its fascination with a mythical, antique New York. Like Piranesi's Rome, Furst's New York is a sublime ruin that can only be evoked.[12]

Dick Tracy's nostalgia is for a gangster-era New York. The film is *The Naked City* with painted shadows, Pop Art without the irony. Stephen Sondheim's incidental music is retro-speakeasy, Milena Canonero's costumes are neo-Carol Lombard, and the film's saturated palette — red, orange, yellow, green, blue, indigo, and violet — suggests Tracy's straightforward, unambiguous morality. Black — the absence of color — cloaks the film's mysterious and evil stranger, known only as The Blank. "From a graphic point of view," cinematographer Vittorio Storaro has noted, "I was trying to be very, very clear, as clear as possible, that life at this moment was a conflict between two energies. One is day, one is night. One is good, one is evil."[13] Richard Sylbert's sets underscore *Dick Tracy*'s nostalgia for such a clear–cut time and place (figs. 6, 7). The villain's headquarters, for example, is part Albert Speer — with the black-and-red color scheme of the Nazi flag — and part Cedric Gibbons, the legendary MGM art director whose sound-stage New York embodied definitive Hollywood-on-the-Hudson.[14]

The Hudsucker Proxy presents yet another nostalgic portrait of New York, this one paying homage to screwball comedies à la Preston Sturges.[15] As the film's narrator says, "You can never tell about the future, but the past . . . that's another story." Largely set in 1958 (but freely borrowing from 1930s and '40s movies), *Hudsucker* offers a familiar parade of New York types and settings: a crowded newsroom with an editor named Smitty, cigar-chomping exec-

utives in Art Deco suites, a savvy career girl with a crackling Katharine Hepburn accent, and a hero struggling for his big break in New York, having arrived by bus from Muncie, Indiana. The film's plot is a capitalist reverie in which labor and management fight each other — the former enslaved in mail-room dungeons, the latter ensconced in sound-stage-scaled boardrooms at the pinnacle of a skyscraper.

Hudsucker's towers self-consciously evoke a long history of cinema iconography. Movies have traditionally ascribed rich and complex associations to skyscrapers — technology, industry, chance, sexual tension, violence. A sable coat falls from a Fifth Avenue penthouse and changes the life of a poor secretary in *Easy Living* (Mitchell Leisen; 1937). A playgirl refuses to dance with a throng of revelers, who feverishly push her to her death from a skyscraper rooftop nightclub in *Gold Diggers of 1935* (Busby Berkeley). From the mast of the Empire State Building, King Kong threatens to destroy the greedy city below (fig. 8), while a love-smitten New York career girl is punished at the landmark's base for a shipboard romance in *Love Affair* (Leo McCarey; 1939) and its 1957 remake, *An Affair to Remember* (Leo McCarey). (Foolishly gazing up in anticipation of meeting her lover on the viewing platform above, she steps into 34th Street to meet an oncoming bus.) And in the concluding moments of *The Fountainhead*, the architect Howard Roark's wife ascends his latest towering creation in an open elevator cab, rising toward her husband standing at its apex, alone and invincible (figs. 9, 11). *Hudsucker* recycles this icon to serve its plot of Capra-esque serendipity: the president's leap to his death from Hudsucker Industries' 45th-floor boardroom coincides with the hero's entry into the building at the beginning of his rise up the corporate ladder.[16]

The constructed urban ensembles of *Batman*, *Dick Tracy*, and *Hudsucker Proxy* represent hermetic versions of the city which offer safety from the real, contemporary one. Their view of New York mythologizes its pre-1960s incarnation — perhaps the last time there seemed to be a cohesion to the city and a hope for its future. Movies also had a narrative logic then. There was no senseless violence. People were killed for

Fig. 8: King Kong *(Merian C. Cooper and Ernest B. Schoedsack; U.S.A., 1933).*

Fig. 9: The Fountainhead *(King Vidor; U.S.A., 1949).* "The Fountainhead" © 1949 Turner Entertainment Co.. All rights reserved.

Fig. 10: Blade Runner *(Ridley Scott; U.S.A., 1982:* Hades Landscape. *Photo: Virgil Murano, Los Angeles.* © 1982, The Blade Runner Partnership.

revenge, for love, for money, but never because they happened to be in the wrong place at the wrong time. Even the young women of *Gold Diggers of 1935* and *Love Affair* suffered moral retribution. It was a time when a heroic New York made sense, and the city itself was the story.[17]

Delirious Los Angeles

New York's decline as the celluloid city of the future followed the city's social and financial upheavals and can be charted against the rise of Los Angeles. Popular myths of Los Angeles — a paradise of booming aerospace industries, sprawling freeways, and leisure amid near-perfect weather — helped promote the postwar city as an urban center on the edge of the twenty-first century. While New York films of the 1980s nostalgically looked back to the city's own cinematic past, films about Los Angeles peered forward with anxiety and dread.

The 1982 release of *Blade Runner* signaled the coming-of-age of Los Angeles as Hollywood's city of the future. Inverting many of that city's most cherished myths about the sunny good life, *Blade Runner*'s fractured, unresolved narrative predicted the most pressing topics of contemporary America, from the Japanizing of the country to urban decay, genetic engineering, and environmental pollution. Although the film's design was no less postmodern than that of *Batman*, its Los Angeles of 2019 — fusing Frank Lloyd Wright, Lang's *Metropolis*, Day-Glo Tokyo, and Las Vegas — offered a new and original synthesis projecting an apocalyptic future. The resulting cyberpunk aesthetic has influenced the look of music videos, television commercials, feature films, nightclubs, and a proposed mall in Times Square. No wonder New Yorkers are suffering a severe identity crisis.[18]

Notes

[1] Sections of this article originally appeared in the *New York Times* on 20 September and 25 October 1992.
[2] Walter Winchell, "Winchell's New York," *Look* (12 January 1954), p.20.
[3] Designed by Stephen Goosson, the film's New York of 1980 required, according to its designer, an immense miniature that filled an entire balloon hangar 125 meters long by 62.5 meters wide.
[4] A Depression dynamo, Crawford's plucky characters possessed the determination to propel her from rags to riches in such films as *Our Blushing Brides* (1930), *Possessed* (1931), *Mannequin* (1938), and *The Women* (1939). As the heroine of *Susan Lenox: Her Fall and Rise* (1931), Garbo suffered her moral fall as the mistress of a shady racketeer while living at the height of material luxury in a skyscraper penthouse, thereby supporting the Puritan adage that forbidden fruit is always sweetest. And Art Deco nightclubs play major roles in such Astaire-and-Rogers musicals as *Follow the Fleet* (1936), *Swing Time* (1936), and *Shall We Dance* (1937).
[5] The opening sequence of *Breakfast at Tiffany's* underscores the blurred line between the "reality" of location shooting and the "artifice" of filming on a sound stage. The sequence's off-beat, bittersweet quality was achieved by juxtaposing Audrey Hepburn's couture evening gown and her modest, delicatessen breakfast. Henry Mancini's haunting score added to the forlorn effect, as did the decision to shoot the actual jewelry store in early morning, when the usually busy corner was deserted.
[6] John Cheever, *The Stories of John Cheever* (New York: Ballantine Books, 1981), p. ix.
[7] The mid-1960s murder of Kitty Genovese, whose cries for help went unanswered by her Queens neighbors, remains one of the most famous accounts of heartless New York and has achieved mythic status.
[8] In the context of New York and the movies, a significant loss to the city's prestige resulted from the construction of the world's tallest skyscraper — Sears Tower — in Chicago (1974).
[9] In *Manhattan*, Allen paid homage to vintage Hollywood with the opening scene's voiceover, a cliché used as well in *The Naked City*, while Scorsese's *New York, New York* is a compendium of movie allusions. In general, Scorsese was deeply influenced by the darker, less candy-colored musicals of such veteran Hollywood directors as George Cukor and Vincente Minnelli, the father of *New York, New York*'s star, Liza Minnelli. Specifically, the New York skyline behind the film's title credits is a reprinted and repainted version of the one that opened *The Man I Love* (1947). Liza Minnelli's role as an up-and-coming singer evoked the career of her mother, Judy Garland, especially the phase that included Cukor's 1954 musical *A Star is Born*. That film influenced *New York, New York*'s somber tone and saturated colors, as did such oddities as the Technicolor *film-noir* musical *My Dream Is Yours* (1949). The frenzied automobile scene in *The Bad and the Beautiful* (1952), directed by Vincente Minnelli, inspired a similar scene in *New York, New York*.
[10] The 1978 publication *Delirious New York*, written by Dutch architect Rem Koolhaas, provides an interesting counterpoint to the films of Allen and Scorsese. Emphasizing the city's development from the turn of the century through World War II, the book celebrates New York's dynamic "culture of congestion" as a model for the future metropolis.
[11] *Batman* press kit (Los Angeles: Warner Bros., 1989), p.9.
[12] The film's Gotham City required a combination of miniatures, matte paintings, and 35

major three-dimensional sets. The film's production dominated the 18 sound stages and 95-acre backlot of the Pinewood Studio outside London. The more than four hundred-meter-long Gotham City street took a hectic five months to build and was reportedly the largest exterior set built in Europe since the 1963 version of *Cleopatra* (Jody Duncan Shannon, "A Dark and Stormy Knight," *Cinefex* 41 [February 1990], pp. 4–33).

[13] Mike Bonifer, *Dick Tracy: The Making of the Movie* (New York: Bantam Books, 1990), p. 54.

[14] Early in the process of conceiving *Dick Tracy*, Sylbert advised director Warren Beatty that the only way to create the generic comic book look he sought would be to build a stylized city. As a result, three blocks of Universal Studio's vintage "New York street" were repainted according to the film's palette. Since these buildings were only three stories tall, elaborate matte paintings were required to expand the city's scope (Glenn Campbell, "Crimestoppers Textbook," *Cinefex* 44 [1990], pp. 24–49).

[15] Sturges wrote and directed such films as *Christmas in July* (1940), *The Lady Eve* (1941), *Sullivan's Travels* (1941), and *The Palm Beach Story* (1942).

[16] *The Hudsucker Proxy* contains two suicidal skyscraper leaps that begin and end the film — both nearly 90 seconds in length. Shots of the skyscrapers, built on a sound stage in a North Carolina film studio, were combined with scenes of the actors suspended on wires and filmed separately. These miniature skyscrapers were oriented vertically for the film's gliding opening sequence through the city; the miniatures were mounted horizontally to accommodate photography of the fall sequences (W.C. Odien, "The Rise and Fall of Norville Barnes," *Cinefex* 58 [1994], pp. 58–81).

[17] It may be no coincidence that movie-related theme shops and restaurants are flourishing on some of the world's most prestigious commercial streets, such as New York's own Fifth Avenue. *Batman* has inspired at least one theme park, at Six Flags Magic Mountain in Valencia, California, where visitors stroll through six acres of fantasy scenery, including "Bruce Wayne/Gotham City Park," "Axis Department Store," and a café entitled "Joker Juices." And in an ironic reversal, New York has inspired "New York, New York," a $350 million casino and hotel planned for Las Vegas. This sanitized New York will include 10 Manhattan skyscrapers built at approximately one-third scale, as well as replicas of the Brooklyn Bridge, the facade of the New York Public Library, and Grand Central Station.

[18] As this article was being completed, a host of new television programs set in New York were being announced for the fall 1995 season, suggesting the persistence of the on-again/off-again love affair between New York and the moving image.

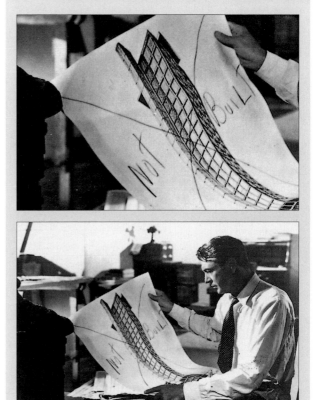

Fig. 11: The Fountainhead *(King Vidor; U.S.A., 1949). "The Fountainhead"* © *1949 Turner Entertainment Co.. All rights reserved.*

Michael Webb

"Like Today, Only More So": The Credible Dystopia of *Blade Runner*

Fig. 1: Filming the pyramid of the Tyrell Co. headquarters for *Blade Runner*. Production Still. *Photo: Virgil Mirano, Los Angeles, Copyright 1982, The Blade Runner Partnership.*

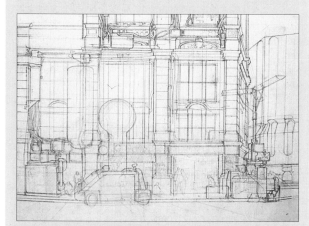

Fig. 2: Syd Mead, Sketch Layout for Street Elevation for *Blade Runner*, 1980. Pencil on paper, 37.9 cm x 25.1 cm. Courtesy of Syd Mead Inc., Los Angeles, USA. Original Art Work created for Ladd Co./Warner Brothers motion picture *Blade Runner* Copyright 1982.

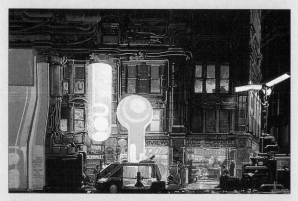

Fig. 3: Syd Mead, Street Set, Elevation for *Blade Runner*, 1980. Gouache on cardboard, 38.1 cm x 25.3 cm. Courtesy of Syd Mead Inc., Los Angeles, USA; Original Art Work created for Ladd Co./Warner Brothers motion picture *Blade Runner* Copyright 1982.

A few films survive initial disfavor on the part of audiences or critics and go on to become icons of their eras. *Metropolis* captured the awed fascination with speed and great size that characterized what we now call the Machine Age and anticipated the Nazi ideology of supermen and slaves. Stanley Kubrick's *2001 — A Space Odyssey* (1968) offered a psychedelic trip into the unknown that has more to do with contemporary drug culture and New Age irrationality than with the impending moon landings. A decade after its 1982 release, Ridley Scott declared that *Blade Runner* "depicts a road we're heading down now — class separation, the growing gulf between rich and poor, the population explosion — and it offers no solutions."[1]

Each of these films represents an autocratic director's personal vision in which the sets and special effects become the principle characters. Their futuristic scenarios provide commentaries on contemporary realities and trends by intent, but also because, as Ernst Gombrich has pointed out, the unfamiliar is always extrapolated from the known.[2] The parallels between *Metropolis* and *Blade Runner* are as striking as their differences. Both draw on medieval cosmology to create a hierarchical universe, with heaven above and hell below; both attempt to address technological innovation and timeless moral issues. Fritz Lang, the German director with training in architecture, proposed an orderly city-state of monumental structures, micro-managed by an authoritarian technocrat, but threatened by incipient rebellion. Scott, the English-born designer, created a city that seems to dissolve into a poisonous smog and that has been relinquished by its power structure, only to survive in a state of anarchy and decay.

Initially, both films were the product of culture shock — specifically, the impact of Manhattan on an impressionable European. For Scott, who had grown up in an England pervaded by American popular culture, the impact of the latter was diffused. After studying to become a stage designer and making an experimental film in London, he won a scholarship that allowed him to work as a graphic designer in New York — where, as he observed, he got the impression of a city on overload, about to descend into chaos.[3] He

returned to London, where he joined the BBC as a set designer and then formed his own company. Over the next 10 years he directed about 3,000 television commercials in Britain and the United States. From that fast-paced period, he remembers the thrill of arriving in New York City by helicopter from Kennedy airport, swooping over the island to land on the roof of the Pan Am Building in midtown. It's an experience that inspired the opening scene of *Blade Runner*, as surely as Lang's first impression of skyscrapers was translated into the opening montage of *Metropolis*.

Scott made *The Duelists* (1977), a critically acclaimed period drama, and achieved a huge popular success with *Alien* (1979) before Michael Deeley, who had produced *The Deer Hunter* (1978), signed him to direct *Blade Runner*. The source was a futuristic detective story, *Do Androids Dream of Electric Sheep?*, by Philip K. Dick. In Dick's story, a nuclear war had blanketed the world with clouds of radioactive dust. Most of the population had fled to colonies on other worlds, where hard and dangerous work was performed by a slave class of androids that had become almost impossible to distinguish from humans. To control their potentially dangerous behavior, they had been programmed to last only four years and had been forbidden to return to earth. Dick's story concerns a bounty hunter's pursuit of six errant androids through the empty buildings of San Francisco and his realization that the creatures he must execute are much like himself.[4]

Essential elements of this story survived eight drafts of a script by Hampton Fancher, who would eventually share the writing credit with David Peoples. Scott considered setting the story in a future metropolis that linked New York and Chicago, but chose Los Angeles as the most convincing locus of urban sprawl and blight. Unlike Dick, he wanted the city of 2019 to be "rich, colorful, noisy, gritty, full of textures and teeming with life. . . I'm trying to make it as real as possible. This is a tangible future, not so exotic as to be unbelievable . . . like today, only more so."[5] Scott wanted to make "a film set forty years hence, made in the style of forty years ago," using futuristic trappings as background to a "familiar Philip Marlowe–Sam

Spade detective story." Androids were rechristened "replicants." What would give *Blade Runner* a resonance that contemporary science fiction films like *Star Wars* (George Lucas, 1977), *Star Trek: The Motion Picture* (Robert Wise, 1979), and *Batman* lacked were the thoughtfulness of the underlying concept, and the layering of images and associations.

In most films, production design is reductive. The unessential is stripped away to simplify the compositions and emphasize the action. Here, it was additive. William Gibson, a cult writer of cyberpunk stories, remarked: "Scott understood the importance of information density to perceptual overload. When *Blade Runner* works best, it induces a lyrical sort of information sickness, that quintessentially modern cocktail of ecstasy and dread."[6] Among the many sources of inspiration for the film, Scott cited William Hogarth's engravings of London street life in the eighteenth century, photos of the teeming markets of New York's Lower East Side, and illustrations from *Heavy Metal*, especially those by the Belgian illustrator Jean "Moebius" Giraud, which he described as "massive, decorative, and brutal." The neon-lit squalor of Times Square and the electrographic jungles of Tokyo and Hong Kong also sparked ideas. But Scott wanted a unified, logical perspective, not an anthology of visual quotations. "Before I bring in a production designer, I like to involve a conceptual illustrator or two," he remarked. "It was a process that worked very well for me on *Alien* when I choose H. R. Giger and Ron Cobb . . . and had them develop a lot of the designs."[7] For this project, he picked Syd Mead, a visual futurist who creates renderings of experimental cars and other products for major corporations.

Mead's first task was to conceptualize the spinner, a computer-guided car that could lift off vertically and fly. Three full-scale mock-ups were built, together with models of different sizes. The assignment soon broadened. "I was hired to design the vehicles," Mead has recalled, but "I started to surround my vehicle sketches with street scenes and architecture — Ridley loved them."[8] (figs. 2, 3, 9) Scott wanted to avoid the sci-fi clichés of "diagonal zippers and silver hair. Films usually present the future as pristine and austere . . .

it's more likely to go the other way."[9] He and his conceptual designer speculated that, in a city of 90 million people, pollution would generate continuous smog and acid rain. Those who could afford to leave would move to "off-world" suburbia or to the security of mile-high towers, abandoning the streets to a multi-ethnic underclass. As wealth drained from the city, it would become too costly to rebuild, so older buildings would be retrofitted with signs and service ducts snaking across their facades. "Everything had to look old, sleazy, and odd," said Mead, "a strange, compacted, crowded look that exaggerates the danger and hopelessness of these people's lives. To me, movies have always been an alternate reality. You just have to adjust it to what people think is real."[10]

Other artists, including illustrator Mentor Huebner, became involved in the process (figs. 4, 5, 6), and as the vision took shape, production designer Lawrence G. Paull was brought in to turn the sketches into sets. Most of the exteriors were shot at night on the back lot of the Warner Bros. Studios in Burbank. The New York street where an earlier generation of *films noirs* had been shot was retrofitted with ducts and neon signs cannibalized from other productions, including Francis Coppola's *One from the Heart* (1982). The set was dressed to suggest an oriental or latino bazaar invaded by armored vehicles and by crowds of extras, including punk rockers, jabbering a strange argot. An advertising blimp flew low overhead. Everything was specially designed, from appropriate stories in the newspapers on vendors' stalls to the instructions on electrified parking meters. Little of this was visible on screen. One is reminded of Erich von Stroheim's legendary excesses in the silent era.

Other scenes were partially shot in downtown Los Angeles in the 1893 Bradbury Building (itself inspired by a science fiction novel) and Union Station (1931–39) — and also at Frank Lloyd Wright's Ennis Brown House in the Hollywood Hills (1923). Each was enhanced with matte paintings to suggest tremendous height and matched to sets built on studio stages. Scott drove his cast and crew to breaking point, ordering sets to be rebuilt before he would shoot, demanding repeated

Fig. 4: Mentor Huebner, Sketch for Blade Runner *(Ridley Scott; U.S.A., 1982):* Exterior Overpasses. *Sepia ink on tissue, 76.2 x 101.6 cm. Private collection, Los Angeles.*

Fig. 5: Mentor Huebner, Sketch for Blade Runner: Exterior Lightning Storm, Base of Tower. *Sepia ink on tissue, 76.2 x 101.6 cm. Private collection, Los Angeles.*

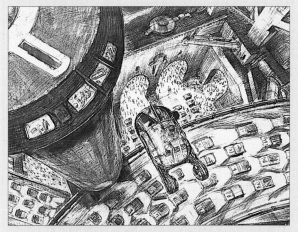

Fig. 6: Mentor Huebner, Sketch for Blade Runner: Exterior Police Headquarters, Spinner Overhead. *Sepia ink on tissue, 76.2 x 101.6 cm. Private collection, Los Angeles.*

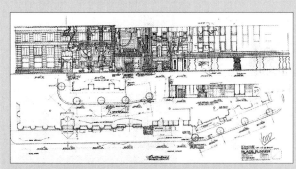

Fig. 7: Bill Skinner, Construction drawing: plan and elevation for construction work on the Warner Bros. backlot for Blade Runner: Exterior Urban Street. *Pencil on graph paper, 91.5 x 152.4 cm. American Museum of the Moving Image, New York City, Gift of David Snyder.*

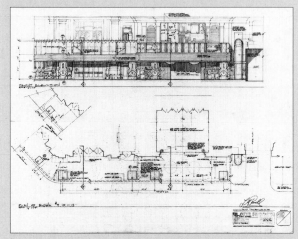

Fig. 8: T. Duffield Jr., Construction drawing: plan and elevation for Construction work on the Warner Bros. backlot for Blade Runner: Exterior Urban Street: Revamp TBS Backlot. *Pencil on graph paper, 91.4 x 101.6 cm. American Museum of the Moving Image, New York City, Gift of David Snyder.*

takes, and keeping everyone on edge. The hostility on the set was palpable and the production was dubbed *Blood Runner*. Harrison Ford, who plays Deckard, the blade runner (bounty hunter) of the title, described it as the worst experience of his life. But he and other actors gave remarkable performances, and Scott's perfectionism paid off on screen.

To a large extent, the look of *Blade Runner* was achieved not on stage nor on the back lot, but in the workshops of the Entertainment Effects Group. This special effects house had been founded, a few years before, by Douglas Trumbull, the technical wizard behind Kubrick's *2001* and Steven Spielberg's *Close Encounters of the Third Kind* (1977). Trumbull and his partner, cinematographer Richard Yuricich, were about to begin work on *Brainstorm*, an ambitious, ill-fated project. But Trumbull agreed to get *Blade Runner* started and then turn over supervision to a colleague, David Dryer.

"Our biggest challenge," Trumbull has said,

> was to develop a feeling of immense scale — the idea of having something like New York with a lot of fifty or sixty story buildings that are part of the landscape; and then, above that, these megastructures that occupy several city blocks and go up many hundreds of stories. And to get that sense of scale with a combination of matte paintings and miniatures . . . lighting and aerial perspective . . . it's just not easy.

What made it possible was that "Ridley can draw what he wants to see, and from that we can extrapolate what's special effects, what's foreground, what's background, and he can then guess at the length of a shot or the angle of a lens."[11] The budget for special effects was $2 million — much less than on other science fiction extravaganzas of that time, and a tiny fraction of what it would cost today. Scott was forced to sacrifice an elaborate introductory sequence that Mead had sketched. Deckard is returning by monorail to the city from a vacation in the desert. He picks up his car at the station, scraping a thick layer of dirt off the windshield, drives onto a 16-lane highway, and is trapped in a traffic jam. He is summoned by radio-phone to police headquarters, leaves the car to be driven home by its automatic pilot,

scales a concrete tower, and is picked up by a spinner. As made, the film begins with an explanatory note, a title — *LOS ANGELES, NOVEMBER 2019* — and an establishing shot that — like the opening montage of *Metropolis* — is powerful, original, and a triumph of the model–maker's art. It also demonstrates how special-effects technology has advanced. Spinners dart like shooting stars across the night sky above a vast industrial zone. Flames spurt from towers; beyond is a vast pyramidal structure, alive with tiny points of light. The transitions in the earlier film were achieved in the camera and on the editing table, as one composition dissolved into another. In *Blade Runner*, each image is a composite of up to 27 separately filmed elements.

Trumbull pioneered the system he calls "motion control" for *2001*, shooting static models of flying machines with a camera that can make repeated passes on a precisely controlled trajectory. For *Blade Runner*, the technology was even more sophisticated. Spinners of different sizes were shot with front and rear lighting, with separate camera passes to record their light trails and faces moving in their windows. These composited images were then superimposed on multiple shots of the industrial landscape, which was dubbed Hades due to its resemblance to a technological hell. The 1.2-by-1.7-meter tabletop model of towers, cut from brass or modeled from plastic foam and lit by fiber optics and from floods below the Plexiglas base, was inspired by a nearby oil refinery. The gushes of flame included frames from Antonioni's *Zabriskie Point* (1970) and footage of a welding torch, projected onto tiny plastic screens suspended above the towers and then reshot. Even when you know how the effects were achieved, the sequence still generates a sense of awe.

To give these model shots a mysterious halation and to simulate atmospheric pollution, filming was done in a smoke studio, which Trumbull had first developed for *Close Encounters*. Diesel fuel was vaporized and pumped into a sealed room, compelling the staff to wear gas masks. This increased some exposures to several hours, and when one model caught fire in a smoke-filled room, the accident was discovered only by chance. Mark Stetson super-vised the model shop and a team that grew from seven to twenty-one. They worked around the clock, com-bining skill and ingenuity in the pro-duction of convincing miniatures. To meet Scott's demand for greater com-plexity in the cityscape, they added anything that was remotely architec-tural — including a spaceship from a previous production and a piece of the burnt model, much as the set decorators crammed the studio street with scavenged hardware and sign-age. All of the models had to be aligned at precise angles to compen-sate for the distortion of wide-angle lenses.

The largest and most impressive model, comparable to the "Stadt-krone" tower in *Metropolis*, was the seven-hundred-story headquarters of the Tyrell Corporation, the interga-lactic manufacturer of replicants and artificial wildlife (since real animals had become a costly rarity.) Trum-bull suggested the form of a stepped Mayan pyramid for the 15-centime-ter-high model that Tom Cranham made from casting resin and acry-lic. Tiny window openings were scratched in the opaque coating on the plastic, allowing light to shine through, and this structure was over-laid with pierced screens of acid-etched brass. Three working elevators ran up its face, and it was flanked by four pairs of canted buttresses. In an early scene, Deckard takes a spinner to the middle of the pyramid and emerges from a miniature elevator into a studio set of a columned hall, with a backlit, animated sun setting behind a painted buttress.

Blade Runner ran over budget, and control of the picture passed to financiers. Test audiences found the story difficult to follow. The finan-ciers called Harrison Ford back to dub a voice-over narration, made cuts, and tagged on an upbeat end-ing. This crude surgery alienated crit-ics and failed to draw the audiences that were standing in line to see *ET — The Extra-Terrestia*, which had opened the previous week. *Blade Run-ner* faded fast.

Nine years later, a Warners exec-utive chanced on the 70-millimeter director's cut of *Blade Runner* in the studio vault. By now, the film had become a legend, and when Warners tested the new version in Los Angeles and San Francisco, it broke theater attendance records. It was re–released nationally without the commentary, with missing scenes restored, and with Scott's ambiguous ending, which suggests that Deckard, who has fallen in love and eloped with an advanced replicant, may be a repli-cant himself.

It's easy to see now that the film was ahead of its time. Bleak and demanding, it was released at the height of the Reagan era, when much of America was being lulled into a state of mindless optimism and greed. Today, it seems prophetic. Illegal immigrants are flooding into south-ern California, and we've begun to confront the moral dilemmas posed by genetic engineering. American cit-ies are in even worse shape than they were a decade ago. Violence is esca-lating. But it is important not to suc-cumb to Spenglerian despair. Cities are shaped by people, and both have great resources of resilience and ad-aptability. Berlin did not become an-other Metropolis; in fact, it is much less divided, economically and socially, than it was in 1927. Los Angeles must not be allowed to ful-fill the apocalyptic scenario of *Blade Runner*.

Notes

[1] Interview with Ridley Scott, Publicity release from The Ladd Company (1982).
[2] Ernest H.Gombrich, *Art and Illusion: A Study in the Psychology of Pictorial Representation* (Lon-don: Phaidon Press, 1960), p. 72.
[3] Don Shay, "Blade Runner: 2020 Foresight," *Cinefex* 9 (July 1982), p. 6.
[4] Philip K. Dick, *Do Androids Dream of Electric Sheep?* (New York: Random House, 1968; Bal-lantine Books, 1982).
[5] *Washington Post*, 27 July 1981.
[6] *Details* (November 1992).
[7] Scott is quoted in Shay (note 3), p. 7 (an authoritative and detailed account, in text and pictures, of the special effects in *Blade Runner*).
[8] *Details* (note 6).
[9] Interview with Scott (note 1).
[10] *Los Angeles Times*, 19 July 1981.
[11] Shay (note 3).

Fig. 9: Syd Mead, Vertical Pan Matte Shot, Street Scene. *Gouache on cardboard, 25.3 x 38.1 cm. Courtesy Syd Mead Inc., Los Angeles. Original Art Work created for Warner Bros. motion picture* Blade Runner. *Copyright 1982.*

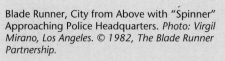

Blade Runner, City from Above with "Spinner"
Approaching Police Headquarters. *Photo: Virgil
Mirano, Los Angeles. © 1982, The Blade Runner
Partnership.*

Das Cabinet des Dr. Caligari
(The Cabinet of Dr. Caligari)

Germany, Decla-Bioscop A.G., 1920

Director: Robert Wiene. *Script:* Carl Mayer, Hans Jano-
witz. *Sets:* Walter Reimann, Walter Röhrig, Hermann
Warm. *Camera:* Willy Hameister. *Cast:* Werner Krauss
(Doctor Caligari), Conrad Veidt (Cesare), Friedrich
Feher (Francis), Lil Dagover (Jane Olfen), Hans Heinz
von Twardowski (Alan), Rudolf Klein-Rogge (criminal).
Premiere: 27 February 1920, Berlin.

A murder becomes visible — as a play of shadows on a gray
wall. And shows once again how something imagined is
more horrible than anything shown. No cinema can compete
with our imagination. That the scream of a raped woman can
be heard, really heard (if one has ears!) in this film — shall
always be remembered about it. — Kurt Tucholsky 1920

Literature: Ernst Angel, "Ein 'expressionistischer' Film," *Die
neue Schaubühne* 2, no. 4 (April 1920), pp. 103–05; Herbert
Ihering, "Das Cabinet des Dr. Caligari," *Berliner Börsen Curier*
(29 February 1920); Kurt Tucholsky, "Tagebuch: Dr. Caligari," *Weltbühne* (11 March 1920); Heinrich de Fries, "Raumgestaltung im Film," *Wasmuths Monatsheft für Baukunst,*
nos. 1–2 (1920–21), pp. 63–75 (see pp. 183–84 of the
present volume); Carl Sandburg, "The Cabinet of Dr. Caligari"
(1921), reprint in Harry M. Geduld, *Authors on Film*
(Bloomington and London: Indiana University Press, 1972),
pp. 47–49; Rudolf Kurtz, *Expressionismus und Film* (Berlin:
Verlag der Lichtbildbühne, 1926); Walter Reimann, "Filmarchitektur – heute und morgen?," *Filmtechnik und Filmindustrie,* no. 4 (1926), pp. 64–65 (see p. 193 of the present
volume); Virginia Woolf, "The Movies and Reality" (1926),
Geduld, 1972, pp. 86–91; *Caligari und Caligarismus* (Berlin:
Deutsche Kinemathek e.V., 1970); R.V. Adkinson, ed., *The
Cabinet of Dr. Caligari: A Film by Robert Wiene, Carl Mayer and
Hans Janowitz* (London: Lorimer, 1972); Lotte Eisner, *The
Haunted Screen* (Berkeley: University of California Press,
1973), pp. 17–27; Siegfried Kracauer, *From Caligari to Hitler:
A Psychological History of the German Film* (Princeton: Prince-
ton University Press, 1974); "Le Cabinet du docteur Caligari,"
Avant-scène du Cinéma 160–61 (July–September 1975),
pp. 8–27; Siegbert Solomon Prawer, *Caligari's Children: The
Film as Tale of Terror* (New York: Da Capo Press, 1988); Mike
Budd, ed., *The Cabinet of Dr. Caligari: Texts, Contexts, Histories*
(New Brunswick and London: Rutgers University Press, 1990);
Jürgen Kasten, *Der expressionistische Film: Abgefilmtes Theater
oder avantgardistisches Erzählkino?* (Münster: MaKs Publika-
tions, 1990); Barry Salt, "From German Stage to German
Screen," in Paolo Cherchi Usai and Lorenzo Codelli, eds.,
Before Caligari: German Cinema 1895–1920, exh. cat. (Porde-
none: Le Giornate del Cinemat Muto, 1990), pp. 402–37; Uli
Jung und Walter Schatzberg, "Ein Drehbuch gegen die CALI-
GARI – Legenden," in *Das Cabinet des Dr. Caligari: Drehbuch
von Carl Mayer und Hans Janowitz* (Hamburg: Edition
Text+Kritik, 1995), pp. 89–108.

Fig. 1: Fleeing from Holstenwall's Citizens, Cesare Leaves the
Abducted Jane on the Bridge.

*Fig. 2: Atelier Ledel/Bernhard, Poster. Lithograph,
127 x 95 cm. Stiftung Deutsche Kinemathek, Berlin.*

1

It is symptomatic that the screenplay of *Das Cabinet des Dr. Caligari* by Carl Mayer and Hans Janowitz was only realized expressionistically because it is set in an insane asylum. The representation of healthy reality is thus opposed to the representation of sick unreality. In other words, Impressionism prevails where one is of sound mind, Expressionism where one is of unsound mind. In other words, insanity as an excuse for an artistic idea [Ihering 1920].

I realized that the sets had to deviate completely in form and design from the usual naturalistic style. The frames, averted from reality, had to acquire a fantastic graphic form. The images had to be like visionary nightmares. No real structural elements could be recognizable. Instead, eccentric painting corresponding to the subject had to dominate the screen. . . Reimann, who applied the Expressionist painting technique in his designs, succeeded with his idea that this subject had to have Expressionist sets, costumes, actors, and direction. . .
Furthermore, I would like to say that sets should remain as background in front of which the action takes place, reflecting it and supporting the actor, who is after all supposed to have the major creative role. In *Caligari* this relationship is reversed. In this single (special) case I will concede that the sets became the major means of expression [Hermann Warm, "Gegen die Caligari Legenden" (ca. 1970), in *Caligari und Caligarismus* 1970].

This Film, *The Cabinet of Dr. Caligari,* is so bold a work of independent artists going it footloose, that one can well understand it might affect audiences just as a sea voyage affects a ship-load of passengers. Some have to leave the top decks, unable to stand sight or smell of the sea. Others take the air and the spray, the salt and the chill, and call the trip an exhilaration . . . .
Cubist, futurist, post-impressionist, characterize it by any name denoting a certain style, it has its elements of power, knowledge, technic, passion, that make it sure to have an influence toward more easy flowing, joyous, original American movies" [Sandburg 1921].

Fig. 3: Walter Reimann, Untitled (Woman on Couch). *Pastel on cardboard, 30.5 x 34.9 cm. University of Southern California, Doheny Memorial Library, Department of Special Collections, Los Angeles.*

Fig. 4: Walter Reimann, Untitled (Café Scene). *Pastel on cardboard, 30.5 x 34.3 cm. University of Southern California, Doheny Memorial Library, Department of Special Collections, Los Angeles.*

Fig. 5: Walter Reimann, "Dr. Caligari Bude." *Pastel on brown paper, 30.4 x 38.1 cm. University of Southern California, Doheny Memorial Library, Department of Special Collections, Los Angeles.*

In January and February 1919, during the days of the Spartacist revolt in Berlin, the as yet unknown screenwriters Carl Mayer and Hans Janowitz wrote the script for *Das Cabinet des Dr. Caligari*. In April 1919, they submitted the screenplay to the producer Erich Pommer, head of the Decla film company. The production of the film, based on a revised version of the script, began in October 1919. The hero, Francis, tells a friend the story of Dr. Caligari, who displays the sleepwalking Cesare in a "cabinet" at the fair in Holstenwall. A series of murders begins in the city. The sleuthing Francis finally exposes Dr. Caligari as the criminal who misuses the sleepwalking Cesare to do the murders. Caligari escapes and disappears into an insane asylum, eventually turning out to be its director. But instead of a morbid play on the dubiousness of state institutions, the tale is eventually revealed as a sick fantasy of the narrating hero. All the characters in his story turn up again at the end in the asylum's inner courtyard, the only structure in the film that displays conventional architectural elements.

In Germany the film was criticized by many for disavowing the Art of Expressionism as the deranged fantasy of a lunatic. After the war, Siegfried Kracauer and Lotte Eisner used this argument to link the film to the subsequent art criticism of the National Socialists. Kurt Tucholsky was fascinated by the "completely unreal dream world" of this film, in which he saw the poetic power of the medium at work. For him, almost completely suppressing realistic representation meant an enormous enrichment of film's suggestive design potential.

Caligari's architectural realization by the set designers Walter Reimann, Hermann Warm, and Walter Röhrig lends it a definitive design principle throughout. A total of 33 different sets were used. The painted views, which distort the sites of the action in perspective and tip them off balance, give the sets a claustrophobic atmosphere in which the actors move like ghosts. The walls of the city streets are covered with enigmatic graffiti. The specifications for the decor determined the camera work and lighting as well. Shadows painted on scenery produced the contrasts between light and dark, while the usually static and neutral camera opened up the sites of the action from the front. Apart from the distorted shapes of the scenery, the obvious artificiality of the sets was programmatic in a more general sense. Reimann felt strongly that film should not try to imitate reality, but should create its own world through the simple means of stagecraft. He repeatedly pointed out the distinct differences between actual architecture and film sets and insisted that the term *film architecture* should be replaced by *film painting*. "In no way are film sets architecture! . . . The film, the art of 'optical' illusion, needs utopia. It needs a set that is utopian space, simulating the atmosphere of a space for the imagination" (Reimann 1926). Only very few of Reimann's sketches for the sets have survived; they are now scattered over four different archives in Paris, Berlin, Frankfurt, and Los Angeles. Warm provided sketches and a number of models for a retrospective exhibition at the Stiftung Deutsche Kinemathek in Berlin in 1963.

No other film exerted as much economic and aesthetic influence on the cinematography of the early Weimar Republic as *Caligari*. Even though the Expressionist film boom following on its success subsided quickly, this film nonetheless opened up new export markets for the German film industry.

P. L.

3

4

5

Fig. 6: Prison Cell.

Fig. 7: Hermann Warm, Prison Cell *(ca. 1963). Colored pencil on cardboard, 26.5 x 35 cm. Stiftung Deutsche Kinemathek, Berlin.*

Fig. 8: Walter Reimann, "Bild für Passage 1". Gouache on paper, 27.5 x 32.5 cm. Stiftung Deutsche Kinemathek, Berlin.

Fig. 9: Courtyard of the Insane Asylum.

Fig. 10: Walter Reimann, Bridge. *Pastel on brown paper, 39.5 x 32.7 cm. Deutsches Filmmuseum, Frankfurt am Main.*

6

7

8

9

Bild, für Passage 1

10

W. Reimann

Das Cabinet des Dr. Caligari

Fig. 11: Dr. Caligari in the Streets of Holstenwall.

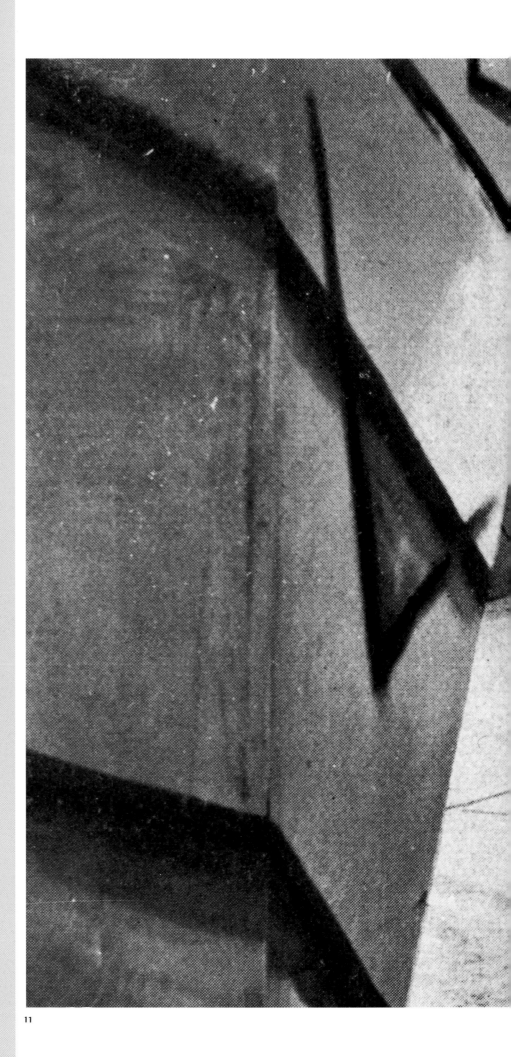

11

Genuine — Die Tragödie eines seltsamen Hauses
(Genuine — The Tragedy of a Strange House)

Germany, Decla Film A.G., 1920

Director: Robert Wiene. *Script:* Carl Mayer. *Sets:* César Klein. *Camera:* Willy Hameister. *Cast:* Fern Andra (Genuine), Ernst Gronau (Count Melo), Harald Paulsen (Percy), Albert Bennefeld (Curzon), John Gottowt (hairdresser), Hans Heinz von Twardowski (hairdresser's apprentice).
Premiere: August 1920, Berlin.

Literature: A. F., "Genuine," *Der Film* 5 (4 September 1920), p. 28; "Genuine," *Freie deutsche Bühne,* no. 3 (12 September 1920); "Genuine," *Der Kinematograph* 14 (12 September 1920); Jgh., "Fern Andra im expressionistischen Film," *Neue Zeit* (4 September 1920); Fritz Olimsky, "Genuine," *Berliner Börsen Zeitung* (5 September 1920); Herbert Ihering, "Porträt César Klein," in *Regisseure und Bühnenmaler* (Berlin: O. Goldschmidt-Gabrielli, 1921), pp. 87–88; Kurt Dingelstedt, "César Klein als Bühnenbildner," *Kunst in Schleswig-Holstein* (1953), pp. 142–53; Rudolf Pfefferkorn, *César Klein* (Berlin: Rembrandt-Verlag, 1962); Johann Schlick, "Cesar Klein, 'Genuine': Ein Beitrag zur expressionistischen Filmarchitektur," *Nordelbingen* 47 (1978), pp. 141–51; Joachim Hauschild, "Cesar Klein: Maler, Entwurfszeichner und Bühnenausstatter," *Weltkunst* 57 (1987), pp. 15–18.

Fig. 1: Josef Fenneker, Poster. Color lithograph 142 x 92 cm. Stiftung Deutsche Kinemathek, Berlin.

Genuine is doubtless one of the weirdest and most fantastic films of early Expressionism. The successful team of scriptwriter Carl Mayer and director Robert Wiene here tried in vain to follow up on the great success of *Caligari.* The painter, stage designer, and interior decorator César Klein was appointed as set designer. The subtitle suggests the intention of incorporating the building in which the action takes place into the bizarre plot as cause and participant. The film, of which only a few copies survive, has not been shown for many years, and its storyline has to be reconstructed from contemporary accounts.

As a member of a mysterious sect, the girl Genuine became accustomed to drinking blood as a child. She is kidnapped by slave dealers and sold to Count Melo, who keeps her captive in his house. Only a hairdresser is allowed to visit her daily. One day, when his apprentice comes instead and falls in love with Genuine, she has the apprentice kill Count Melo. Yet, after a brief love affair she yearns for other men and for the blood of the apprentice. But before he too is murdered, he manages to escape. He returns to take revenge on Genuine, killing her and then himself, just before the police rush into the house.

Contemporary critics commented extensively on the set designer's efforts. Like *Caligari, Genuine* was made exclusively in the studio. Here, too, the artificiality of the architecture was emphasized to stress the alien, synthetic psychological world of the plot. However, there is less use than in *Caligari* of spatial depth, sequences of movement, and various lighting conditions, substituting instead a more two-dimensional treatment of the floor, walls, and ceiling. As we know from César Klein's preliminary drawings, the lively Expressionist sets were designed in powerful colors. And although he experimented with a number of sketches in black and white, he could not prevent the sets from appearing overdone and disjointed to a number of critics. "The paintings by César Klein may testify to new expressive possibilities, but their much too rich imagination obscures the clarity of the image in a splendid confusion of decor and costumes. . . With its artificially bizarre audacity, this presentation suffocated the emotion the actor made one feel," wrote a contemporary critic ("Genuine," *Der Kinematograph* 1920). For the development and discussion of Expressionist film and its attempt to represent psychological space, *Genuine* is an important counterpart to *Caligari.* Because of the lack of a framing narrative, there was no opportunity here to write off the Expressionist decor as the vision of someone mentally ill. Conservative critics doubted that Expressionism was justified in such a case (Jgh. 1920); others claimed that *Genuine* stood at the beginning of a new epoch in artistic filmmaking (A. F. 1920).

> Genuine lives in a subterranean glass house filled with magic trees, the splendor of glittering mirrors, luxurious beds, strange furnishings. The house itself has extensive halls, quiet enclosed gardens, dark rooms full of fabulous knick-knacks, and exotic curios. . . The town is a dream town with curious boutiques, narrow little lanes, rough people. Around the town there is a magic forest. . . This forest is a masterpiece one would like to own as a painting, and at the same time utterly characteristic of what Wiene actually wants. . . Wiene creates a forest out of cardboard and canvas. He does without nature because he wants to present a fairy tale, and thus he achieves a strength of atmosphere even beyond the best works by Schwind [the nineteenth-century Romantic painter Moritz von Schwind]. We have here the first poet who gives film style, the first maestro who masters the material fully [A. F. 1920].

D.N.

GENUINE

MIT

FERN
ANDRA
REGIE
ROBERT WIENE

PLAKATKUNSTANSTALT
DINSE & ECKERT
BERLIN S.O. 16

3

4

Fig. 3: César Klein, Genuine's Throne. *Colored pencil on paper, 25 x 32 cm. Theaterwissenschaftliches Institut der Universität Köln.*

Fig. 2: César Klein, Interior design for Marmorhaus movie theater, Berlin, 1913.

Fig. 4: César Klein, Genuine's Throne. *Black and white water-color on paper, 25 x 32 cm. Theaterwissenschaftliches Institut der Universität Köln.*

Fig. 5: Genuine with the Barber's Assistant.

Fig. 6: In the Barbershop.

5

6

Algol

Germany, Deutsche Lichtspielgesellschaft, 1920

Director: Hans Werckmeister. *Script:* Hans Brennert, Friedel Köhne. *Sets:* Walter Reimann. *Cast:* Emil Jannings (Robert Herne), John Gottowt (goblin), Hanna Ralph (Maria), Ernst Hofmann (Reginald Herne). *Premiere:* 3 September 1920, Berlin.

Literature: "Algol," *Der Film*, no. 37 (11 November 1920), p. 25; "Algol," *Der Kinematograph*, no. 713 (September 1920); "Algol," *Illustrierte Filmwoche*, no. 36 (1920), p. 1; Balthasar [Roland Schacht], "Kinol," *Freie Deutsche Bühne*, no. 41 (19 September 1920), pp. 87–90; Christian Flüggen, "Algol," *Deutsche Lichtspielzeitung*, no. 39 (18 September 1920), p. 7; Lothar Knud Fredrik, "Algol," *Film-Kurier* (4 September 1920); Heinrich de Fries, "Raumgestaltung im Film," *Wasmuths Monatsheft für Baukunst*, nos. 1–2 (1920–21), pp. 63–75 (see pp. 183–84 of the present volume); Herman G. Scheffauer, "The Vivifying of Space" (1924), reprint in Lewis Jacobs, ed., *Introduction to the Art of the Movies* (New York: Noonday Press, 1960), pp. 76–85; Walter Reimann, "Filmarchitektur — Filmarchitekt?!," *Gebrauchsgraphik*, no. 6 (1924–25), pp. 3–13 (see pp. 193 of the present volume); Lotte Eisner, *Vingt ans de cinéma allemand 1913–1933*, exh. cat. (Paris: Centre National d'Art et de Culture George Pompidou, 1978), p. 45; Ilona Brennicke and Joe Hembus, *Klassiker des deutschen Stummfilms 1910–1930* (Munich: Goldmann, 1983), pp. 171–72; Francis Courtade, *Cinéma expressioniste* (Paris: H.Veyrier, 1984), pp. 119–21; Jürgen Kasten, "Algol — Tragödie der Macht," *Neue Züricher Zeitung* (25–26 December 1987); Frank Kessler, "Les Architectes-peintres du cinéma allemand muet," *Iris*, no. 12 (1991) p. 47–54.

Fig. 1: Walter Reimann. Algol Machine, *1920. Reconstruction by Michael Brown, 1995. Wood, metal, wire, 22.8 x 45.7 x 63.5 cm. Photo: Michael Brown.*

Fig. 2: Robert Herne Looking out over Hernestadt from His Office. *Frame enlargement by Gerhard Ullmann, Munich.*

Fig. 3: The Algol-Machine. *Frame enlargement by Gerhard Ullmann, Munich.*

Fig. 4: The Hall of Power. *Frame enlargement by Gerhard Ullmann, Munich.*

Fig. 5: In Front of the Hall of Power. *Frame enlargement by Gerhard Ullmann, Munich.*

Although publicity strategists tried to profit from *Caligari*'s success and presented *Algol* shortly afterwards in a similar style, the two films are virtual opposites in their stylistic methods. While *Caligari* is distinguished by the uniform, highly artificial treatment of the sets (also designed by Walter Reimann), *Algol* provides a daring mixture of painted interiors, outdoor takes, and documentary material. An amazing wealth of locations, visual angles, and atmospheres results from this different approach.

The coal miner Robert Herne is entrusted by a Mephistophelian goblin with a small machine that runs without electricity and is powered by rays from the distant planet Algol. Herne lets himself be tempted by the prospect of becoming rich and powerful with this machine. Twenty years later, power lines from Herne's empire cover the whole world. Yet, his wealth has not made him happy. The people he loved have moved to the small, neighboring agrarian state. Pursued by the envy and greed of his fellow men, he finally despairs of his power, destroying his central engine room and getting killed himself.

At first glance, Reimann's set designs may seem obvious in the way they reflect the characters. The goblin lives in the bizarre landscape of the Algol Star or in a crooked garret on earth, and Robert Herne works in a severely decorated office, while his unstable son Reginald lolls among soft pillows, curtains, and colorfully speckled wall paper. The colonnade of the engine room along which Herne hurries toward his doom makes the inevitability of his route visible by means of perspective foreshortening. "In the end Jannings can hardly get through," mocked one critic (Fredrik 1920). But what all these spaces have in common is that they illustrate Reimann's particular conception of the functions of film architecture, about which he published impassioned statements in several articles between 1924 and 1926. As in *Caligari*, he continued the wall decoration onto the floor, emphasizing the alien, painterly aspect of the space in *Algol*. Contemporary rooms are depicted: the office of an industrial magnate, his residential spaces, and, above all, a large machine room. Nevertheless, these interiors are clearly only painted and never attempt to simulate real architecture. Even the machines deliberately resemble wood and cardboard, playfully decorated with painted ornament. Thus, Reimann's design style was clearly part of a program independent of the film in question. The distorted and "expressionistic" forms that were typical for *Caligari*, however, are rare in *Algol*. The landscape on the star itself, reminiscent of contemporary work by Hermann Finsterlin, is the most striking example. Even here, though, the formal language of Expressionism was used to evoke the Other — in this case, an alien, threatening creature.

Other references to contemporary architectural ideas can be found, especially in the view from Robert Herne's office. In the foreground are high, vaulted machine rooms; above them, a shimmering, crystalline structure towers before the night sky. Immediately after the war, young Expressionist architects had designed a number of tall, visionary communal buildings and utopian glass cathedrals as symbols of a new spirituality. From 1920 on, more and more conservative architects had adopted these ideas and propagated large office towers as symbols of a new nationalism. The industrial cathedral outside Robert Herne's window represents this transition. Its formal language is that of the idealistic Expressionist architects; its function in the film is that of a symbol for a highly industrialized, imperialistic state. Reimann imagined Herne City as a futuristic city of high-rises in which countless brightly lit skyscrapers towered above the deep canyons of the streets. The choice of locations in the film was loaded with political meaning. Robert Herne is shown living in the Neue Orangerie at Sanssouci, the summer residence of the German emperors, and is thus symbolically connected with the recently abandoned Prussian monarchy. The happier life, the film suggests, is led in the peaceful, agrarian neighboring state, thus taking a position in the heated debate about Germany's future following its defeat in World War I.

D. N.

1

2

3

4

5

Fig. 7: Walter Reimann, Drawing for Algol: Hernestadt.

Fig. 8: Hermann Finsterlin, "Architectural Landscape," 1919. Oil and pencil on carton, 75 x 74 cm. Deutsches Architektur-museum, Frankfurt am Main.

Fig. 9: The City's Silhouette. Frame enlargement by Gerhard Ullmann, Munich.

Fig. 10: Reginald Herne and Yella Ward in a Rooftop Café. The Skyscrapers of "Hernestadt" in the Distance.

Fig. 11: Robert Herne's Son Reginald Awaits His Father's Death.

7

Fig. 6: On the Algol Star. Frame enlargement by Gerhard Ullmann, Munich.

8

9

10

11

Der Golem,
wie er in die Welt kam
(The Golem, how it came into the world)

Germany, Projektions-A.G. Union, 1920

Directors: Paul Wegener, Carl Boese. *Script:* Paul Wegener, Henryk Galeen. *Sets:* Hans Poelzig, Marianne Moeschke, Kurt Richter. *Camera:* Karl Freund. *Cast:* Paul Wegener (The Golem), Albert Steinrück (Rabbi Löw), Lyda Salmonova (Mirjam, his daughter), Ernst Deutsch (assistant), Otto Gebühr (the emperor), Lothar Müthel (Count Florian).
Premiere: 29 October 1920, Berlin.

Literature: Andrej, "Ein Gespräch mit Paul Wegener: Einführendes zum Golem," *Film-Kurier* (20 October 1920); Herbert Ihering, "Der Golem," *Berliner Börsen Kurier* (31 October 1920, morning ed.); Paul Westheim, "Eine Filmstadt von Poelzig," *Das Kunstblatt* 4, no. 11 (November 1920), pp. 325 ff; Heinrich de Fries, "Raumgestaltung im Film," *Wasmuths Monatsheft für Baukunst,* nos. 3–4 (1920–21), pp. 63–75 (see pp. 183–84 in the present volume); John R. Clarke, "Expressionism in Film and Architecture: Hans Poelzig's Sets for Paul Wegener's 'The Golem,'" *Art Journal* 34, no. 2 (Winter 1974–75), pp. 115–24; Ilona Brennicke and Joe Hembus, *Klassiker des deutschen Stummfilms, 1910–1930* (Munich: Goldmann, 1983), pp. 63–68; *Der dramatische Raum: Hans Poelzig Malerei Theater Film,* exh.cat. (Krefeld: Krefelder Kunstmuseen 1986); Wolfgang Pehnt, "La porta sul prodigioso — Hans Poelzig's Film Sets for 'Der Golem', 1920," *Domus* no. 688 (November 1987), pp. 80–84; Julius Posener, *Hans Poelzig: Reflections on His Life and Work* (New York, Cambridge: Architectural History Foundation, MIT Press, 1992), pp. 143, 150.

Poelzig's main concern was not to design an historically accurate milieu but to find the right form to correspond to the strangeness of the subject matter. One can note the skill with which he creates three-dimensional depth in the nooks and crannies of the streets and squares, something that was still unusual in films of that time (1920). With a plastic freedom that disregards simple structural considerations, he lends an intense eloquence to the facades, doors, turrets, windows, oriels. In an interior he takes the vaulting beyond the limits of the structurally possible, places mysterious staircases and corridors in such a way that light and shadow become ghoulish decorations. At the time, the era of silent films, he said himself with dry sarcasm that at least the houses should "speak Yiddish" — a joyous spirit of invention fills the sinister and gloomy world (Theodor Heuss, 1939 in: Posener 1992).

Fig. 1: The Synagogue in the Ghetto.

Henryk Galeen's script sets the medieval legend of the Golem, a clay figure with the power to protect the Jewish people from harm, in the sixteenth–century Prague ghetto. When Rabbi Löw sees that the stars are predicting danger for his people, he fashions a huge Golem with the help of his assistant and brings the clay figure to life by magic. The Golem saves the emperor's life, and an imperial decree expelling the Jews is successfully prevented. However, when the Golem is misused by the Rabbi's assistant for an act of personal revenge, the figure is transformed into a raging monster and sets fire to the ghetto. Only the innocent trust of a little girl calms him down, making it possible for the rabbi to stop the conflagration with a magic incantation.

Contemporary critics celebrated this film as a milestone in set design. This was also due to the fact that for the first time a prominent architect had designed the sets. Hans Poelzig, who had arrived on the scene before World War I with powerfully romantic, expressive buildings, had caused a sensation in 1919 with his redesign of a former circus building into a large theater in Berlin. Together with his future wife, Marianne Moeschke, he had not only transformed the foyers into elegantly lit cavelike spaces but had also realized a spectacular architectural vision in the auditorium by installing light bulbs behind countless concentric rows of overlapping stalagtites, thus creating a magical shower of various shades of color. Never before had theatrical space and technology been blended so convincingly into an illusionistic whole.

The sets for *The Golem* are thoroughly permeated with the working methods and means of the architect. Poelzig turned the ghetto into a labyrinthine settlement of clay buildings. Historical verisimilitude was not the basis for this choice of material; it was intended to illustrate, in addition to notions of timelessness and closeness to nature, the unity of the Jewish community with the Golem. As Paul Wegener put it, "It is not Prague that my friend the architect Poelzig built. Rather it is a poem of a city, a dream, an architectural paraphrase on the theme of the Golem. The lanes and squares are not meant to recall anything real; they are meant to create the atmosphere the Golem breathes" (Andrej 1920).

Poelzig showed this intimate relationship by making his clay architecture appear to have been twisted and formed by hand. These structures and some of the interiors were modeled three-dimensionally by Moeschke after Poelzig's drawings and subsequently built full–size out of wood, canvas, and clay on the Tempelhof field in Berlin. A total of 54 buildings was constructed; the indoor takes were made in the studio. "Thus an architecture was created which is eloquent in a unique way. . . It has its own life, life which an architect's spirit projected into it. The volumes have become expressive in the hands of the modeler, they have received momentum, a gesture, a face" (Westheim 1920).

The ghetto was deliberately made to appear unified without architectural hierarchies. Neither the synagogue nor Rabbi Löw's house stand out especially from the other structures. This timeless, earthbound architecture is contrasted in the film with the architecture of the imperial court. The wildly ornate, highly stylized structures of the latter correspond with the frivolous and disrespectful attitude of the courtiers. Poelzig here applied one of the most powerful dogmas of the modern movement, which, at least since Adolf Loos's famous article "Ornament and Crime" (1910), had equated rich ornamentation with social decadence and superficiality.

According to contemporary critics, the value of Poelzig's sets extended far beyond the immediate occasion of the film: "We are certain that if we had not become a poor nation, we should make this Poelzig give our cities a new physiognomy, and we have no doubt that Poelzig would be the architect capable of making this Post–Wilhelmine period hold its own for posterity. . . He was able to conjure up a world of the imagination, diversely animated, agitated and agitating, out of nothingness" (Westheim 1920).

D. N.

Fig. 3: Hans Poelzig, Design for a poster showing the interior of the synagogue.

Fig. 4: Hans Poelzig, Sketch for a concert hall in Dresden, 1918. Charcoal and colored pencil on cardboard, 32.2 x 25.8 cm. Architekturmuseum, Frankfurt am Main.

Fig. 5: In the House of Rabbi Löw.

Fig. 6: At the Emperor's Court.

Fig. 7: The Ghetto on Fire.

Fig. 2: Hans Poelzig, Interior of the Grosses Schauspielhaus, Berlin, 1919.

Von Morgens bis Mitternachts
(From Morning til Midnight)

Germany, Ilag-Film Berlin, 1920

Director: Karlheinz Martin. *Script:* Herbert Juttke, Karl-heinz Martin, based on a play of the same title by Georg Kaiser. *Sets:* Robert Neppach. *Camera:* Carl Hoffmann. *Cast:* Ernst Deutsch (cashier), Erna Morena (lady), Roma Bahn (daughter, beggar girl, cocotte, mask, Salvation Army woman), Heinrich von Twardowski (young man), Eberhard Wrede (bank director), Frida Richard (grandmother).
Premiere: Mid 1922, Munich.

Literature: Georg Kaiser, *Von Morgens bis Mitternachts* (Berlin: S. Fischer, 1916); Heinrich de Fries, "Raumgestaltung im Film," *Wasmuths Monatshefte für Baukunst* 5 (1920–21), pp. 63–78 (see pp. 179–81 of the present volume); Rudolf Kurtz, *Expressionismus und Film* (Berlin: Verlag der Lichtbild-bühne, 1926); *Von Morgens bis Mitternachts* (Munich: Film-museum, 1993); Fred Gehler, "Der Raum des Dichters — Georg Kaiser 'Von Morgens bis Mitternachts,'" in Klaus Krei-meier, ed., *Die Metaphysik des Decors: Raum, Architektur und Licht im klassischen deutschen Stummfilm* (Marburg: Schüren, 1994), pp. 10–21.

Fig. 2: In the Lady's house.
Fig. 3: The Cashier's House.
Fig. 4: In the Brothel.

Fig. 1: At the Salvation Army.

From morning til midnight: the unusual course of a day in the life of a bank clerk who tries to break out of his petty, monotonous world for once in his life. The hopelessness of his undertaking is registered in his actions. He cannot offer the money he has embezzled to his adored demi-mondaine, who had applied unsuccessfully at the bank for a loan to buy a painting, and this money cannot provide him with any prospect of changing his personal situation. He escapes from his cramped domestic conditions with an outing to the city of B. There, he enters a world of leisure characterized by superficiality. Six-day bicycle races, a gambling den, a bar, and a nightclub — all the sites of pleasure and vice are now open to him thanks to money, but they remain empty and desolate. Thus, his escape becomes his passion. In his imagination, the women he meets have the face of death. A woman from the Salvation Army, in whom he confides in his ultimate despair, calls the police in order to collect the reward. The bank clerk evades the law by shooting himself. In the closing sequence, his dead body merges with the enormous cross in the Salvation Army meeting hall for a final "Ecce Homo" image.

Von Morgens bis Mitternachts belongs, together with *Caligari,* to the outstanding testimonies of cinematic Expressionism, even though this film never reached the contemporary public in Germany. Despite intensive advertising and the launching of production bulletins in the trade press, it found no distribution there and was apparently only screened in private and special showings. This is reported in a review of a screening in Munich in mid-1922 which especially emphasizes the power of the painted sets in the film. It was shown in December 1922 at the Hong-za movie theater in Tokyo and received well by the critics. For a long time, *Von Morgens bis Mitternachts* was presumed lost, but a copy survived at the National Film Center in Tokyo.

The screening history of *Von Morgens bis Mitternachts* sheds a telling light on the status of the artistically ambitious film in the commercially oriented film industry of the early Weimar Republic. Although subsequent productions created under the catchword of Expression-ism, such as *Genuine,* attempted to imitate *Caligari* stylistically, the film adaptation of Georg Kaiser's play of the same name by Karlheinz Martin moved a long distance away from briefly festering Caligarism. While *Caligari* had made use of a framing narrative to justify the dreamy atmosphere of the images with a realistic point of departure, Martin's representation remains in a self–contained fantasy world from the start. The architectural critic Heinrich de Fries presented the differences in design between *Von Morgens bis Mitternachts* and *Caligari* in a comparative analysis:

> Once again, the conception of space in the film *Von Morgens bis Mitternachts* will be briefly described: abstract space, colorless and incorporeal impressions, no exploitation of perspective, but only the impression of background surfaces, no effects of light or shade, but black and white treatment. Confirmation of the nonexistent. The space as a passive, reticent entity not alive or active on its own [de Fries 1920–21].

In congenial teamwork, the set designer Robert Neppach and cameraman Carl Hoffmann heightened the painterly aspect of the architecture. Painted and constructed sets blend with the characters: "The figures have abandoned their organic shape, are fragments, formal elements of the decorative idea, they contribute to shaping the pictorial space, are torn apart by spots and stripes of light which have been painted on them" (Kurtz 1926).

The various architectural and dramatic motifs of *Caligari* and *Von Morgens bis Mitternachts* make clear that the Expressionist film does not conform to a consistent stylistic concept, but tends to present an individually differentiated aesthetic realization each time.

P. L.

2

4

3

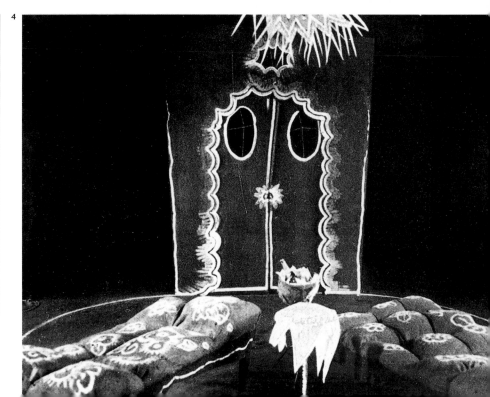

Die Strasse
(The Street)

Germany, Stern Film G.m.b.H., Ufa, 1923

Director: Karl Grune. *Sets:* Ludwig Meidner, Karl Goergen. *Camera:* Karl Hasselmann. *Cast:* Eugen Klöpfer (civil servant), Lucie Höflich (his wife), Aud Egede Nissen (whore), Anton Edthofer (pimp), Leonard Haskels (small-towner).
Premiere: 29 November 1923, Berlin.

Literature: "Film Kritik: Die Straße," *Film – Kurier* (30 November 1923); "Kunstbauten zur 'Straße,'" *Neue illustrierte Filmwoche*, no. 14 (1923), p. 215; "Nächtliche Großstadtstrasse im Film," *Film-Kurier*, no. 7 (8 January 1924); Publicity Release "Die Strasse" (Berlin: Hansa Film Verleih, 1924); Siegfried Kracauer, *From Caligari to Hitler: A Psychological History of the German Film* (Princeton: Princeton University Press, 1947); Lotte Eisner, *The Haunted Screen* (Berkeley: University of California Press, 1973), pp. 252–56; Werner Sudendorf, "Das sporadische Genie: Die Stummfilme Karl Grunes 1919–1929," in Helmut G. Asper, ed., *Wenn wir von gestern reden, sprechen wir über heute und morgen: Festschrift für Martha Mierendorff zum 80. Geburtstag* (Berlin: Edition Sigma, 1991), pp. 13–24.

Fig. 1: Cover of the program by Erich Godal. Stiftung Deutsche Kinemathek, Berlin.

Fig. 2: By the River.

Fig. 3: In the Street.

This is the story of a night in the big city, lived and suffered through by the hero, a minor civil servant, who is seduced by the lights and temptations of the street. At dusk, he leaves his wife and his secure bourgeois home to immerse himself in a one-night adventure. In the morning, disappointed and defeated, he returns to his wife, who, without a word dishes up last night's reheated soup for him. Instead of the adventures he had thought he was missing, the nocturnal city entangled him in an endless series of threatening situations, humiliations, and fatal misunderstandings.

What had suddenly awakened the hero's appetite for adventure were images of street life. In a famous scene at the beginning of the film, the shadows of passersby are projected into his dim living room. When he looks out the window, he sees the twilit city as a whirl of superimposed promises. Having been drawn outdoors, the hero looks in shop windows and restaurants and finally follows a lady. But his enthusiasm soon gives way to awkward timidity, and the city's buildings take on a strange, threatening character. In one famous sequence, the big eyeglasses advertising an optician's shop cast searching looks at him just as he falls into a prostitute's trap.

Karl Grune's film is an eloquent example of the sort of grappling with urban experiences that played an important role in the cultural self-definition of the Weimar Republic. The collaboration of the painter Ludwig Meidner, who had already acquired a reputation before World War I as a brilliant delineator of dynamic urban scenes, was of great importance for the film.

Grune and Meidner were concerned with exposing the period's enthusiasm for big cities as an illusion. The street, which presents itself at first as a bright, shining temptation, turns out to be completely different in the hero's own experience of it. Suddenly, it appears not only commonplace but also dark, unsafe, and bedeviled. Meidner created buildings with massive walls and small windows, dark lanes, and crooked backyards. The speeding traffic is more threatening than intoxicating. The idyllic skyline with small, twinkling houses by the river is obviously as false as the relationship between the awkward hero and the whore sitting on a bench facing it. Thus, the film is also a subtle parable about the promises of illusion achieved by the means used in film itself and about temptation followed by disenchantment.

The profound fascination exercised by the theme of the city street, extending far beyond the immediate occasion of the film, is evident in numerous contemporary reviews. Often enough, the disillusioning ending of Grune's film was lost sight of completely. Especially for the grandiose opening montage, he was praised as the "poet of the night, of the inferno" and for his "pathos of the everyday": "In Grune's film, the street was conceived as a stimulating, provocative factor, driving the blood to ecstasy — like an injection of some dangerous stimulant. . . The street is not just any location for the film, it is the characteristic site of the pictorial vision for film today" ("Nächtliche Großstadtstrasse" 1924). As another reviewer put it "To some extent the real world in this film has the reality of the supernatural. Grune does not present an environment with its details, but shows the essentials, the quintessence, one might say, the idea of the respective atmospheres where this nocturnal adventure leads" (Film-Kurier 1923). Some people even claimed to see an ominous reflection of the times in this film: "And now the vision of the street . . . the grimace of an age that sacrifices its soul to business and stuns itself with wild capers. The dance of death of an epoch that overstrains its voice so as not to have to hear its own wailing" ("Film Kritik" 1923). After World War II, Siegfried Kracauer interpreted this tendency matter-of-factly as an early withdrawal from the progressive leanings of the time: "Instead of recognizing the values of anarchistic life, the film deprecates them in that it designates the street as an area where the law of the jungle rules and people look for happiness in play and superficial sexual affairs" (Kracauer 1947).

D. N.

Die Nibelungen

(The Nibelungs)
Part One: Siegfried
Part Two: Kriemhilds Rache (Kriemhild's Revenge)

Germany, Decla-Bioscop-Ufa, 1924

Director: Fritz Lang. *Script:* Thea von Harbou. *Camera:* Carl Hoffmann, Günther Rittau. *Sets:* Otto Hunte, Erich Kettelhut, Karl Vollbrecht. *Music:* Gottfried Huppertz. *Cast:* Paul Richter (Siegfried), Hans Adalbert von Schlettow (Hagen), Margarethe Schön (Kriemhild), Hanna Ralph (Brunhilde), Theodor Loos (König Günther).
Premieres: 14 February 1924 (part 1), 26 April 1924 (part 2), Berlin.

1

Literature: Herbert Ihering, "Die Nibelungen," *Berliner Börsen Kurier* (15 February 1924); Fritz Lang, "Worauf es beim Nibelungen Film ankam," *Ufa press release* (1924); Kurt Pinthus, "Das Tagebuch," *8-Uhr Abendblatt* (3 May 1924); Erich Kettelhut, "Erinnerungen," unpublished manuscript, ca. 1960, Archive Stiftung Deutsche Kinemathek, Berlin; Lotte Eisner, *The Haunted Screen* (Berkeley: University of California Press, 1973), pp. 151–70; idem, *Fritz Lang* (London: Secker and Warburg, 1976), pp. 69–81; Victoria M. Stiles, *The Siegfried Legend and the Silent Screen: Fritz Lang's Interpretation of a Hero Saga, Literature/Film Quarterly* 4 (1980); Rob Edelman, "Die Nibelungen," in Frank N. Magill, ed., *Magill's Survey of the Cinema: Foreign Language Films,* vol. 2 (Englewood Cliffs: Salem Press, 1982), pp. 803–05; Reinhold Keiner, *Thea von Harbou und der deutsche Film bis 1933* (Hildesheim: Georg Olms Verlag, 1984), pp. 84–90; Graham Cooper, "Form and Fable: The Influence of German Industrial Art on Fritz Lang's Die Nibelungen," *Performing Arts Annual* (1986), pp. 4-37; Sabine Hake, "Architectural Hi/stories: Fritz Lang and The Nibelungs," *Wide Angle* 12, no.3 (July 1990), pp. 38–57; Hein-B. Heller, "Man stellt Denkmäler nicht auf den flachen Asphalt," in Joachim Heinzle and Anneliese Waldschmidt, eds., *Die Nibelungen* (Frankfurt am Main: Suhrkamp, 1991), pp. 351–96; Dieter Bartetzko, "Bauhaus der Träume: Babelsberger Filmarchitekturen," in Michael Töteberg and Klaus Kreimeier, eds., *Die Nibelungen* (Berlin: Deutsches Historisches Museum, 1992), pp. 5–15; Angelika Breitmoser–Bock, *Bild, Filmbild: Schlüsselbild: Zu einer kunstwissenschaftlichen Methodik der Filmanalyse am Beispiel von Fritz Langs Siegfried* (Munich: Schaudig, Bauer, Ledig, 1992); Michael Esser, "Zombies im Zauberwald: Die Nibelungen von Fritz Lang," in Hans-Michael Bock and Michael Töteberg, eds., *Das Ufa Buch* (Frankfurt am Main: Zweitausendeins, 1992), pp. 142–45; Heide Schönemann, *Fritz Lang: Filmbilder, Vorbilder* (Potsdam: Edition Hentrich, 1992).

2

Fig. 1: Otto Hunte, Sketch for *Die Nibelungen, 1. Teil: Siegfried: "Bridge between Two Towers." Gouache on paper, approx. 42 x 60 cm.* Signed: O. Hunte. *Deutsches Filmmuseum, Frankfurt am Main.*

Fig. 2: Erich Kettelhut, Sketch for *Die Nibelungen, 1. Teil: Siegfried: "Brunhild's Castle in the Lake of Fire." Pencil and colored Pencil on paper. 28 x 48 cm. Stiftung Deutsche Kinemathek, Berlin.*

Fig. 3: Erich Kettelhut, Sketch for *Die Nibelungen, 1. Teil: Siegfried: "Brunhild's Castle in the Lake of Fire with Northern Lights." Pastel on paper, 49 x 64 cm. Stiftung Deutsche Kinemathek, Berlin.*

Fig. 4: The Cathedral at Worms.

3

The film version of the "Nibelungen-lied," which had been raised to the status of German national epic in the Romantic era, was the most ambitious production of Ufa to date. The screenplay reduces the epic source to a skeletal plot that revolves around the polarities of good and evil, love and hate, innocence and malevolence. Siegfried becomes the victim in the first part of the film. He leaves the lonely wood in which he learned the blacksmith's craft from Mime and fights his way through a magic forest to Worms, toward the court of Günther and his sister Kriemhild. On his way, he plunders the Nibelungen treasure guarded by Alberich and appropriates his magic hood. Siegfried kills a dragon and bathes in its blood, making himself invincible, except at a small spot on his back, which a fallen leaf covers accidentally. Thus armed, Siegfried is victorious in further challenges and wins a tournament to obtain Kriemhild's favor. The grim Hagen of Troye becomes his bitter rival. Intrigue and revenge escalate to the first climax, the insidious murder of Siegfried. In *Kriemhilds Rache*, Kriemhild marries Etzel, the leader of the Huns. With their help, she takes horrible revenge on her family for Siegfried's death, getting killed herself in the process.

The vision of the Middle Ages as a supposedly better period in German history provided an escape for many from an apparently hopeless modern age after World War I. Thea von Harbou and Fritz Lang dedicated *Die Nibelungen* "to the German people" in the opening credits and "to the prestige of German culture and civilization, from whose most noble root the saga of the Nibelungen has sprung," as Lang explained on the occasion of the screening of the second part. This was clearly a reference to the psycho-political situation after the war. The architecture and decor of the film underscore this claim with a contemporary medieval vision. Clear, cool interiors and architecture, along with plain geometrical ornament, dominate the scenes at Worms, in contrast to the fantastic vision of Brunhild's castle in the lake of fire and the more "primitive" architecture of rounded forms and wild, expressionistic ornament for the culture of the Huns. These qualities evoke the beginnings of modernist style at the turn of the century, the arts and crafts of the

early Bauhaus, and also, the colorful fantasies of Expressionist architects. The critics emphasized the superiority of the film design over the ability of the actors:

> Thus, the curious thing happens that . . . what is almost not sensed in the epic becomes the artistically most valuable aspect of the film: the pictorial element, the scenery, the idyllic atmosphere, the movement. Fritz Lang was a painter and is still a painter now. . . Therefore the best parts of the film are not the actual Nibelungen incidents, but that which is draped colorfully around this horrible story [Pinthus 1924].

In the fall of 1922, preparations for the production began with lengthy and exhaustive production meetings at Lang's home. The entire technical and artistic team was present. Cameramen, set designers, costume designers, and makeup artists worked on this *Gesamtkunstwerk*, for which Lang prescribed the stylistic tenor. He wanted to capture four different worlds in one stylistic whole: "the world of Worms," a world of refined culture, contrasting with the world of Siegfried, "the cathedral of the forest, the meadows lying in the twilight, the gnarled trees in which ghostly, elflike Alberich, the lord of the dwarfs, dwells," as well as "the world of Brunhilde, Isenland, northern lights, alien, pale, icy air" and "the world of the Huns and Etzel, the Asian, the lord of the earth" (Lang 1924). Every frame, every detail of the decor was discussed thoroughly before Lang wanted to be shown the first designs. Otto Hunte drew them, in part during all-night sessions. These designs formed the basis for conferences in which, besides the architecture, the lighting and camera work were discussed. Then, they were handed over to Erich Kettelhut to be worked out further. He completed the technical drawings and calculated the proportions according to the dimensions agreed upon.

Many of Hunte's and Kettelhut's architectural drawings have been preserved in the Stiftung Deutsche Kinemathek, Berlin, and the Cinémathèque Française, Paris. While not identical with stills, they demonstrate all the characteristics and requirements of film scene composition. Not only do the rooms and architecture appear strictly composed and conceived in detail in these

Fig. 5: Siegfried in the Forest.

5

Fig. 7: Erich Kettelhut, Construction drawing for the filming of the model of Brunhild's Castle. Ink, watercolor on paper, 28 x 48 cm. Stiftung Deutsche Kinemathek.

Fig. 8: Otto Hunte, The Castle at Worms. *Sketch for* Die Nibelungen, 1. Teil: Siegfrieds Tod. *Gouache on cardboard, approx. 42 x 60 cm. Signed:* O. Hunte. *Deutsches Filmmuseum, Frankfurt am Main.*

Fig. 9: In Burgundy's Castle.

Fig. 10: Erich Kettelhut, Sketch for Die Nibelungen, 2. Teil: Kriemhild's Rache: Hagen and Volker Keeping Night Watch. *Pastel on paper, 50 x 65 cm. Stiftung Deutsche Kinemathek, Berlin.*

drawings; Nature is also subjected to symmetry and artifice. Kettelhut, who documented the shooting precisely in his memoirs, wrote of the take of the magic forest, through which Siegfried rides toward the courtly world:

> We began with the construction of the forest on the grounds. I'm saying construction on purpose, because this construction was not grown architecture, but a cathedral created by mysterious forces. Its treetrunks over two meters in circumference reached up without branches into a twilight gloom. The roof, which was never visible, let single broad shafts of sunlight illuminate the darkness. This forest was discussed for a long time in the production meetings [Kettelhut ca. 1960].

P. L.

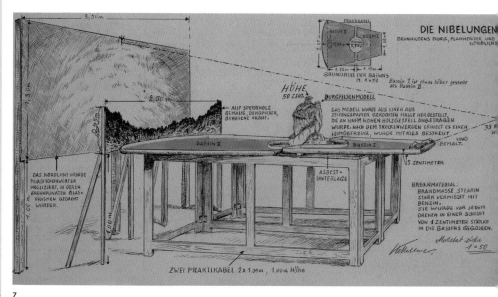

7

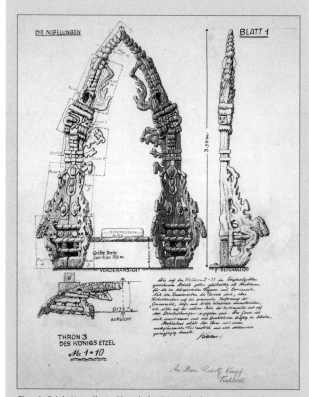

Fig. 6: Erich Kettelhut, Sketch for Die Nibelungen, 2. Teil: Kriemhild's Rache: King Etzel's Throne. *Ink, pencil and sepia wash on paper, 41 x 56 cm. Stiftung Deutsche Kinemathek, Berlin.*

NIBELUNGEN · 1.TEIL Burg zu Worms

8

9

10

L'Inhumaine
(The Inhuman One)

France, Cinégraphic, 1924

Director: Marcel L'Herbier. *Script:* Pierre MacOrlan. *Sets:* Robert Mallet-Stevens, Alberto Cavalcanti, Fernand Léger (laboratory), Claude Autant-Lara (winter garden), Pierre Chareau (light fixtures and furniture), Jean Puiforcat, René Lalique, and Jean Luce (decorations). *Camera:* Georges Specht, Jean Letort. *Cast:* Georgette LeBlanc (Claire Lescot); Jacques Catelain (Einnar Norsen); Philippe Herriat (The Maharajah Djorah).
Premiere: July 1924, Paris.

Literature: Adolf Loos, "'L'Inhumaine': Histoire féerique," *Neue Freie Presse* (29 July 1924); Robert Mallet-Stevens, "Architecture et Cinéma," *Les Cahiers du Mois,* no. 16–17 (1925), pp. 95–98; Robert Mallet-Stevens, *Le Décor moderne au cinéma* (Paris: Massin, 1928); Michel Louis, "Mallet-Stevens and the Cinema 1919–1929," in Hubert Jeanneau and Dominique Deshoulières, eds., *Robert Mallet-Stevens, Architecte* (Brussels: Editions des Archives d'Architecture Moderne, 1980); Richard Roud, *Rediscovering French Film* (Boston: Little, Brown and Co., 1983); Christiane Louis, "La velocità . . . la notte/Speed . . . Night: Rob. Mallet-Stevens' Architecture for 'L'Inhumaine,' 1924," *Domus,* no. 689 (December 1987), pp. 80–84; Luc Wouters, "Cinema and Architecture," in Jean François Pinchon, ed., *Rob. Mallet-Stevens, Architecture, Furniture, Interior Design* (Cambridge, MA: MIT Press, 1990), pp. 91–107.

It is undeniable that cinema has a marked influence on modern architecture; on the other hand, modern architecture contributes its artistic share to cinema. Modern architecture does not just offer cinematographic decor, but it leaves its imprint on the mise-en-scène, it overflows its frame; architecture plays. (. . .)
Modern Architecture is essentially photogenic: large plans, straight lines, sober ornaments, unified surfaces, clear contrast between light and shade: which better background could one dream of for images in motion, which better contrast to display life itself? In the near future, the architect will be the indispensible colloborator of the set designer [Mallet-Stevens 1925].

Fig. 1: Fernand Léger, The Laboratory.

The plot of *L'Inhumaine*, a mishmash of science fiction, love story, and thriller, chronicles three days in the lives of the glamorous, notorious soprano Claire Lescot, the "inhuman one" of the title, and two rivals for her affection, Einnar Norsen, an engineer who is the hero of the story, and the Maharajah Djorah, the villain. The story opens with a dinner party at Lescot's sleekly luxurious villa. She cold–heartedly plays Norsen and Djorah against each other, inducing Norsen to feign his suicide in a successful attempt to win her. Norsen gives the reformed Lescot a tour of his laboratory, which features such marvels as a device that enables her not only to broadcast her singing around the world on radio but also to see on a television screen the delighted reactions of listeners from Chicago to Paris. This inspires the jealous Djorah to murder Lescot, and — to further torment Norsen — leave her body at his laboratory. Little does Djorah know that the lab contains a subterranean room, the purpose of which is the revival of the dead. In a dramatic sequence of quick-cuts and montage which recalls the creation of Maria the robot in Fritz Lang's *Metropolis,* the lab comes alive with moving machinery, bubbling chemicals, and superimposed views of lightning and static electricity. Lescot appears to revive.

The Viennese architect Adolf Loos, reviewing *L'Inhumaine* in 1924, was much impressed: "It is a stunning poem to modern technique," he wrote. Not all viewers were so enthusiastic. What critics objected to was, first, the disparity between the rather conventional melodramatic plot and the *avantgarde* production design and, second, the disharmony between the different ideas pursued by the different set designers. Mallet-Stevens's stark, geometrical exteriors — very much in tune with his own architectural production at the time — were thought to clash with Cavalcanti's extravagant Deco interiors, Autant-Lara's pseudo-expressionistic winter garden, and Léger's intricately geometrical lab machines. This convergence, if not collaboration, is precisely what fascinates us about the film today. In an interview published in 1968, Marcel L'Herbier emphasized not the plot but the set designs: "We wanted it to be a sort of summing up, a sort of resumé of everything which made up the research

into form in France two years prior to the famous Decorative Arts Exhibition" (Louis 1980). An early sequence in the film, in which a tuxedoed Norsen in his sports car pulls up at Mallet-Steven's moderne villa, seems to encapsulate that moment's fascination with new technology and design, stylishly applied.

The film's use of elaborate interior sets and exterior models is striking, but of equal interest is its dramatic use of existing Parisian architecture. The opera singer Lescot's performances are at the Théâtre des Champs Elysées, built and designed in 1911 by Auguste Perret, with facades attributed to Henry van de Velde. This solid and — by 1924 — slightly time-worn building provides a contrast to the sleekly moderne artificial sets used elsewhere in the film. While the villa of Lescot, featured prominently at the beginning of the film, and Norsen's isolated lab, featured at the end, could be said to represent the heroine and hero, the theater, featured at the middle of the story, represents a sort of conventional, urban, neutral ground between them. L'Herbier introduces the theater by panning across the allegorical relief statues by Antoine Bourdelle on the decorated front facade (which itself became an influence on the design of cinema facades in the 1920s and '30s). However, two of the most dramatic scenes of the film take place in what appears to be the alley behind the theater. From here, Perret's massive reinforced concrete structural system is visible, the grid of concrete members filled in only by brick or translucent window panels. It is against this framing grid, and particularly on either side of the windows, that Lescot is pursued by the jealous Djorah after her performances. In one scene, we see his shadow through the window, identifiable by his top hat and distinctive cane. While the other shadows move, Djorah's remains still. His hand reaches toward us eerily to touch the window, becoming a distinct silhouette. The gray, weather-beaten surfaces of the back street contrast with the brightly lit, sleek, black and white surfaces of the villa and lab. The theater and, by extension, the city around it offer not only a neutral space but also a menacing environment. While Lescot has complete control of events at her villa, and Norsen of events at his lab (and

[A]ll previous sensations are overshadowed by the scenes of recalling from the dead. The architect — it is France's most modern master Mallet–Stevens — together with the director has created breathtaking images, an ode to the monumentality of modern and utopian technique. We know similar achievements from the mise–en–scène of "The Makropolous File," the utopian drama of the Çapek brothers, which the painter Kiesler decorated. But here, in addition, we encounter the unlimited depth of space, the ever–changing places of action, and the undertakings of the engineer and his helpers, which are close to lunacy. This impression on the eye is similar to a musical impression, and Tristan's cry "Do I hear the light?" becomes true. The impression of these last images was overwhelming. One left the theater under the impression that one had witnessed the birth of a new art. An art that appeals to parts of our cerebral system, whose artistic yearnings had remained unfulfilled up to now [Loos 1924].

while L'Herbier himself has greater control of the sequences filmed on the artificial stage sets), the characters become subject to danger and confusion once they leave these modern, isolated havens for the city. This contrast seems to confirm the observation made by Le Corbusier and Pierre Jeanneret (in a proposal for an unbuilt pavillion at the 1925 *Exposition des arts décoratifs*) that "the 'street' is only a mummified grimace faced with the phenomenon of the car. The city is no more than an anachronism menacing our physical and moral health."

Léger, who filmed his own abstract exercise in cinema, *Ballet mécanique*, at the same time that he worked on *L'Inhumaine*, observed of 1920s cinema that it was "encumber[ed] by literature, and sentimentality" (Roud 1983). This was arguably true of *L'Inhumaine*. Mallet-Stevens noted in 1928 that modern architecture was used by filmmakers "exclusively for places of debauch-

ery: nightclubs or boudoirs of the demi–mondaine, which would allow one to suppose that the admirable efforts and researchers of painters, decorators, and architects are good only to surround those of ill–repute" (Mallet-Stevens 1928). *L'Inhumaine* did little to counter these observations. The critic Pierre Bourgeois wrote of the film in 1924: "On the one hand there is the intellectual side, a synthetic interpretation of moral and physical elements; and on the other, the commercial side, a melodramatic expression of emotions. The two forces are locked in combat from beginning to end" (Louis 1980). Such combat is far from unfamiliar to today's movie-goers, particularly those interested in films with elaborate sets and architectural references. While *L'Inhumaine* may ultimately have succumbed, it succumbed with exuberant, unpolished, jazzy, and eclectic style.

T. d. M.

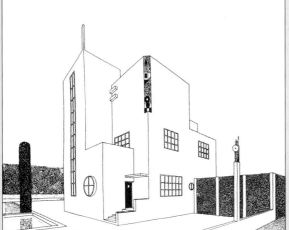

Fig. 2: Robert Mallet-Stevens, Design for a House, *1923.*

Fig. 3: Auguste Perret, Théâtre des Champs Elysées, *Paris 1911.*

Fig. 4: Robert Mallet-Stevens, Model of the Engineer's House.

Fig. 5: Robert Mallet-Stevens, The Engineer's House.

Fig. 6: Set by Claude Autant-Lara, Alberto Cavalcanti.

Fig. 7: Set by Robert Mallet-Stevens.

4

5

6

7

Das Wachsfigurenkabinett
(The Waxworks)

Germany, Neptun-Film A.G. for Ufa, 1924

Director: Paul Leni. *Script:* Hendrik Galeen. *Sets:* Paul Leni, Fritz Maurischat. *Camera:* Helmar Lerski. *Cast:* Emil Jannings (Harun al Rashid), Conrad Veidt (Ivan the Terrible), Werner Krauß (Jack the Ripper), Wilhelm Dieterle (the poet/Assad/a Russian prince), John Gottowt (proprietor of the waxworks booth).
Premiere: 13 November 1924, Berlin.

Literature: Rudolf Kurtz, *Expressionismus und Film* (Berlin: Verlag der Lichtbildbühne, 1926), p. 79; Siegfried Kracauer, *From Caligari to Hitler: A Psychological History of the German Film* (London: D. Dobson, 1947; reprint, Princeton: Princeton University Press, 1974); John D. Barlow, *German Expressionist Film* (Boston: Twaine, 1982), pp. 103–09; Ilona Brennicke and Joe Hembus, *Klassiker des Deutschen Stummfilms, 1910–1930* (Munich: Goldmann, 1983), pp. 292–30; Hans-Michael Bock, *Paul Leni: Grafik, Theater, Film,* exh. cat. (Frankfurt am Main: Deutsches Filmmuseum, 1986); *Das Wachfigurenkabinett: Drehbuch von Henrik Galeen zu Paul Lenis Film von 1923,* with an introductory essay by Thomas Koebner and material about the film by Hans-Michael Bock (Munich: Edition Text+Kritik, 1994).

Fig. 1: Jack the Ripper Sequence: View over the Roofs of the City towards the Fair.

Fig. 2: Jack the Ripper Sequence: The Caroussel.

The plot of *Das Wachsfigurenkabinett* tells of a young man hired by the owner of a wax museum to write descriptions of the exhibited figures for the public. After completing the stories of Harun al Rashid and Ivan the Terrible, the young man collapses in exhaustion at his desk in the museum. In his dreams, the wax figure of Jack the Ripper comes to life and pursues him and his girlfriend, the daughter of the booth's proprietor, through the expressionistically distorted streets of the town.

While the stories of Harun al Raschid and Ivan the Terrible were set in their respective exotic and historical surroundings, both the fair, where the wax figures are exhibited and where the story begins, and the final nightmare were designed in expressionistic fashion, with distorted architecture and eerily lit spaces. Clearly, Leni's film, generally considered the last of the expressionist experiments, responded to *Caligari,* which had initiated that style. Werner Krauß, who had played Caligari, was cast here as Jack the Ripper. A fair is the point of departure here as well, and a framing narrative is the connecting link and junction to reality. Many felt that *Caligari* had harmed Expressionism's reputation by dismissing it as the dream world of the insane. Leni's approach, on the other hand, explores the possibilities of an Expressionist filmic language. The town and the fairground where the story of the waxworks begins are represented with exactly the same distorted angularity as the young scribe's nightmares. An uneasiness with apparent reality remains after his awakening. Siegfried Kracauer remarked, "As dreams usually reveal the compulsions of the dreamer, the dream character of the Jack the Ripper episode arouses the suspicion that Jack and his accomplices are not meant to be mere figures of the past but the tyrants among us" (Kracauer 1947). Leni, with the help of his cameraman, Helmar Lerski, played with the potential of the new medium, leaving behind the conventional, rigid lighting and camera work indebted to theater that characterized *Caligari.* For several scenes, the actors had to act in front of dark velvet curtains to allow the later superimposition of separate takes. Among these were filmed sequences of Leni's drawings, which blended directly with the moving images.

This speeding, close pursuit, nothing but Krauß's calmly rigid face all the time, and two timid, fleeing young people, takes place among spatial catastrophes, among walls that bend, divide, crumble — among flashes of light which seem to smash the architecture into dazzling pieces. Natural shape is recklessly abandoned, and the bound and released dimensions of surfaces and lines, walls and bodies, stresses and projections are sensualized; nothing but power wanting to explode, the heaving of highly animated architecture into space, the voraciousness of openings, and the dizzying flight of stairs. Leni decorated this clear, controlled architecture, as it were, with light. The light, distilled from a thousand sources, creates feverish dreams in space, underscores every curve, runs along broken lines, creates depths without backgrounds, conjures up blackness on crooked walls so they seem to rise higher. The technical possibilities of the camera are harnessed, photographing images into each other and over each other, in order to liberate the mobility of forms in space from conventional bonds and elevate it to a metaphysical sphere. Means and materials are so confidently subordinated to a powerful decorative will that the audience accepted these very remote and subtle scenes with huge applause.
Expressionism attained this success because it subordinates its means to a psychological purpose. It becomes applied art. Leni masterfully drew this function out of it, thus creating a wealth of applications for Expressionism in film [Kurtz 1926].

D. N.

1

2

3

4

Fig. 3: *Paul Leni,* Jack the Ripper Sequence. The Panopticum, *Charcoal on paper, 19.5 x 25.4 cm. British Film Institute, London.*

Fig. 4: *Paul Leni,* Jack the Ripper Sequence. *Charcoal on paper, 34.9 x 30.5 cm. British Film Institute, London.*

Fig. 5: *Paul Leni,* Jack the Ripper Sequence. *Charcoal on paper, 34.9 x 30.4 cm. British Film Institute, London.*

Fig. 6: *Paul Leni,* Jack the Ripper Sequence. *Charcoal on paper, 35.5 x 30.5 cm. British Film Institute, London.*

Fig. 7: Jack the Ripper Sequence: In the Streets of the City.

5

6

7

Der letzte Mann
(The Last Laugh)

Germany, Union–Film der Ufa, 1924

Director: F.W. Murnau. *Script:* Carl Mayer. *Sets:* Robert Herlth, Walter Röhrig. *Camera:* Karl Freund. *Cast:* Emil Jannings (porter), Mary Delschaft (daughter), Max Hiller (bridegroom), Emilie Kurz (aunt), Hans Unterkircher (manager).
Premiere: 23 December 1924, Berlin.

Literature: Willy Haas, "Der letzte Mann," *Film-Kurier* 303 (24 December 1924); idem, "Was wird gebaut? Ein Besuch im Ufa–Gelände Neubabelsberg," *Film-Kurier* 169 (19 July 1924); G.V. Mendel, "Der letzte Mann," *Lichtbildbühne*, no. 152 (31 December 1924), p. 20; "Le Dernier des hommes," *Mon ciné* (12 November 1925), pp. 10, 11, 17; Lotte Eisner, *Murnau* (Berkeley: University of California Press, 1973), pp. 154–58; Michel Marie, "Une Première: Le Découpage intégral du 'Dernier des hommes' en continuité photographique," L'*Avant-Scène du Cinéma*, 190–91 (July–September 1977), pp. 45–84; David A. Cook, *A History of Narrative Film* (New York: Norton, 1981), pp. 120–25; Ilona Brennicke and Joe Hembus, *Klassiker des deutschen Stummfilms, 1910–1930* (Munich: Goldmann, 1983), pp. 114–18; Colin Loader, "Social Language in The Last Laugh," *Film and History* 18, no. 2 (May 1988), pp. 39–49; Luciano Berriatúa, *Los Proverbios chinos de F.W.Murnau* (Madrid: Instituto de la Cinematografía, 1990), pp. 236–73.

Der letzte Mann is generally considered to be an early milestone in the history of motion pictures, with an enormous influence on later productions. The story tells about an old hotel doorman who is demoted to the position of a toilet attendant and who has to put up with the scorn of his neighbors until a gift of money from a wealthy American guest makes him a rich man. Presented entirely without subtitles, the film stands out due to its cinematographic description of psychological aspects of the main character's sufferings, of shame, despair, spiteful glee, drunkenness, and fear. Three elements above all make this depiction convincing and contributed to the widespread impression that the film represented one of the first full realizations of the new medium's potential: the achievement of its star, Emil Jannings; the virtuoso and novel mobile camera work, which went hand in hand with daring superimposition effects and montage techniques; and, finally, the psychological role of architecture in the film.

Murnau and his set designers spent enormous energy and funds on the erection of the sets and also on the creation of a metaphorical language of architectural elements. The crucial moment when the doorman is told of his degradation and loses his uniform is seen through the panels of a glass door, making his shame visible to outsiders. Shortly afterwards, when he pilfers his livery in order to appear in dignity at his daughter's wedding the multi-storied hotel that the doorman had so proudly represented leans threateningly toward him. What appear at first to be two opposite poles of urban life — the brightly lit, huge palatial hotel downtown in the midst of lively traffic and the narrow backyard of a tenement block — soon prove to be two sides of the same coin, inseparable from each other. In the porter's fevered, drunken dreams after the party, the backyard and the hotel lobby blend; an elevator glides up and down in a corner of the tenement block, and a revolving door grows to threatening proportions.

Both the hotel itself and the buildings across the street are shown as enormous skyscrapers. Unusual at a time where there were hardly any buildings in Berlin higher than five stories, skyscrapers were often cited as symbols of American capitalism (and as such they act here as representations of the heartlessness of the great city). At the same time, however, skyscrapers were discussed by German architects and planners, who advocated an alternative style for high-rise buildings and a different urbanistic treatment. The sets by Herlth and Röhrig reflect these debates and present a skyscraper architecture that is astonishingly sober and unornamented.

Several of Herlth's sketches for the film have survived at the Cinémathèque Française in Paris. They range from technical drawings for the trick photography to conceptual sketches of individual scenes which seem to envision lighting and camera angles as well.
D.N.

Fig. 1: Set under construction.

Fig. 2: Production shot: Building the backyard set.

Fig. 3: The Hotel. *Sketch by Robert Herlth.*

Fig. 4: In Front of the Hotel.

1

2

3

4

[T]his is something completely different again, completely new — something which, although Lupu Pick tried it first, F.W. Murnau carried through here with stunning radicality, taking all the consequences: the running, dancing, pirouetting camera, performing acrobatics, actually twisting around in its movements. No one in America has dared to do that yet. Like the eye of the beholder, who also "approaches" something strange — no, it's different: like the eye of a creative writer, in which a spark has been lit at the sight of some small, insignificant close-up in a backyard. And now he struggles for the totality of the scene. To accompany the big face of a grinning old proletarian woman, he must have the whole desolate interior facade of the tenement block, all four sides of the yard, also the leaden gray city sky above, also the balconies, where an old dusty rug is being beaten, as well as the bumpy, dirty pavement littered with garbage. He has to have it all together — but all somehow relating again to the grinning toothless witch's face, dominating everything at the moment, determining everything, symbolizing everything, this whole world of desolation, dust, and oppression . . . Murnau's architect Röhrig completed a second large structure besides this for the same film: the facade of the metropolitan hotel the size of the Berlin Kaiserhof or Vienna's Imperial — a really gigantic hotel, with an adjoining city street and an outdoor structure in perspective above an American city [Haas, "Was wird gebaut," 1924].

There was a telegram from Hollywood addressed to Ufa, asking what camera we had used to shoot the film. It added that in the USA there was no such camera, and no town to compare with the one in our film. . . We had been helped by our use of perspective models, too. In order to make convincing the sequence where the man who thinks he is the most important person in the hotel whistles to summon motor cars, the hotel behind him had to appear enormous, at least thirty storeys high. So we used a model. This was a technique that was already known, but it had rarely been used with such success. . .
The view, or rather "background", seen from the revolving door was managed by means of a perspective shot of a sloping street 15 meters high in the foregroung diminishing to 5 in the "distance". The street ran between model skyscrapers as much as 17 meters high — this again caused Hollywood a good deal of astonisment.
To make the "perspective" work we had big buses and Mercedes cars in the foreground; in the middle-ground middle sized cars; and in the background small ones, with behind them again chidren's toy cars. Farthest of all, in front of the shops, we had crowds of "people" cut out and painted and moved across the screen on a conveyor belt [Robert Herlth, quoted in: Eisner 1973].

Fig. 5: Robert Herlth, Sketch for the construction of the street scene in front of the hotel. Pencil on tracing paper, approx. 21 x 28 cm. Cinémathèque Française, Musée du Cinema, Paris.

Fig. 6: Set under construction.

Fig. 7: The Skyscrapers across the Street from the Hotel. Frame enlargement by Dietrich Neumann.

Fig. 8: Robert Herlth, Sketch for Der letzte Mann: The Doorman Loses His Position.

Fig. 9: The Hotel Tower Bends Down to Threaten the Doorman. Frame enlargement by Dietrich Neumann.

Fig. 10: The Former Doorman as Restroom Attendant.

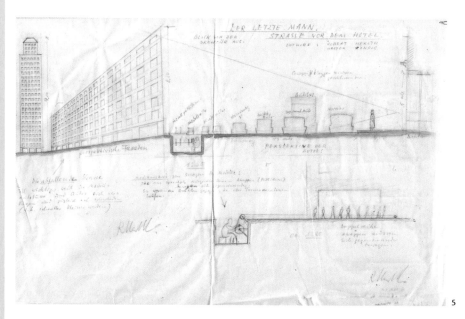

5

6

7

8

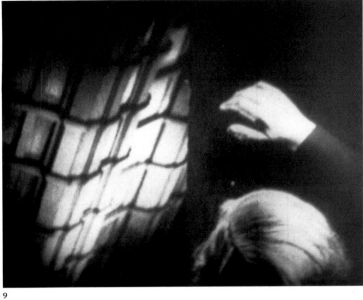

9

10

Aelita — Queen of Mars

(Originally released as
Aelita: The Revolt of the Robots)

U.S.S.R., Mezhrabprom-Rus, 1924

Director: Jakov A. Protazanov. *Script:* Feodor Otsep and Alexei Faiko, after Alexei Tolstoy's novel *Aelita or The Decline of Mars.* *Sets:* Sergei Kozlovsky, Isaac Moisseyevitch Rabinovich, Victor Simov, Alexandra Exter. *Camera:* Yuri A. Zhelyabuzhsky, Emil Schuneman. *Cast:* Nicholai Tsereteli (Loss, Spiridanov), Valentina Kuindzhi (his wife), Iuliia Solntseva (Aelita), Nicholai Batalov (Gussev), A. F. Pergonets (Ihoshka), Konstantin Eggert (Tuskub), V. A. Jornadsky (Gor). *Premiere:* 25 October 1924, Moscow.

Literature: Alexei Tolstoi, *Aelita or The Decline of Mars* (1922) (Ann Arbor: Ardis Publishers, 1985); Mordaunt Hall, "The First Lady of Mars," *New York Times* (26 March 1929); Alexander S. Birkos, *Soviet Cinema: Directors and Films* (Hamden, CN: Archon Books, 1976), pp. 90–91; Michael Louis, "Aelita, ou le rêve de l'homme ridicule," *Archives de l'architecture moderne* 11 (1977), pp. 34–49; Milka Bliznakov, "The Realization of Utopia: Western Technology and Soviet Avant-Garde Architecture," in William C. Brumfield, ed., *Reshaping Russian Architecture: Western Technology, Utopian Dreams* (Cambridge, MA: Woodrow Wilson International Center of Scholars, 1990), pp. 145–63; Peter Kenez, *Cinema and Soviet Society, 1917–53* (Cambridge and New York: Cambridge University Press, 1992), pp. 46–47; Denise Youngblood, *Movies for the Masses: Popular Cinema and Soviet Society in the 1920s* (New York: Cambridge University Press, 1992).

This film is far more interesting to read about than to gaze upon. The producers had quite a good if a none too fresh idea, but it is worked out with a certain apathy, possibly because the Russians did not detect any opportunity to spread a little propaganda. The very passages that one conjures up in one's imagination are not in the film. Instead there are many scenes with queer settings and martians sparsely costumed in spiked hats and celluloid or metal garments. . . . There are weird stairways, which look as if they were made of thin wood or cardboard, and the tinting of the film destroys what depth there might be to the very ordinary photography. The film is short, for which one feels thankful, but, short as it is, it seems too long [Hall 1929].

The Ship landed by a tall, heavy, gloomy building, like a pyramid, of blood-red and black stone. On the broad staircase, among the square columns that narrowed toward the top and only reached a third of the way up the building, stood a group of Martians . . . Gussev looked in awe at the turbulent square, multicolored from all the clothing, the multitude of wings flapping overhead, the massive gray or black-red buildings, and the transparent outlines of towers beyond the roofs. What a city, now I call this a city! [Tolstoi 1922].

Aelita illustrates the growing fascination with science fiction novels in the young Soviet state. It was among the earliest science fiction films as well as one of the very first films to come out of revolutionary Russia and had great success at home and abroad. In fact, it was the most discussed Russian film until Sergei Eisenstein's *Battleship Potemkin* (1925). The director, Jakov A. Protazanov, was a successful filmmaker in Russia even before the Revolution. Like many Russians intellectuals (among them Tolstoi, the author of *Aelita* [1922], and Alexandra Exter, the set designer), Protazanov left Russia in the turbulent years after the October Revolution for the centers of the European avant–garde, Paris and Berlin. After being called back to Moscow in 1923 by the Rus film studio, he proceeded to make ten silent films in the next six years, beginning with *Aelita.* According to the program brochure, Protazanov shot 22,000 meters of film for the 2,841–meter picture and employed a cast and crew of thousands. *Aelita* was among the most expensive Russian films of its time.

The film centers on the young Russian communications engineer Loss, who is immensely interested in space travel and is secretly working on plans for a spaceship to Mars. In his fantasies, he sees the Martian queen waiting for him. Returning from his work, he becomes worried about the faithfulness of his wife and, suspecting an affair with a tenant, shoots her in a moment of jealousy and then runs away. An intense daydream follows, in which Loss sees himself building his rocket and escaping to Mars with his friend Gussev. En route, they discover a stowaway, Detective Kazlovsky, ready to arrest Loss for murder. On Mars, Loss immediately falls in love with the beautiful but powerless Queen Aelita. Having watched him kiss his wife through her telescope, she has eagerly been awaiting his arrival to learn more about this earthly habit. Confronted with social injustice on Mars, Loss and Gussev stir up a revolution among the slaves who work in gigantic underground factories, and a Soviet republic is established on the red planet. Aelita, however, betrays the freedom movement. Disappointed, Loss kills her and finally awakens. He finds himself at the Moscow railroad station

and decides to return home, where, greeted by his wife, he realizes that his shot had missed her. The suspected tenant in the meantime has been arrested for fraud. Loss decides to stop daydreaming, burns the blueprints for his spaceship, and goes back to work to build the new Soviet Union.

Although Protazanov clearly took a less adventurous route in his use of cinematic language than his contemporaries Dziga Vertov or Sergej Eisenstein, *Aelita* is innovative in its narrative and creative in its montage of realistic and dream sequences, and it features remarkable sets and costume designs. As is often the case, the set design is somewhat independent of the narrative. Although Martian society is presented as feudal and dictatorial (a metaphor for prerevolutionary Russia), the Martians' technical devices and the design of their metropolis have an exciting, clean, modernistic character that contrasts favorably with the overcrowded and haphazard life of Moscow. In fact, their metropolis bears a certain resemblance to the models of a future socialistic city designed by Alexander Vesnin and Ludmilla Popova for the 1921 October celebrations in Moscow. Both feature tall spires, tremendous arches, and ample wiring for successful communication. Some of Exter's drawings from the early '20s reveal her interest in similar urban visions. The asymmetrically curved, inclined, overlapping walls of the interior spaces seem influenced by *Das Cabinet des Dr. Caligari*, Cubist painting, and contemporary theater decoration. Even the subterranean caves in which an army of helmeted slaves works are spacious and reveal enormous machines with armatures and expressively painted giant flywheels. Among the many compelling inventions in the Martian city is a fan–door, operating like a camera's shutter, which leads to the "tower of radiant energy" in which the telescope is installed. Equally important is the occasional use of architecture as a symbol of the old system. When the travelers from Earth praise their revolution at home a liberated Russian worker is seen underneath the flaming inscription *October 25, 1917* crushing models of classical architecture with a hammer and forging a sickle out of his chains.

D. N.

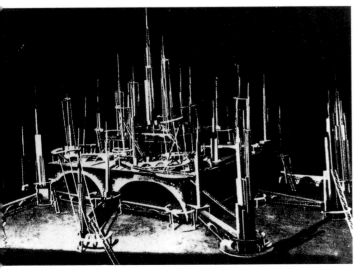

Fig. 1: Alexander Vesnin and Ludmilla Popova, Models of a future socialistic city designed for the October celebrations in Moscow in 1921.

Fig. 2: I. Rabinowitsch, Model for the Martian City.

Fig. 3: Alexandra Exter, Dynamic City, 1921.

Fig. 4: Martian Architecture.

Fig. 5: In the Martian City.

Metropolis

Germany, Universum Film A.G., 1927

Director: Fritz Lang. *Script:* Thea von Harbou, based on her novel. *Sets:* Otto Hunte, Erich Kettelhut, Karl Vollbrecht. *Camera:* Karl Freund, Günther Rittau. *Cast:* Brigitte Helm (Maria), Alfred Abel (Joh Fredersen), Gustav Fröhlich (Freder, Joh Fredersen's son), Rudolf Klein-Rogge (Rotwang), Fritz Rasp (the thin man), Theodor Loos (Josaphat), Heinrich George (Groth). *Premiere:* 14 January 1927, Berlin.

Literature: Thea von Harbou, *Metropolis* (1926), reprint (Berlin: Ullstein, 1984); Otto Hunte, "Der Baumeister von 'Metropolis,'" *Illustrierter Film-Kurier* (1927); Karlernst Knatz, "Der Weltfilm der UFA: Fritz Langs Metropolisfilm," *Tägliche Rundschau* 47, no. 16 (11 January 1927); "Metropolis," *Reichsfilmblatt*, no. 11 (1927), p. 17; H.G. Wells, "Mr. Wells Reviews a Current Film," *New York Times Magazine* (17 April 1927), pp. 4, 22; Luis Buñuel, "Metropolis," *Gazeta literaia* (1927–28); Erich Kettelhut, "Erinnerungen," unpublished manuscript, ca. 1960, Archiv Stiftung Deutsche Kinemathek, Berlin; Lotte Eisner, *The Haunted Screen* (Berkeley: University of California Press, 1973), pp. 223–36; Siegfried Kracauer, *From Caligari to Hitler: A Psychological History of the German Film* (Princeton: Princeton University Press, 1974); Ilona Brennicke and Joe Hembus, *Klassiker des deutschen Stummfilms 1910–1930* (Munich: Goldmann, 1983), pp. 134–42; Reinhold Keiner, *Thea von Harbou und der deutsche Film bis 1933* (Hildesheim: Georg Olms Verlag, 1984), pp. 91–100; Donald Albrecht, *Designing Dreams: Modern Architecture in the Movies* (London and New York: Thames and Hudson, 1986), pp. 153–57; Helmut Weihsmann, *Gebaute Illusionen: Architektur im Film* (Vienna: Promedia, 1988), pp. 171–77; Paolo Antonelli and Romana Schneider, "Metropolis in Vitro," *Domus* 717 (June 1990), pp. 74–80; Heide Schönemann, *Fritz Lang: Filmbilder, Vorbilder* (Berlin: Verlag Edition Hentrich, 1992), pp. 68–91; Dietrich Neumann, "The Urbanistic Vision in Fritz Lang's *Metropolis*," Thomas W. Kniesche, Stephen Brockmann (eds.), *Dancing on the Volcano: Essays on the Culture of the Weimar Republic* (Columbia, SC: Camden House, 1994) pp. 143–162; Gerhard Vana, "Modell und Mimesis: Zum Problem der Dimension in der Architektur am Beispiel von Fritz Langs *Metropolis*" (Ph.D. diss., Technical University, Vienna, 1994).

Fig. 1: Erich Kettelhut, "The Tower of Babel." Oil on cardboard, 43.6 x 55.2 cm. Stiftung Deutsche Kinemathek, Berlin.

Despite many justified objections about weaknesses of the plot, *Metropolis* counts as one of the most expressive testimonies of its age, an example of its political conflicts, hopes, fears, and enthusiasm for technology and American ways. Above all, *Metropolis* is a film of powerfully expressive architectural metaphors, a gallery of contemporary visions, and an important turning point in the development of film architecture. The story centers on Freder, his love for the working girl Maria, and the conflict with his father, Joh Fredersen, the almighty ruler of the huge city of Metropolis, who has armies of slaves laboring underground at gigantic machines. Searching for Maria, Freder sees for the first time the underground machine halls and the life-threatening labor conditions. When his father discovers Freder's love for Maria, who acts as a Christian priest to the workers, he has a robot lookalike constructed who deeply confuses Freder by seeming to betray him. The robot, out of control, starts a revolt among the workers. Only after the resulting destruction of the machines, the near death of thousands of women and children, and the rescue of his son from mortal danger is Joh Fredersen willing to become a more humane ruler.

As he had for *Die Nibelungen* and *Testament des Dr. Mabuse* (The Testament of Dr. Mabuse; 1922), Fritz Lang worked with the three set designers Erich Kettelhut, Otto Hunte, and Karl Vollbrecht on *Metropolis*. Having had architectural training himself, Lang often intervened emphatically in the design process. By a unique stroke of luck, not only are single sketches for *Metropolis* preserved, but an astoundingly clear, eloquent series of drawings by Erich Kettelhut from 1925–26 has also survived in the Stiftung Deutsche Kinemathek, Berlin, and the Cinémathèque Française, Paris. With these drawings, the prehistory of the famous view down into the abyss of the city's busy streets unfolds almost cinematographically. In addition, the manuscript of Kettelhut's memoirs sheds light on the collaboration among the director, scriptwriter, and set designers.

For Kettelhut and Hunte, the design of an architectural vision was a completely new task. They had never before conceived buildings

When the sun sank behind Metropolis, so that the houses became mountains and the streets valleys, when the streams of a light that was so cold it seemed to crackle, burst out of all the windows, from the walls of the houses, from the roofs and out of the belly of the city, when the silent blaring of the advertising lights arose, when the spotlights began to play on the New Tower of Babel in all the colors of the rainbow, the buses became chains of light, the small cars become rushing light-fish in a waterless deep sea, while from the invisible harbor of the subway an eternally constant magic glow surged forth, crossed by hasty shadows — then the cathedral stood in this unbounded ocean of light which dissolved all shapes in its shine, as the only dark thing, black and persevering, and seemed in its lack of light to separate from the earth and rise up higher and higher, and seemed in this maelstrom of tumultuous light to be the only thing tranquil, the only thing prevailing [Von Harbou 1926, p. 18].

There was, for example, the Tower of Babel, final image of a grandiose vision, which had begun with the building of the tower, with hundreds of slaves pulling an enormous block of ashlar through the desert sand. Otto Hunte's design for the completed tower was reminiscent of well-known design by old masters. I had drawn a tapered cone with a wide ramp circling upwards around it toward the top. Lang preferred Otto's idea, the cameraman Karl Freund mine; the opinions of the others were equally divided on both sides. My design looked more primitive, stranger, Otto's was somewhat more representative and easily understandable. In addition, Lang himself had also built a model for the top for the tower that was similar to Hunte's design. . . The discussion eventually settled on psychologizing details, became irrelevant and aggressive. Fritz Lang and Thea von Harbou decided in the end according to their own preferences [Kettelhut, ca. 1960].

Fig. 2: Erich Kettelhut, "1. Version." Ink on paper, 30.7 x 40.2 cm. Stiftung Deutsche Kinemathek, Berlin.

Fig. 3: Erich Kettelhut, "2. Version." Gouache on grey paper, 30 x 39 cm. Stiftung Deutsche Kinemathek, Berlin.

Fig. 4: View of the City.

that had no direct models. Two of Kettelhut's early drawings show entire city quarters rising like continuous mountain ranges. The detailed drawing *City of the Sons* reveals how Kettelhut planned the precise position of some of the film's locations: The domed glass house of the "pleasure garden" is visible at the top left; the statues lining the stadium shine at the top right. Kettelhut and Hunte's efforts soon concentrated on the view into the city streets underneath the "New Tower of Babel." The first version of downtown Metropolis Kettelhut drew is amazingly idyllic: traffic flows smoothly on several levels; plenty of parking spaces are provided. Pedestrians stroll among skyscrapers and look at window displays. A Gothic cathedral stands in the background as the focal point of the city, surrounded by the narrow, old houses of the wealthy middle class. This is probably how everyone in 1925 imagined a German city would look in the not too distant future. For the skyscrapers in the foreground, Kettelhut relied on the visions of his architect colleagues, who had produced numerous ideal designs during the period of forced inactivity due to the economic crisis. Probably most impressive is the curved glass building in the middle ground to the left, which could easily be mistaken for the frequently published design of a glass skyscraper by Mies van der Rohe. The central role of the cathedral in this drawing reflects Thea von Harbou's novel on which the film was based, in which "a small Gothic sect" resists the assault of new machine idols, who have names like Huitzilopochtli and Durgha. The German Gothic cathedral (it is no coincidence that it looks like Cologne Cathedral in Kettelhut's drawing) is presented as a bastion against the assault of modernity and the decadence of foreign cultures.

How this conception gradually yielded under Lang's direction can be deduced from Kettelhut's preliminary drawings. With a thick brown pencil, Lang crossed out Kettelhut's carefully detailed first version of the cathedral twice and wrote beside it: "Away with the church; Tower of Babel instead." With this terse comment, he not only left behind eloquent evidence of his directing style but also determined new priorities for the appearance of the set, making it refer to the contemporary discus-

sion regarding urban planning. The silhouettes of future cities, many architects argued at the time, should be dominated not by church towers, but by modern "temples of work," i.e. skyscrapers. In Kettelhut's second version, the cathedral has in fact disappeared and is replaced by an impressive multi-story concrete cone carrying an airplane landing platform. The city center has become even more peaceful and inviting. It continues to be framed by variously shaped buildings in the unornamented style of the avant-garde. We can only imagine, since there is no documentary evidence, that Lang put his foot down a second time at this point. It must have become obvious that a film plot about an inhumane ruler, the conflict between father and son, and, finally, the catastrophic destruction of the subterranean living quarters and machine rooms could not be mounted in such a friendly setting. Along similar lines, Kettelhut's early sketch for the "Hall of the Machines" shows them situated in a light-filled hall with large windows. Later, it was decided to place the machines underground and turn the main generator into a threatening altar for human sacrifices.

But how was a future city of oppression and exploitation to look? Kettelhut made use of several sources. In the film, the memory of the biblical Tower of Babel is revived in a dream sequence obviously based on Pieter Bruegel's famous painting of 1563. Photos of canyon-like streets in New York where, it was said, office employees never saw the daylight had been very popular in architecture magazines especially since World War I. Kettelhut introduced such streets on a scale that exceeded anything that existed in America at the time. He devoted much attention to the tower in the background, finally giving it an overwhelming, massive, threatening form. This tranformation appears to have been a reflection of contemporary debate in Germany. The massive forms of the monumental structures often cited in this context awakened memories of German imperialism, and interestingly, *Metropolis* was celebrated as a national demonstration of strength. However, the final scene of reconciliation between the ruler and the oppressed in the film takes place on the steps of the cathedral. Its role as the heart of Metropolis, which had

2

3

4

Fig. 5: Erich Kettelhut, "In the Elevator." Oil and gouache on cardboard, 30 x 41 cm. Stiftung Deutsche Kinemathek, Berlin.

been so curtly negated in Kettelhut's first drawing, was restored.

Kettelhut's preparatory work demonstrated that set design had to create more than just a background. It had to accompany the plot, underlining and commenting on it, and, beyond that, could refer to contemporary architectural debate. The young director and film critic Luis Buñuel was the first to recognize that the sets for *Metropolis* succeeded in this way. After the Spanish premiere in 1927, he wrote, "Now and forever the architect will replace the set designer. Film will be the faithful translator of the architect's boldest dreams" (Buñuel 1927–28). Kettelhut easily mastered a variety of drawing styles and executed his work in ink, colored pencil, watercolor, gouache, and oil, sometimes referring to the construction of the sets in the margins. A number of his paintings were used directly in the film. *Dawn* was part of the opening montage, the night view of the Tower of Babel (Fig. 1) belonged to an elaborate trick sequence, in which beams of light were shown moving up and down the facade of the tower. This was shot frame by frame in a stop-motion sequence; a new position for each beam was painted onto the varnished surface between each shot. For the impressive view into the street "canyon," a six-meter-deep perspectival model was built out of wood, plaster, canvas, and cardboard. The effect of motion was again achieved by shooting frame by frame and by individually advancing each car, airplane, train, and elevator between each shot.

D. N.

Fig. 7: The Machine.

Fig. 6: Filming downtown.

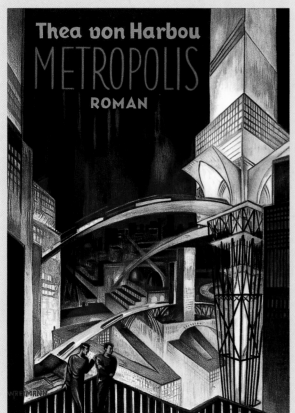

Fig. 8: Walter Reimann, Cover design for Thea von Harbou's novel Metropolis *(Berlin, 1926), ca. 1925. Color print on cardboard, 55 x 39 cm. Signed: W. Reimann. Deutsches Filmmuseum, Frankfurt am Main.*

Fig. 9: Boris Bilinski, Poster for the French premiere. Kunstbibliothek, Berlin.

Fig. 10: Pieter Bruegel the Elder, "The Building of the Tower of Babel," 1563. Oil on panel, 114 x 155 cm. Vienna, Kunsthistorisches Museum.

Fig. 11: The Tower of Babel.

Fig. 12: Erich Kettelhut, "Dawn." Oil and gouache on cardboard, 39 x 54.5 cm. Stiftung Deutsche Kinemathek, Berlin.

Fig. 13: Erich Kettelhut, "City of the Sons." Colored pencil and grey wash on paper, 30.7 x 40.2 cm. Stiftung Deutsche Kinemathek, Berlin.

12

13

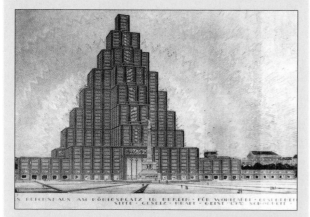

Fig. 14: Otto Kohtz, Project for federal office building for Berlin, 1920. Pencil, pen and ink, wash on cardboard, 49.5 x 70 cm. Plansammlung Technische Universität Berlin.

Fig. 17: Erich Kettelhut, "City from Above with Tower, Image No. I." Gouache on cardboard, 39.2 x 52.6 cm. Stiftung Deutsche Kinemathek, Berlin.

Fig. 19: In the Pleasure Garden.

Fig. 20: The Stadion.

Fig. 18: Erich Kettelhut, "Hall of the Machines: View from Above." Gouache and colored pencil on cardboard, 27.5 x 36.5 cm. Cinémathèque Française, Paris.

Fig. 15: Mies van der Rohe. Glass Skyscraper, 1922.

Fig. 16: E. Haimovici, R. Tschammer, and A. Caroli. Project for trade fair tower, Leipzig, 1920.

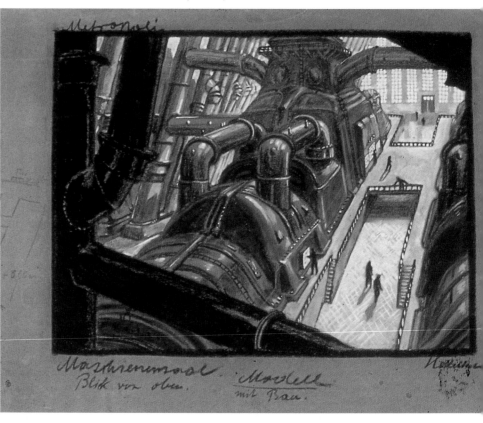

19

20

Sunrise

U.S.A., Fox, 1927

Director: F.W. Murnau. *Script:* Carl Mayer, based on Bernhard Sundermann's novel *Die Reise nach Tilsit.* *Sets:* Rochus Gliese. *Camera:* Karl Struss, Charles Rosher. *Cast:* George O'Brian (man), Janet Gaynor (woman), Garet Livingston (woman from the city). *Premiere:* 29 November 1927, Los Angeles.

Literature: Hermann Sudermann, *Litauische Geschichten* (Stuttgart: Cotta, 1918); Arnold Höllriegel, "Hollywood sucht den 'europäischen' Film," *Berliner Tageblatt,* no. 589 (19 December 1926); C. Adolph Glassgold, "Sunrise," *Arts* 12 (November 1927), pp. 282–83; "Sunrise Brings a New Day to the Movies," *Literary Digest* (3 December 1927); Dorothy B. Jones, "Sunrise: A Murnau Masterpiece," *Quarterly of Film, Radio and Television* 9 (1954–55), pp. 238–62; Molly Haskell, "Sunrise," *Film Comment* (Summer 1971), pp. 16–19; Lotte Eisner, *Murnau* (Berkeley: University of California Press, 1973), pp. 167–85; Robin Wood, "Murnau's Midnight and Sunrise," *Film Comment* 5 (May–June 1976), pp. 4–19; Mary Ann Doane, "Desire in 'Sunrise,'" *Film Reader* 2 (1977), pp. 76 ff; Steve Lipkin, "Sunrise: A Film Meets Its Public," *Quarterly Review of Film Studies* 2 (August 1977), pp. 339–55; Nestor Almendros, "Sunrise," *American Cinematographer* (April 1984), pp. 28–32; Dudley Andrew, *Film in the Aura of Art* (Princeton: Princeton University Press, 1984,) pp. 28–58; Luciano Berriatúa, *Los Proverbios Chinos de F.W. Murnau* (Madrid: Filmoteca Española, 1990), pp. 395–461.

Hundreds and hundreds of workmen, Mexicans in huge sombreros swarming around like ants, are in the process of building the main square of a city. The facades are already standing, and my knowledge of film tells me that nothing but these sculpturally structured facades, with their windows and oriels and balconies and shutters, will be erected. But it's unbelievable, the thought is too tremendous. . . The streetcar tracks are already laid, along which real streetcars will travel, and two elevated railways are waiting to begin operation. Coffee shops, banks, office buildings, and department stores are already identifiable. A church in the Schinkel style with severe columns is just being completed [Karl Friedrich Schinkel, 1781–1841, important classicist architect in Germany, D. N.]. The whole thing is not an American city square, but a European one, yet so modern you could freeze; it seems all to be made of stone and steel and glass . . . Murnau, the blonde giant, looks at me with his impenetrable smile. "In my film," he says, "you will hardly be allowed to notice this square and these cars once the great emotional conflict between the two people begins. All this is only decoration, background — only America can provide this, although it's not even the most important thing [Höllriegel 1926].

Fig. 1: Erich Mendelsohn, Mosse Haus, Berlin, 1922.

Fig. 2: The main city square at night in the rain.

Based on a 1917 novel, the film describes a crucial conflict in the life of a farm couple. The farmer is seduced by a vacationing woman from the city and with the prospect of a better life there is persuaded to kill his wife on a boat trip. A bundle of twigs he hides in the boat is intended to assure his survival after the feigned accident. At the decisive moment, however, he does not have the heart to carry out the deed and continues the boat trip with his wife to the city on the opposite shore of the lake instead. Their shared experiences there reconcile the young couple. On the return trip across the lake at night, a storm capsizes the boat. The man swims ashore. Although his wife cannot be found at first, she is finally rescued. The bundle of twigs is what saves her life.

Sudermann's novella, in which the man dies in the storm, but his wife gives birth to a son nine months later, is mainly about the development of the heroine's complex emotions and the contrast between city and country. Murnau created a brilliant parable about the dangers and attraction of the modern city. The urban temptress uses descriptions of the fast, entertaining life there as her lure. "Come to the city!" the title shouts, and fragmentary images of advertising lights and jazz trumpeters, of skyscrapers and a fast ride through a crowded street, whirl across the screen. Yet, after the abandoned murder attempt, when the couple gradually return to mutual trust and openness, it is precisely this colorful and exciting experience that reconciles them. Together, they manage the threatening swarm of traffic and discover the amenities of various shops and amusements. And only the modern architecture of the city provides locations, it seems, that constitute an adequate background for the complex emotional strands of the plot.

In one of the most moving scenes in the film, the two protagonists cower at a coffee shop table in the city and very slowly find their way out of fear, remorse, and despair back to openness and forgiveness. In his novel, Sudermann had set this scene in a narrow room in a dark café. Here the man's exposed guilt and the fragility of newly gained trust are complemented by the brilliant choice of decor and virtually illustrated architecturally: the walls of the coffee shop are completely

1

transparent. Janet Gaynor and George O'Brian are literally sitting in a glass house, its modernity not only unparalleled in 1926 but also a timeless metaphor for the power of film architecture.

The architecture of the city, which Murnau had built at tremendous expense on the Fox studio grounds in Culver City, California, is worthy of closer inspection. Designed by Rochus Gliese before his arrival in the United States, the set is equipped with the typical attributes of a modern big city: streetcars, frenzied traffic, neon lights, and an elevated railway. Its uncompromised architectural modernity however is not comparable with that of any existing city of the time. Only the plain, classical church can be identified as a historical building. Everything else is an assembly of simple unadorned facades of glass and concrete, seemingly reflecting the contemporary debate about a future architecture in Germany. Erich Mendelsohn's Mosse Building in Berlin (1922) provided the model for a large cantilevered canopy. Gliese's sketches reveal his familiarity with the contemporary preference for glass curtain walls, simple cubic forms and horizontally protruding floor slabs. *Sunrise* served as a testing ground for current architectural ideas, and it brought modern architecture to America, just ahead of Richard Neutra's Lovell House in the Hollywood Hills (1927–29) and Le Corbusier's first visit to New York (1927).

D. N.

Fig. 5: In the Restaurant.

Fig. 6: Production shot with Janet Gaynor. The elevated train station is visible in the background.

Fig. 7: In the Cafe.

Fig. 8: The city square in daylight.

5

6

Fig. 3: Rochus Gliese, Sketch for Sunrise. Charcoal on paper (reproduction of drawing; original is missing). Courtesy of Kevin Brownlow, London.

Fig. 4: Rochus Gliese, Sketch for Sunrise. Charcoal on paper (reproduction of drawing; original is missing). Courtesy of Kevin Brownlow, London.

7

8

Asphalt

Germany, Universum Film A.G., 1929

Director: Joe May. *Script:* Fred Mayo [Joe May],
Hans Szekely, Rolf E. Vanloo. *Sets:* Erich Kettelhut.
Camera: Günther Rittau. *Cast:* Gustav Fröhlich
(Officer Holk), Betty Amann (Else Kraemer), Albert
Steinrück (Police Chief Holk), Else Heller (his wife),
Hans Adalbert von Schlettow (Consul Langen),
Hans Albers (a thief).
Premiere: 11 March 1929, Berlin.

Literature: Hans Feld, "Ein Wunderwerk der Filmarchitektur:
Die Asphaltstrasse im Film-Atelier," *Film-Kurier*, no. 263
(2 November 1928); "Nächtliche Großstadtstraße im Film,"
Film–Kurier, no. 7 (8 January 1928); Felix Henscheidt,
"Asphalt," *Reichsfilmblatt* (16 March 1929), p. 12; "Joe May
auf dem 'Asphalt,'" *Kinematograph* 23 (12 March 1929),
no. 60; Erich Kettelhut, "Asphalt," *Reichsfilmblatt* (9 March
1929); Raca [Siegfried Kracauer], "Asphalt," *Frankfurter Zeitung*, no. 235 (28 March 1929); Wolfgang Jacobsen, "Schim-
merndes Schwarz und leuchtendes Weiß: Betty Amann in Joe
Mays 'Asphalt,'" in Hans-Michael Bock and Michael Töteberg,
Das Ufa Buch (Frankfurt am Main: Zweitausendeins, 1992),
pp. 248–49; Peter Mänz, "Modernität als Handwerk," in
Michael Töteberg and Klaus Kreimeier, eds., *Asphalt — Ufa
Magazin*, no. 7 (Berlin: Deutsches Historisches Museum,
1992), pp. 8–12; Gero Gandert, *Der Film der Weimarer Republik 1929* (Berlin and New York: Walter de Gruyter, 1993),
pp. 29–33.

Asphalt was considered by contemporary critics as a "typical example of
artificially elevated pulp fiction"
(Raca 1929). Eros and seduction as
the cause for the disintegration of
authority form the framework of this
melodrama. A jewel thief, Else, is
handed over to a policeman to be
booked. She persuades the officer to
accompany her to her apartment
first, so that she can fetch her pass-
port. There, she seduces him. The
policeman falls in love with her; the
catastrophe runs its course. At the
climax of the dramatic entangle-
ment, the enamored officer kills a
sinister associate of the lady. He con-
fesses his misdeeds to his father, a
retired chief of police, who hands his
son over to the authorities. In the
end, Else exonerates the policeman
in court, his right to self-defense clears
him of the charge, and she goes to
jail herself. Justice has been satisfied.
The purification of the thief provides
the prospect of a happy ending.

The story itself is not what raises
Asphalt to the status of a late classic
of German silent film, however.
Rather, it is the composition and the
teamwork of the artistic ensemble
responsible for the unique contemporary atmosphere of this ambitious
Ufa production. The producer, Erich
Pommer, just back from the United
States, had brought the actress Betty
Amann with him. Her lascivious,
sensual game of seduction was fully
exploited by the director, Joe May.
Gustav Fröhlich, Fredersen's son in
Metropolis, as the policeman Holk is
scarcely inferior to Amann. But in
the end, even the acting achievements and May's superb production
style seem merely clever compared to

the spectacular sets by Erich Kettelhut and the photographic art of
Günther Rittau.

Rittau's contributions are mani-
fested immediately in the opening
sequences, when he condenses
images of asphalt workers into a visual fireworks display of multiple
exposures. The title of the film in-
scribes itself into the frames over this
graphic pattern. *Asphalt* stands as a
synonym for urbanity, haste, and
vitality. The experience of Ruttmann's documentary exploration
of the city in *Berlin, die Sinfonie der
Großstadt* (Berlin, Symphony of a
Great City [Walter Ruttmann; 1927])
is integrated into this film.

Kettelhut joined the production
just before the start of shooting. The
producers had first intended Robert
Herlth to design the sets, but there
were disagreements with Joe May,
who was notorious for his choleric
nature. Herlth withdrew, leaving preliminary drawings that are interesting to contrast with the architectural
solutions by Kettelhut. Herlth's
urban streets suggest the sober formal language of classic modern
architecture. In a strictly centralized
perspective construction, tall, extensive store windows line a pavement
converging on infinity. Kettelhut's
urban street provides a denser, still
somewhat visionary view. Advertising lights, overlapping architecture,
thronging crowds, and traffic all
present the animated metropolitan
flair that was expected of contemporary Berlin. Erich Mendelsohn's Universum cinema (1926–28) appears in
Kettelhut's sketches, as does a glassed-
in pedestrian bridge recalling the Zoo
or Friedrichstraße railroad stations.

Fig. 1: Production shot.

Fig. 2: Rudi Feld, Filming Asphalt *in the Studio, 1928. Oil on
canvas, 83.5 x 65 cm. Stiftung Deutsche Kinemathek, Berlin.*

In earlier years, it would have been taken for granted that a complex of such large dimensions would have been built outdoors. The large, exemplary studios of Ufa, however, equipped with the latest technical inventions, inspired us to abandon tradition and erect the structural complex inside the studios despite its size. . .

All these difficulties of construction seemed minor in view of the requirements of the script to build the street in the way the pedestrian's eye sees it: sometimes faster, then slowly again, wandering past moving and immobile things, stopping here and there, looking ahead or sideways, lifting upwards or sweeping into the distance. . . The powerfully animated optical effect led me to depart from designing the set in the often customary way as a complete picture from my fixed point of view. Rather, it had to be my aim to provide interesting details and views everywhere for the panning lens. . . In the eye of the camera (audience), which, freed of all restraints, can move at will through the sets, the whole thing is resolved into the intended, animated image of a city street [Kettelhut 1929].

Thus, the studio street for *Asphalt*, developed in a former airplane hangar in Staaken, extended in perspective through the huge doors in order to create the illusion of a broad horizon. Rudi Feld, head designer at Ufa's publicity department, produced an oil painting of this extraordinary set seen from the overhead cranes in the studio. According to the production bulletins, the set was 15 meters wide and 230 meters long, with a thin layer of asphalt. Shop windows broken up by shop entrances and showcases lined the street. In order to make the set as authentic as possible, the windows were decorated by leading Berlin firms, which were allowed to advertise with their logos in exchange. Due to the use of a crane, the camera had a previously unknown mobility. It tracked at length through the street using a bird's-eye perspective, emphasizing the architecture's value as a showpiece and intervening dramaturgically in the action. The street scenes in *Asphalt* represent the last highlights of virtuoso silent film architecture. Rudi Feld's enormous billboard adorning the theater for the Berlin premiere, equipped with electric lights and moving vehicles, carried that architecture back into the streets.

P. L.

Fig. 3: Erich Kettelhut, Design for the city street, 1928. (Film-Kurier, 1929).

Fig. 4: Robert Herlth, Design for the city street, 1928. Pencil on paper, 25 x 35.2 cm. Stiftung Deutsche Kinemathek, Berlin.

Fig. 5: Robert Herlth, Design for the city street, 1928. Pencil on paper, 22.5 x 28.5 cm. Stiftung Deutsche Kinemathek, Berlin.

Fig. 6: Production shot.

Fig. 7: Advertisements for the premiere of the film at the theater, 1928. Photograph by Hans Casparius.

4

5

Just Imagine

U.S.A., Fox, 1930

Director: David Butler. *Script and Songs:* DeSylva, Brown, and Henderson. *Sets:* Stephen Goosson. *Cast:* El Brendel (Single O), Maureen O'Sullivan (LN–18), John Garrick (J–21), Marjorie White (D–6), Frank Albertson (RT–42), Hobart Bosworth (Z–4), Kenneth Thomson (MT–3).
Premiere: October 1930, Los Angeles.

Literature: Harvey Wiley Corbett, "The Coming City of Set-back Skyscrapers," *New York Times* (29 April 1923), Sec. 4,5; Douglas Hodges, "Just Imagine," *Examiner Herald World* (18 October 1930); John Dedgelman,"'Just Imagine' Is Packed with Strange Sights for 1930 Eyes," *L.A. Record* (4 October 1930); Mordaunt Hall, "A Clever Film Fantasy," *New York Times* (30 November 1930); "Just Imagine," German newspaper clipping, 22 December 1930, Stiftung Deutsche Kinemathek, Berlin; "New York in 1980," *New York Times*, (16 November 1930); John Brosnan, *Future Tense: The Cinema of Science Fiction* (New York: St. Martin's Press, 1978), pp. 40–41; Frederick Pohl, "The Demi–Docs: 'Just Imagine' and 'Things to Come,'" in Danny Peary, ed., *Omni's Screen Flights/Screen Fantasies* (Garden City: Doubleday, 1984), pp. 90–96;. Donald Albrecht, *Designing Dreams: Modern Architecture and the Movies* (London and New York: Thames and Hudson, 1986), pp. 162–64.

Fig. 1: New York in the Future.

In *Just Imagine*, probably the first science fiction musical ever, New York City is presented fifty years into the future as a completely different city with an entirely changed skyline and urban organization, nine levels of traffic, private airplanes for everyone, and a number of (then) astonishing technical amenities, such as televisions, pills for nourishment, and rocket travel to Mars. The citizens are identified by numbers. The film's protagonist, Single O, is reawakened in a laboratory (not unlike Rotwang's chamber for the duplication of Maria in *Metropolis*) from his 50-year state of suspended animation after having been hit by a golf ball in 1930. He witnesses the love story of J–21, who will only be allowed to marry his girlfriend LN–18 by the state authorities once he has proven his distinction by piloting a famous inventor's spaceship to Mars and returning safely (with Single O as a stowaway).

Filmed in 1929, when the celebrated architectural delineator Hugh Ferriss published his collected drawings of visionary setback skyscrapers under the title *Metropolis of Tomorrow*, the film's sets make clear reference to Ferriss's compelling vision. Skyscrapers of up to two hundred stories are placed far enough apart to let light into the deep canyons between them, the different traffic levels seem well ordered, and the buildings gleam with electricity, thus providing images of a healthy, prosperous, and enjoyable future. Stylistic unity has been achieved, as no traces of earlier historic buildings are to be seen. Apart from Ferriss's influence, other architectural references include "skyscraper bridges" as designed by Raymond Hood in 1929, or even the recently completed, setback Chrysler Building and Bank of Manhattan (1929), as well as the Empire State Building, which was nearing completion in 1930. Set designer Stephen Goosson's slender towers, however, are by far more elegant than their built predecessors; their facades are dissolved into rows and rows of brightly lit windows.

Thus, Depression–plagued America was presented with a confident, very *American* view of the future. Clearly meant as a response to the much–discussed success of *Metropolis* (as was sourly noted by the German critics), the film not only aimed at surpassing its predecessor's design extravaganzas by erecting the vast city miniature (reportedly 85 meters long and 25 meters wide) in a huge dirigible hangar; it also clearly attempted to respond to the German film's brooding view of future technology and urban life with a cheerful and authentically American answer. Whereas Ferriss had depicted the evolution of the set-back skyscraper as a natural process of crystallization, the architectural historian Francisco Mujica had argued that the similarity of such buildings to Mesoamerican pyramids made them distinctly and historically American.

The setback regulation of the New York Zoning Law of 1916, which had begun to transform architecture in the United States during the 1920s, had been enthusiastically welcomed as the long-awaited advent of a specifically American form of architectural modernism. "What we are getting now is something utterly new and distinctive," the New York architect Harvey Wiley Corbett had written in 1923.

> And its effect will be felt on the architecture of the whole world. The setback style will go down in history along with the Gothic, the Classical and the Renaissance. . . The new type of the city with its innumerable spires, towers and domes, set back from the cornice line, will provide a fascinating vision. All the novelty in the world brought under a larger scheme [Corbett 1923].

Whereas contemporary American reviewers of *Just Imagine* were divided in their opinions about the strength of the plot and the success of the melodies, they all agreed on the breathtaking imagery of the sets, designed, as the *Examiner Herald World* put it, "in an ultra modern style unrevealed heretofore by the most ultra of ultramodern artists."

D. N.

Fig. 2: Hugh Ferriss, Sketch for The Metropolis of Tomorrow *(1928): "The Business Center." Pencil on paper, 73.7 x 88.9 cm. Columbia University, Avery Architectural and Fine Arts Library, New York.*

Fig. 3: Sky Rendezvous.

Fig. 4: Laboratory.

Fig. 5: On Mars.

2

3

4

5

The Black Cat

U.S.A., Universal Studios, 1934

Director: Edgar G. Ulmer. *Script:* Edgar G. Ulmer, Peter Ruric. *Sets:* Edgar G. Ulmer. *Camera:* John Mescall. *Cast:* Boris Karloff (Hjalmar Poelzig), Bela Lugosi (Vitus Werdegast), David Manners (Peter), Jacqueline Wells (Joan).
Premiere: May 1934, Los Angeles.

Literature: "The Black Cat," *New York Times*, 19 May 1934, p. 18; Peter Bogdanovich, "Interview with Edgar G. Ulmer"; Myron Meisel, "Edgar G. Ulmer: The Primacy of the Visual," in Todd McCarthy and Charles Flynn, eds., *Kings of the Bs* (New York: E.P. Dutton, 1975), pp. 377– 409; 147– 64; Paul Mandell, "Edgar Ulmer and the Black Cat," *American Cinematographer* (October 1984), pp. 34 – 47; "Le Chat noir," *L'Avant-scène cinéma* 338 (March 1985), pp. 20 – 51.

Fig. 1: The House of Hjalmar Poelzig.

Fig. 2: Poelzig and Werdegast on the Staircase.

Fig. 3: The Black Mass.

Fig. 4: Hjalmar Poelzig and His Wife.

Referring only very remotely to a story by Edgar Allan Poe, the film portrays the bizarre adventures of a young couple on their honeymoon in Hungary, where they meet the mysterious Vitus Werdegast, on his way to settle an old account with a wartime rival. In need of shelter during a storm, they follow their companion to the isolated country house of the architect Hjalmar Poelzig. In the course of a single night, they witness murder, incest, a Satanic mass, and torture, before managing to escape from the exploding house at the last minute.

The Black Cat, little known to date, has rightfully been dubbed one of the most unusual and enigmatic films of the '30s. As a so–called B picture — that is, both low-budget and low-brow — it was shot very quickly. The director and set designer was the Austrian Edgar G. Ulmer, a stage designer for Max Reinhardt in Berlin as a young man, who had assisted in the decor for a series of films, including Henrik Galeen's *Golem*. Ulmer eventually went to America as F.W. Murnau's assistant art director. Despite all the inconsistencies in the plot, Ulmer's film nevertheless is quite complex, full of personal, cinematographic, and contemporary historical references.

At a time when films often promoted modern architecture as a major attribute of fast-paced, modern life, here it became a distinctive feature of European decadence, a direct result of the horrors of World War I. Hjalmar Poelzig's ultramodern villa with Corbusier-style ribbon windows is located above a World War I cemetery on the walls of the ruined fortress of Marmaro. "A masterpiece of construction built upon the ruins of a masterpiece of destruction," wryly comments the visitor Werdegast in the film. That an architect should embody the abysmally evil main character, who displays his murdered mistresses in glass coffins next to which he celebrates Satanic masses, was unusual enough. But that he should be named after Hans Poelzig, one of the most respected German architects of the day, can probably only be interpreted as a tasteless joke or some personal act of revenge. (Ulmer knew Poelzig from his Berlin period; they had met while working on *Der Golem*.) Inside the architect's house in *The Black Cat* are the most modern, brightly lit rooms, which

Hans Poelzig himself, as Ulmer declared later, would not have designed in as modern a fashion until about 20 years later (Bogdanovich 1975).

The film is full of references to the accomplishments of German silent films of the preceding years. Like the hypnotized Cesare in *Caligari*, Hjalmar Poelzig arises stiffly from his bed when the strangers arrive at night. The black mass he celebrates in the cellar of his supermodern house satirizes Maria's masses in the catacombs of *Metropolis*. The bus driver who brings the travelers to Poelzig's house has an uncanny resemblance to Emil Jannings in *Der letzte Mann*. Classical music accompanies the terrors on screen, ranging from Schubert's *Unfinished Symphony* to Franz Liszt's Piano Sonata in B Minor and Bach's Toccata and Fugue in C Major. What was considered by many to be a wicked, shameless film, mercilessly satirizing celebrated European achievements in modern architecture, classical music, and film, became the most successful Universal Studios film of 1934.

D. N.

2 3

4

Things to Come

England, London Film Productions
(released by United Artists), 1936

Director: William Cameron Menzies. *Script:* H.G. Wells, based on his book *The Shape of Things to Come.* *Sets:* Vincent Korda. *Camera:* George Périnal. *Cast:* Raymond Massey (John, Oswald Cabal), Ralph Richardson (The Boss), Edward Chapman (Pippa Passworthy/Raymond Passworthy), Margareta Scott (Roxana Black/Rowena Black), Sir Cedric Hardwicke (Theotocopulos). *Premiere:* 21 February 1936, London.

Literature: H.G. Wells, *The Shape of Things to Come* (London: Cresset Press, 1935, reprint Boston: Gregg Press, 1975); Alistair Cooke, "Mr. Wells Sees Us Through," *Listener* (18 March 1936), pp. 545–46; Kenneth Fearing, "The Screen: A Voice from the Past," *New Masses* (5 May 1936), p. 27; "Mr Wells Looks . . . at *Things to Come*," *Time* (6 April 1936), pp. 43–46; H.G. Wells, "Rules of Thumb for *Things to Come*," *New York Times* (12 April 1936, sect. IX, p. 4); Mark van Doren, "After the Next War," *Nation* 142 (29 April 1936), p. 560; Sibyl Moholy-Nagy, *Experiment in Totality* (Cambridge, MA: MIT Press, 1969), p. 129; Timothy Travers, "The Shape of Things to Come: H. G. Wells and Radical Culture in the 1930s," *Film and History* 6, no. 2 (May 1976), pp. 31–36; John Brosnan, *Future Tense: The Cinema of Science Fiction* (New York: St. Martin's Press, 1978), pp. 55–61; "H.G. Wells, Things to Come," in *Magill's Survey of the Cinema: English Language Films, 1st ser.*, vol. 4, 1980; Frederick Pohl and Frederick Pohl IV, *Science Fiction Studies in Film* (New York: Ace Books, 1981), pp. 78–90; Terence Senter, "Moholy-Nagy's English Photography," *Burlington Magazine* 123, no. 944 (November 1981), pp. 659–71; Fredrick Pohl, "The Demi Docs: *Just Imagine* and *Things to Come*," in Danny Peary, *Omni's Screen Flights/Screen Fantasies* (Garden City: Doubleday, 1984), pp. 90–96; Donald Albrecht, *Designing Dreams: Modern Architecture in the Movies* (London and New York: Thames and Hudson, 1986), pp. 162–63; Paola Antonelli, *"Things to Come: La transparenza del futuro,"* *Domus*, no. 719 (September 1990), pp. 90–97; Christopher Frayling, *Things to Come* (London: British Film Institute, 1995).

Fig. 1: The Interior of the City.

In 1936, the renowned science fiction author H.G. Wells became involved in creating a futuristic film based on his own screenplay called *The Shape of Things to Come.* Wells made clear from the beginning that he understood his efforts to be an answer to Fritz Lang's *Metropolis,* distributing a memo to the members of the crew (and subsequently publishing it in the *New York Times*) in which he wrote: "As a general rule you may take it that whatever Lang did in *Metropolis* is the exact contrary of what we want done here" (Wells 1936).

The film surveys a century in the life of an English "Everytown", beginning in 1936. After a devastating war and long decades of suffering due to disease and the rule of despots, technology and reason finally lead to the erection of a new "Everytown" in 2036. A dispute over the pros and cons of progress and technology develops when a rocket is launched to explore the moon.

Set designer Vincent Korda's friend the artist Fernand Léger was asked by Wells to supply the special effects and architectural settings for the film. But Léger's drawings, reminiscent of his own 1924 film *Ballet mécanique,* were not approved by Wells, and the architect Le Corbusier was asked to submit designs. He declined. In the end, Vincent Korda designed the settings himself, adopting some of Le Corbusier's formal ideas from his book *Towards a New Architecture,* which had been published in English in 1927.

In an attempt to recognize recent advances in avant-garde filmmaking in the movie, the former Bauhaus professor and photographer Lászlò Moholy-Nagy was asked by Korda to participate. Korda had known Moholy-Nagy since 1930 and had been impressed with his short abstract film *Lightplay.* Moholy-Nagy helped to create the central sequence showing the construction of the new Everytown in 2036. In the editing process, a lot of Moholy's material was discarded, however. He had not only created abstract sequences of moving geometric patterns to illustrate the profound changes that led to the building of the new city but also designed his own version of a city of the future, consisting of transparent cones and glass-clad skeletal towers. These towers are clearly reminiscent of his Bauhaus colleague Mies van der Rohe's curvilinear glass skyscraper of 1922. Mies's consciously anti-monumental response to the heavy towers of his conservative German colleagues was adopted by Moholy-Nagy as a response to the massive towers of Lang's *Metropolis.* As Sybil Moholy-Nagy later remembered, her husband had wanted to "eliminate solid form. Houses were no longer obstacles to, but receptacles of man's natural life force, light. There were no walls, but skeletons of steel, screened with glass and plastic sheets" (Moholy-Nagy 1969). The material he used for his transparent cones and skyscrapers was a new display plastic called Rhodoid, which came in sheets, rods, or tubes and a thousand different colors.

Wells's urban concept was quite literally the antithesis of Lang's highrise city. He explored the fundamental dichotomy between the vertical towers of a skyscraper city and their counterpart in the form of a gigantic subterranean cave (a contrast Lang had already employed by juxtaposing the world of the rulers with Maria's catacombs). In the final section of *Things to Come,* the old Everytown has vanished completely, the surface of the earth has been returned to Nature, and the new Everytown is located in a gigantic underground cavern. The skyscrapers of New York, Lang's departure point, remain but a faded memory in *Things to Come,* only to be seen in educational films. "What a funny place New York was," says one little girl, "all sticking up and full of windows."

Korda's design for Everytown in 2036 adopted the unornamented, minimalistic horizontality of the modern movement and its streamlined successors. What to us seems to foreshadow American hotel lobbies of the 1970s was recognized as a unique vision of compelling visual power by many contemporary reviewers, who otherwise had little patience for Wells's long and heavily moralizing play: "And the achievement of '*Things to Come*' is no more and certainly no less than the ingenious hours spent around little white models by William Menzies, Vincent Korda, and George Perinal. Without tossing a penny, I should say that Vincent Korda is the hero of the piece" (Cooke 1936).

D.N.

Things to Come's vision of future civilization consists of beehive cities built into monster excavations — whether underground or in the sides of mountains I cannot say, since the photography at this point becomes very trick. The point is that the cities lie somewhere out of the sun, which according to one of the wise men is a poor thing at best, shining down there or in there, wherever it is, the people of the future manufacture their own light rays as we do our central heat; and bask athletically in glass houses. . . Try as I did to think otherwise, I could only think that living there would be like living in an electric ice box, you on your tray and I on mine. The whole picture was for me intolerably prosy and grotesquely unconvincing. I was confirmed in a former suspicion, namely, that the future is the dullest subject on earth [van Doren 1936].

Everytown of the year 2054 will be dug into the hills. It will not be a skyscraper city. . . The old town itself under the open sky has disappeared and given place to a few terraces and exterior structures. There are unfamiliar architectural forms, grass slopes and formal trees. It is very tranquil and beautiful, the apotheosis of Everytown. A few aeroplanes of novel structure pass across the sky. Along a wide highway flows an almost noiseless traffic of streamlined vehicles that come and go through a great entrance, far more brightly lit than the world outside [Wells 1935, pp. 92, 106].

Fig. 2: Vincent Korda, Sketch of the Entrance to Everytown in 2036.

Fig. 3: Leaving Town.

Fig. 4: Building the City.

Fig. 5: László Moholy-Nagy, Preliminary Design Study for the City of the Future.

Fig. 6: Everytown Destroyed.

Fig. 7: Lessons about Skyscrapers.

3

4

6

7

Lost Horizon

U.S.A., Columbia Studios, 1937

Director: Frank Capra. *Script:* Robert Riskin, based on the novel by James Hilton. *Sets:* Stephen Goosson with Cary Odell, Lionel Banks, and Paul Murphy. *Camera:* Joseph Walker. *Cast:* Ronald Colman (Robert Conway), Jane Wyatt (Sondra), Edward Everett Horton (Alexander P. Lovett), John Howard (George Conway), Thomas Mitchell (Henry Barnard), Margo (Maria), Isabel Jewell (Gloria Stone), H.B. Warner (Chang), Sam Jaffe (High Lama).
Premiere: 3 March 1937, Los Angeles.

Literature: James Hilton, *Lost Horizon* (New York: Morrow and Co., 1933); "Lost Horizon," *Life Magazine* (14 December 1936); "Lost Horizon," Columbia Pictures press kit (1937); Sidney Skolsky, "Lost Horizon," *Chicago Times*, (17 March 1937); "Denverites Nominate Outstanding Buildings," *Architectural Record* 86, no. 6 (December 1939), p. 10; Edward Connor, "Revisiting Lost Horizon," *Screen Facts*, no. 2 (1963), pp. 50–55; Frank Capra, *The Name above the Title* (New York: Macmillan, 1971); Charles J. Maland, *Frank Capra* (Boston: Twayne Publishers, 1980), pp. 98–101; Harold Meyerson, "Lost Horizon," in *Magill's Survey of Cinema, English Language Films* 1st ser., vol. 3 (1980), pp. 1006–8; Robert Sennett, *Setting the Scene: The Great Hollywood Art Directors* (New York: Harry N. Abrams, 1994), pp. 144–49.

Fig. 1: The Courtyard of the Lamasery.

Frank Capra's highly successful film describes the last-minute escape of a small group of Westerners from Baskul in China during a civil war. They are flown out of the country, not, however, in the direction they anticipated. Among them are Robert Conway, the designated British ambassador to China, and his brother George. In the Tibetan mountains, the plane crashes during the pilot's attempt to land. The surviving passengers are met by a native search party and are led over icy, seemingly impassable mountains to the Valley of the Blue Moon, called Shangri–La. In this deep valley, they find a mild climate and a small settlement of natives and Europeans, who, due to the valley's remoteness, only rarely have contact with the outside world. They live in a peaceful religious community under the guidance of a high lama, a former Belgian priest. Because of the climatic conditions in the valley and a lifestyle free from struggle, the inhabitants age much more slowly than their counterparts outside; their high lama is already more than two hundred years old.

While awaiting appropriate transportation to enable them to complete their journey, the travelers make friends (and find lovers) among the inhabitants. Robert Conway is selected to succeed the high lama after the latter's death. However, his brother's beautiful new girlfriend, Margo, who has been living in Shangri-La since 1888 and has been longing to return to the outside world, convinces George Conway that the lamasery is a fraud. George and Margo embark on a journey out of the valley, unwillingly accompanied by Robert. Shortly after they leave, Margo starts to age rapidly and soon dies. George kills himself. Robert marches on and, after a long and dangerous journey, finally arrives in London. His passionate longing for Shangri-La, however, is so strong that he soon travels back to Tibet to try to find the Valley of the Blue Moon again.

On the brink of World War II, foreshadowed by the Spanish Civil War, and in the middle of the Depression, Frank Capra presented the ultimate escapist utopia — "the most convincing dream in modern fiction," according to *Life* magazine (*Life Magazine 1936*). *Lost Horizon* cost $2.5 million to make, an unsurpassed figure for Columbia Studios in those

1

Fig. 2: Raymond Harry Ervin, *House for Harry E. Huffman, Modeled after the Set for* Lost Horizon. *Photo: Hyskell. © The Architectural Record.*

Fig. 3: *The model of the lamasery and the surrounding mountain range on Columbia's studio lot.*

Fig. 4: *Cary Odell, Sketch for the lamasery courtyard.*

days. The enormous expense was in part due to the elaborate set, which earned an Academy Award for Stephen Goosson. According to a Columbia press release,

> It is regarded as the largest individual unit set ever to be built in Hollywood. Occupying a space of more than a thousand feet in length and five hundred feet wide, the set comprises a gigantic lamasery surrounded by mountains and a great patio, the center of which is occupied by a large pool with fountains playing their sparkling water on hundreds of water lilies. More than two miles of pipe had to be laid for this practical fountain and real flowers and grass were planted in this great garden with climbing flowered vines creeping over the spotless white monastery. Two hundred doves were oriented to the set weeks in advance of the actual shooting as an added touch of beauty ["Lost Horizon" 1937].

The architecture of Shangri-La presented a very particular challenge for Goosson, who had only a few years earlier depicted a futuristic New York City in *Just Imagine*. As the centerpiece of Shangri-La, the lamasery had to serve as a metaphor for the timeless synthesis of East and West, peace of mind, moderation, and human kindness. Neither European historical or contemporary styles nor indigenous Tibetan ones seemed appropriate. Hilton's novel did not offer much help, since the style of the lamasery is not described in much detail. Goosson found his answer in the recent European and American architectural avant-garde, skillfully blending elements of the formal language of the European modernists and Frank Lloyd Wright with vague notions of the luxury that is amply described in the novel. He replaced the indigenous blue-tiled roofs that Hilton mentions with flat, cantilevered roofs that emphasize horizontality. The unornamented white cubic buildings are reminiscent of the style of Le Corbusier or Robert Mallet-Stevens and have ribbon windows at the corners and simplified white columns without base or capital. The symmetrical layout of the central courtyard with the lily pond, the deep overhanging eaves, and the emphasis on horizontality all owe a debt to Wright's architecture, for example his 1915 Imperial Hotel in Tokyo.

Goosson's choice revealed the influence of contemporary rhetoric. The architects of the modern movement had insisted again and again that their approach was not just a passing fashion, but in fact marked the end of stylistic change, the final goal of a long development process, the end of history. They not only claimed for their work qualities such as purity, honesty, and simplicity but also considered it part of a future global culture, an international style, that ignored political, economic, and cultural boundaries. In the film, the high lama considers his Shangri-La settlement to be just such a synthesis of the achievements of humankind: "I determined to gather all things of beauty and culture I could, and preserve them here," he explains to his visitors.

Shangri-La's architecture marks one of the very few instances in which a film set directly influenced real, built architecture. The "Shangri-La" residence of Harry E. Huffman, designed by Raymond Harry Ervin for a site in the Rocky Mountains near Denver, Colorado, was voted the second most outstanding building in that city in 1939.

D. N.

2

3

4

The Fountainhead

U.S.A., Warner Bros., 1949

Director: King Vidor. *Script:* Ayn Rand, based on her 1934 novel. *Sets:* Edward Carrere. *Camera:* Robert Burks. *Cast:* Gary Cooper (Howard Roark), Patricia Neal (Dominique), Raymond Massey (Gail Wynand), Kent Smith (Peter Keating), Robert Douglas (Ellsworth Toohey), Henry Hull (Henry Cameron), Ray Collins (Roger Enright), Paul Stanton (The Dean).
Premiere: July 1949, Los Angeles.

Literature: Ayn Rand, *The Fountainhead* (New York: Bobbs–Merrill Co., 1943); "Architecture and Love in Mix–Up," *Cue* (9 July 1949); "The Fountainhead," *Christian Science Monitor* (14 July 1949); "Ayn Rand Replies to Criticism of Her Film," *New York Times* (24 July 1949); Bosley Crowther, "In A Glass House: Reckless Ideas Spouted by the *Fountainhead*," *New York Times* (17 July 1949); "The Current Cinema: Down with Beaux Arts," *New Yorker* (16 July 1949); Aline Mosby, "Real Architects Flunk Colleague Gary Cooper," *Courier Journal, Louisville, Kentucky* (28 July 1949); George Nelson, "Mr. Roark Goes to Hollywood," *Interiors* 108, no. 9 (1949), pp. 106–11; "The Fountainhead," *Citizen* (24 January 1950); Julia Johnson, "The Fountainhead," in Frank N. Magill, ed., *Magill's Survey of the Cinema: English Language Films,* 2nd ser., vol. 2 (Englewood Cliffs: Salem Press, 1981), pp. 828–31; Andrew Saint, *The Image of the Architect* (New Haven: Yale University Press, 1983), pp. 1–18; Donald Albrecht, *Designing Dreams: Modern Architecture in the Movies* (London and New York: Thames and Hudson, 1987), pp. 168–74; Edward Gunts, "The Fountainhead at 50," *Architecture* 82, no. 5 (1993), pp. 35–37.

Throughout the centuries there were men who took first steps down new roads armed with nothing but their own vision. The great creators — the thinkers, the artists, the scientists, the inventors — stood alone against the men of their time. Every great new thought was opposed. Every great new invention was denounced. But the men of unborrowed vision went ahead. They fought, they suffered and they paid. But they won [Howard Roark in *The Fountainhead*].

Fig. 1: Model of the Wynand Building on Table in the Foreground. *"THE FOUNTAINHEAD"* © *1949 Turner Entertainment Co. All rights reserved.*

The Fountainhead can claim to represent the epitome of an architecturally significant film. The main character is an architect, there are a large number of inventive sets responding directly to contemporary architectural discourse, and the film presents a very specific, and much discussed, idea of the role of the architect in society.

Howard Roark is presented as a young architect who has been dismissed from college because of his unwillingness to compromise in architectural matters. Whereas his classmate Peter Keating becomes a successful, though undistinguished, architect, Roark insists on executing commissions according to his own ideas, giving up a desperately needed contract when he learns that he is expected to change the facade to a more conventional design. He is forced to work as a day laborer in a quarry. Finally, he gets the chance to design a skyscraper in Manhattan for the independently minded Roger Enright. When Keating, overloaded with work, asks Roark to help him, he agrees to design a low-cost federal housing project, Cortland Homes, under Keating's name, with the strict condition that his design must not be changed. When the project is compromised, Roark dynamites the almost-finished structure. A heated public debate follows. Gail Wynand, a bitter and cynical newspaper tycoon, defends Roark in his paper, but eventually has to give up his position to end a boycott by his readers. In a long speech in the courtroom ("probably one of the longest speeches ever to be spoken on the screen" according to the *Christian Science Monitor*), Roark defends his action, wins over the jury, and is acquitted. Wynand, the humiliated newspaper man, commissions him to design an enormous skyscraper in his name and then commits suicide. His wife, Dominique, who has been having a love affair with Roark, is finally free to marry him.

Ayn Rand's immensely successful novel and the less successful film served as demonstrations of her philosophy of "objectivism," whose central element is the defense of absolute personal freedom and uncompromising individuality. She was inspired in the creation of the figure of Roark by the architect Frank Lloyd Wright, who had recently returned to center stage in the architectural

profession with such highly publicized buildings as Falling Water (1936) and the Johnson Wax Factory (1936–39). Both of these buildings served as models for some of the designs in the movie. The old architect Henry Hull, Roark's unsuccessful teacher, who in his last moments utters the words "Form always follows function," is an homage to Louis Sullivan, one of America's most respected architects and Wright's teacher before the turn of the century. The highly publicized Chicago Tribune Competition of 1923 seems to have served as useful source material for art director Edward Carrere. Whereas the traditional designs of Roark's more successful colleagues refer stylistically to Raymond Hood's and other American entries, European projects such as the Dutchman Bernard Bijvoet's horizontally layered design seems to have influenced Roark's own Enright skyscraper. This building also features a wing with a resemblance to the flat glass slab of the UN Building in New York, which was just nearing completion in 1949.

For the purposes of the film, pompous historicist architecture stands for artistic impotence and weakness of character, while the strict and simple forms of European modernism stand for uncompromising individuality. Reality — and Rand's novel — was more complex. European architects like Bijvoet would probably have been comfortable with some form of collectivism, and the UN Building was purposefully conceived in a group design process. In the novel, the hero's struggle for integrity was symbolic of the striving for more genuine and honest *American* architecture. Rand had clearly differentiated between Roark's style (modelled on Wright's late Arts and Crafts idiom) and stark European *Modernismus.*

The great surprises in the film are the unbuilt projects that Carrere designed for Henry Hull. They surpass Roark's in boldness and visual power and can stand as independent, rather progressive designs, employing heavy concrete volumes in proto-Brutalist fashion or starkly displaying their structural framework.

When the film was released, the critical response was almost unanimously negative. The architectural press maliciously pointed out structural problems with the enormous cantilevers in Roark's residential

Fig. 2: Raymond Hood, Winning Entry for Chicago Tribune Competition, 1922.

Fig. 3: Bernard Bijvoet, Entry for Chicago Tribune Competition, 1922.

Fig. 4: Howard Roark's Wynand Building in New York City. *"THE FOUNTAINHEAD" © 1949 Turner Entertainment Co. All rights reserved.*

Fig. 5: Alternative Projects Are Presented to Gail Wynand. *"THE FOUNTAINHEAD" © 1949 Turner Entertainment Co. All rights reserved.*

Fig. 6: Walter Gropius in Front of His Chicago Tribune Competition Entry, 1922.

Fig. 7: Frank Lloyd Wright in Front of the San Francisco Call Tower Building. © Pedro Guerrero.

Fig. 8: Howard Roark with the Model for a Skyscraper. "THE FOUNTAINHEAD" © 1949 Turner Entertainment Co. All rights reserved.

designs (Nelson 1949). Apart from noting Cooper's wooden performance and several weaknesses of the plot, the criticism sparked a debate around the notion of genius and the question of an artist's absolute right to his work, even if it meant destroying someone else's property. But even if Rand's portrayal of an architect as an unfailing artistic genius was exaggerated, it was not far from the truth. There were plenty of images of contemporary architects in the pose of proud creators to inspire Carrere. Wright himself was obviously flattered by Rand's attention. He wrote to her in 1945: "Your thesis is the great one. Especially at this time. Your grasp of the architectural ins and outs of a degenerate profession astonishes me." Wright designed an (unexecuted) house for Rand in 1946. However, when the movie was released and Roark was unanimously criticized for dynamiting the Cortland Homes project, Wright stated: "I do not want to become identified with it. I agree with its thesis, the right of an artist to his work, but I think she bungled it. It is a treacherous slant on my philosophy. She asked me to endorse the book, but I refused" ("The Fountainhead" 1950). The prominent builder Victor Gruen said in an interview, "People will be afraid to go to modern architects. They'll stick to Chippendale" (Mosby 1949).

The appeal of *The Fountainhead* for the general public is undiminished: a hundred thousand copies are still sold each year. Warner Bros. is working with producer James Hill on a remake of the movie. In a recent review of the book to commemorate its 50th anniversary, *Architecture,* the journal of the American Institute of Architects felt it necessary to be outspoken in its rejection of the central concept:

> Many of the nation's design issues involve correcting mistakes made by the Howard Roarks of the world. . . The key to reading *The Fountainhead* today is not to see Howard Roark as a role model, but as the ultimate bad boy of American architecture. Rand's 50-year-old depiction of the architectural profession has grown more and more out of sync with reality; there is no room in the profession for Howard Roark today [Gunts 1993].

D.N.

6

7

132

Fig. 9 and 11: Edward Carrere's Drawings of a Residence and a House for Gail Wynand. "THE FOUNTAINHEAD" © 1949 Turner Entertainment Co. All rights reserved.

Fig. 10: Frank Lloyd Wright, "Cottage Studio for Ayn Rand," Hollywood, 1946. Copyright © 1995 The Frank Lloyd Wright Foundation.

Fig. 12: Howard Roark and Henry Hull. "THE FOUNTAINHEAD" © 1949 Turner Entertainment Co. All rights reserved.

9

10

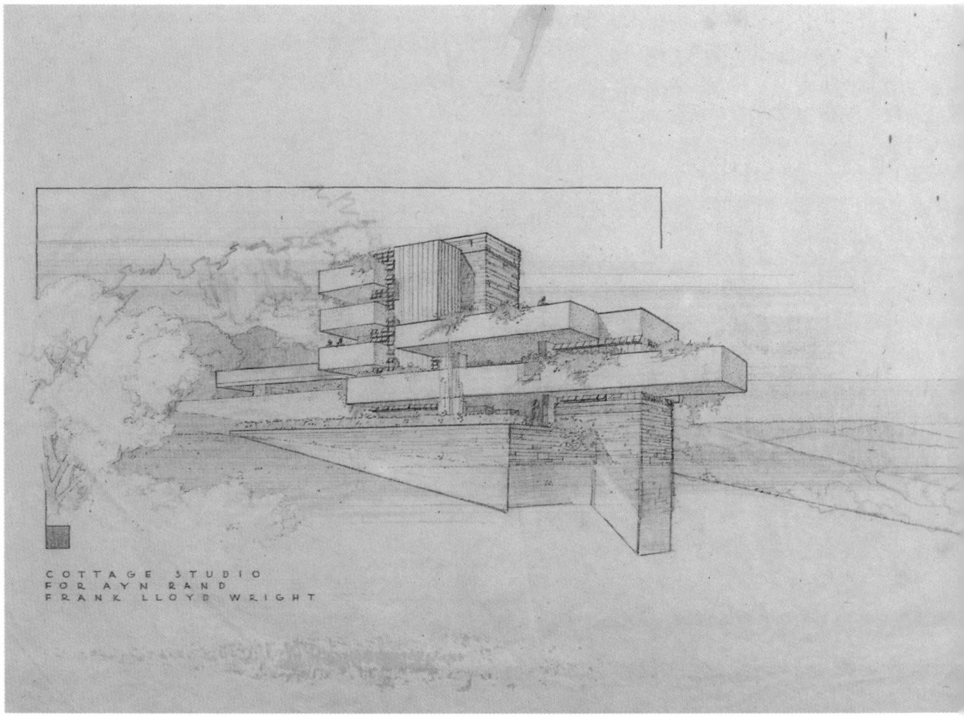

11

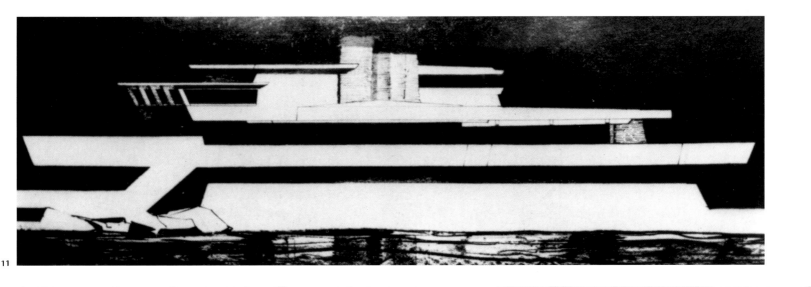

12

Mon Oncle
(My Uncle)

France, Spectra Films/Gray Films/Alter Films (AA), 1958

Director: Jacques Tati. *Script:* Jacques Tati, Jacques Lagrange, Jean L'Hote. *Sets:* Jacques Lagrange. *Camera:* Jean Bourgoin. *Cast:* Jacques Tati (M. Hulot), Jean Pierre Zola (Charles Arpel), Adrienne Servantie (Mme. Arpel), Alain Becourt (Gerard Arpel). *Premiere:* April 1958, Paris.

Literature: "My Uncle, Mr. Hulot," *Cue* (8 November 1958); Richard W. Nason, "M. Tati in Praise of Innocence and Smiles," *New York Times* (2 November 1958); "Slapstick Comedy," *New York Times* (9 November 1958); "The Torment of Mr. Tati," *Life* (17 November 1958); "Talking Shop," *Hollywood Reporter* (7 January 1959); Jean-André Fieschi and Jean Narboni, "Le Champ large," *Cahiers du cinéma*, no. 199 (March 1968), pp. 6–22; Penelope Gilliatt, "The Current Cinema: Jacques Tati," *New Yorker* (28 August 1971), pp. 58–61; Brent Maddock, *The Films of Jacques Tati* (Metuchen: Scarecrow Press, Inc., 1977), pp. 63–75; Lucy Fischer, *Jacques Tati: A Guide to References and Resources* (Boston: G.K. Hall and Co., 1983); Gordon Walters, "Mon Oncle," in Frank N. Magill, ed., *Magill's Survey of the Cinema: Foreign Language Films*, vol. 5 (Englewood Cliffs: Salem Press, 1985), pp. 2085–86; Michel Chion, *Jacques Tati* (Paris: Cahiers du Cinéma, 1987), pp. 43–65; Marc Dondey, *Jacques Tati* (Paris: Editions Ramsay Cinema, 1989), pp. 124–80.

Fig. 1: The House of M. Arpel.

A series of scenes showing encounters between M. Hulot and his little nephew serve as the basis for Jacques Tati's subtle settling of accounts with the excesses of modernity. M. Hulot regularly picks up his nephew Gerard Arpel from his parents' ultramodern villa and brings him to the cozy Parisian suburb of St. Maur. Here, there are coffee shops and greengrocers, and children play typical suburban games. M. Hulot lives in a romantic attic apartment in an absurdly crooked old building. He can only manage to reach it via the complicated ascent and descent of a whole series of different stairways. By contrast, in the Arpels' house, which is part of a new development, modern design rules. The presence of a large number of modern labor-saving inventions has led to a compulsively restricted lifestyle. These two spheres are clearly separated from each other by filmic means. Warm colors and the sounds of a Parisian suburb accompany the images from M. Hulot's world. Sharp colors and the racket of mechanical devices distinguish the Arpels' house. On his way to his nephew's home in the new development, M. Hulot has to climb over the ruins of old Paris. With a careful gesture, he puts a broken brick back into place. In his own surroundings, he is confident and un-self-conscious, but in the Arpels' modernist, sterile, mono-functional environment, he stumbles from one mishap to another.

M. Arpel, M. Hulot's brother-in-law and president of a plastics company, tries in vain to find him a job. Equally in vain, he tries to involve M. Hulot in a conversation with a neighbor woman at a garden party in order to turn the eccentric outsider into a successful fellow citizen. The strict and unimaginative businessman awkwardly strives to win the affection of his son Gerard, who much prefers to be with his unconventional uncle. Only at the end, when Hulot is eventually sent to a new job in the country, does Arpel appear to have learned from the carefree cheerfulness of his brother-in-law. He succeeds in making his little son laugh for the first time.

An infinite wealth of details in the film refers directly to design classics that were still being celebrated and glorified in the '50s. In the white, cubic, terribly impractical modern house, the car has the most important place, and the purchase of a garage door is a cause for celebration. The house alludes to the cubic white houses of the French modernists, probably above all to the aesthetics developed by Le Corbusier in the '20s, which still had a utopian and futuristic flavor, especially for the general public. An entire street in the new development seems to consist of similar uniformly stuccoed housing cubes. Perhaps this refers to the rue Mallet-Stevens, a street built by the Parisian architect Robert Mallet-Stevens in 1926–27. In search of a bed late one drunken night, Hulot tips a curved bench over sideways. In this way, he produces a clever take-off on the lounge chair designed by Le Corbusier and Charlotte Perriand in 1929. The Arpels' uninviting garden, containing, in addition to precisely bordered lawns, colored gravel beds and strictly geometrical pools, may allude to the short-lived fashion for modernist gardens during the '20s in France. As Jacques Lagrange, Tati's artistic collaborator, later recalled in private conversations, the film elicited furious responses from members of the architectural profession, who felt they had been ridiculed in public. Arpel and his wife try earnestly to conform to the specifications of their architect and submit to the strict formalism of their building. With sharp irony, Tati revealed the transformation in meaning of the forms of classical modernism from avant-garde statement to petit-bourgeois fashion item. At the same time, he mocked an important by-product of modernism that had been the theme of *The Fountainhead* 10 years earlier: the position of the architect as an unchallengeable dictator of taste in the lives of his clients. Tati was well aware of how his choice of characters could be read as an interpretation of architecture. Commenting on M. Arpel's house, he said, "if one had given the same house to simpler and more intelligent people, everything would have been different" [Fieschi and Narboni 1968].

Mon Oncle won the Special Jury Prize at the Cannes Film Festival in 1958 and an Oscar as the best foreign film in 1959.

D. N.

Fig. 2: M. Hulot in his Apartment.

Fig. 3: M. Hulot Struggles with the Gate at M. Arpel's House.

Fig. 4: Robert Mallet-Stevens, Rue Mallet-Stevens, Paris, 1926–27. .

Fig. 6: M. Hulot on his Way to M. Arpel.

Fig. 7: Jacques Lagrange, "Villa Arpel", color pencil and acrylic paint on transparent paper, c. 45 x 80 cm.

Fig. 8: Outside M. Arpel's House.

Fig. 9: M. Hulot's Chaise Longue.

6

7

Fig. 5: Le Corbusier and Charlotte Perriand, Chaise Longue for the Salon d'Automne, 1929.

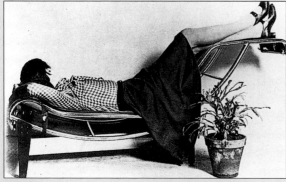

Playtime

France, Specta Films, 1967

Director: Jacques Tati. *Script:* Jacques Tati and Jacques Lagrange. *Sets:* Jacques Lagrange. *Camera:* Jean Badal and Andréas Winding. *Cast:* Jacques Tati (M. Hulot), Barbara Dennek (Claudia), Jacqueline Lecomte (Claudia's friend), Léon Doyen (Porter), Georges Montant (M. Giffard), John Abbey (M. Lacs), Valérie Camille (M. Lacs's secretary), Henri Piccoli (gentleman). *Premiere:* 17 November 1967, Paris.

Literature: Jean-André Fieschi, "Le Carrefour Tati," *Cahiers du cinéma* 199 (1968), pp. 24–28; idem and Jean Narboni, "Le Champ large: Entretien avec Jacques Tati," *Cahiers du cinéma* 199 (1968), pp. 6–22; Vincent Canby, "Playtime, a Funny Film, and Tati's Most Brilliant," *New York Times*, 28 June 1973; Jonathan Rosenbaum, "Tati's Democracy," *Film Comment* 9, no. 3 (May–June 1973), pp. 36–41; Lucy Fischer, "Beyond Freedom and Dignity: An Analysis of Jaques Tati's Playtime," *Sight and Sound* 45, no. 4 (Autumn 1976), pp. 234–39; Brent Maddock, *The Films of Jacques Tati* (Metuchen: Scarecrow Press, Inc., 1977), pp. 76–95; Kristin Thompson, "Playtime: Comedy on the Edge of Perception," *Wide Angle* 3, no. 2 (1979), pp. 18–25; Lucy Fischer, *Jacques Tati: A Guide to References and Resources* (Boston: G.K. Hall and Co., 1983); Dave Kehr, "Playtime," in Frank N. Magill, ed., *Magill's Survey of the Cinema: Foreign Language Films,* vol. 5 (Englewood Cliffs: Salem Press, 1985), pp. 2456–60; Michel Chion, *Jacques Tati* (Paris: Cahiers du Cinéma, 1987); Marc Dondey, *Jacques Tati* (Paris: Editions Ramsay Cinéma, 1989), pp. 184–212; Andrea Kahn, "Playtime with Architects," *Design Book Review* 24 (1994), pp. 22–29; Michel Wolf, "Tativille," *Visions urbains: Villes d'Europe à l'écran,* exh. cat. (Paris: Centre Georges Pompidou, 1994), pp. 35–41; Jacques Kermabon, "Tati architecte: La Transparence, le reflet et l'éphémère," *CinémAction,* no. 75 (1995), pp. 134–37.

Playtime is a gloriously funny movie about a Paris so modern it does not yet exist, a Paris composed entirely of streets like our Avenue of the Americas, hemmed in by efficiently beautiful glass-and-steel towers in which, if we are quick about it, we may see momentary reflections of Sacre Cœur, the Arch of Triumph or the Eiffel Tower [Canby 1973].

Fig. 1: Production Shot. On Location in Tativille.
© *CEPEC/ PANORAMIC.*

As the architecture critic Andrea Kahn put it recently, "Jacques Tati's *Playtime* is a movie where architectural material, matters pertaining to architecture as well as to architecture's matter, has a starring role" (Kahn 1994). In a continuation of some of the themes of *Mon Oncle*, Tati's *Playtime* is mainly a film about modern architecture and the influences of modern technology. Tati foregoes any conventional narrative and instead presents a series of carefully orchestrated events that revolve around the visit to Paris of a businessman (M. Hulot) who crosses paths with a group of American tourists. They meet coincidentally, lose sight of each other, and meet again. At the "Royal Garden" restaurant, M. Hulot sees the tourists and makes the acquaintance of the charming Claudia. During the course of the evening, the atmosphere in the prematurely opened restaurant shifts from stiff elegance to energetic interactivity, due to the malfunctioning of the establishment and frantic attempts by the architect, manager, and waiters to improve the situation. Early the next morning, the tourist group returns to the airport; the shy M. Hulot buys a small bouquet for Claudia.

Such a summary cannot do justice to the film's intention and its strange, intense presence on the screen. Rightly called "one of the keystones of modern filmmaking (Kehr 1985), *Playtime* developed a revolutionary approach to narrative structure and cinematographic space and presents a humorous but lucid comment on modern architecture. Prominent film historians have emphasized the fact that Tati succeeded in creating a new stage in the development of cinematic language. The stylistic triad of the long shot, the long take, and deep-focus photography helped to introduce a different level of spectator consciousness. Tati's frames are usually filled with an abundance of details, figures, and subplots that all happen simultaneously. The viewer, presented with choices about what to watch, is liberated to a certain degree from passive submission to the director's decisions. As Tati put it in 1968, he expected "a little more attention and a little more imagination on the part of the spectator" (Fischer 1976). This approach also frees the viewer to observe the architecture of the

1

Fig. 2: Grand Ensemble Paris Sarcelles, 1959–66.

set with a greater degree of attention.

The nondescript modern architecture that Tati humorously presents lacks poetry and originality, and is also profoundly confusing and intimidating. Searching for his partner, M. Giffard, Hulot gets lost frequently in offices that seem to have an abundance of similar circulation spaces and glass-enclosed waiting rooms. Glass, the most cherished material of the modern movement, is shown to be absurdly deceptive, acting either as a reflector or as an invisible barrier

Playtime is, of course, also a film about Paris. Whereas in *Mon Oncle*, Tati presented a convincing comparison between the new suburbs and the charming older quarters, the city is now solely represented by "Tativille," a grim vision of Paris in the near future, with badly designed, modernistic skyscrapers and housing projects. All that the tourists see of such sites as the Eiffel Tower and the Arc de Triomphe are reflections in windows or doors that open accidentally. Paris is identified as participating in the "International Style" that makes all parts of the globe look alike — exemplified by a travel agency's display window in which destinations as far apart as London and Mexico City are advertised with the same image of a featureless modernistic skyscraper. Tati appears to have been reacting directly to recent developments in Paris, which included a number of large-scale urban projects such as the huge glass-clad office buildings at the Gare Montparnasse (1958–64) and suburban developments such as the infamous Sarcelles (1959–66).

The scenes in the Royal Garden restaurant offer Tati's answer to the evils of modern society and the sterility of modern architecture. The restaurant itself serves as a metaphor for the city, which is exemplified in typical Tati fashion by a somewhat incapacitated visitor who tries to find his way out by studying the marble patterns on the wall, mistaking them for a street map. Things improve when the visitors take matters into their own hands. The disintegrating ceiling panels and collapsing dividers are rearranged to create new spaces, in which a different, joyful atmosphere prevails. The spirit of poetic anarchy which Tati offers as a response to the rigid patterns of commercial modernism foreshadows the best moments of creativity during the May 1968 revolution. In the bus on her way out to the airport, Claudia holds the small bunch of lilies of the valley from M. Hulot. Suddenly, she realizes that the flowers look like miniatures of the streetlamps outside. At a crowded traffic circle, cars, trucks, and motorcycles circulate as if on a giant carousel. Even among the devices of modern life, Tati tells us, there are elements of mystery, awe, and poetry.

Tati spent an enormous budget creating his artificial Tativille on a lot outside Paris with full-scale building facades and a whole collection of miniatures of modernistic skyscrapers that could be moved about on rails. He built a temporary city using 50,000 cubic meters of concrete, 3,200 square meters of carpentry, and 1,200 square meters of glass. A critic wrote in 1968:

> From the beginning the director seems like an architect, and one of the boldest of them (as daring as Gaudi, as pure as Frank Lloyd Wright). Piece by piece, panel by panel, he constructs a fantastic, blueish metropolis out of glass and iron, which he populates afterwards according of his choreography, like Nietzsche's dancing God. . . It is not enough that such a city looks nice; it has to function, has to be inhabitable (red lights, elevators, heating, neon signs etc.). In populating this chessboard logically and mysteriously, Tati proves to be a better strategist than De Mille, a better choreographer than Berkeley. This sequence of spatial-temporal mechanisms is among the most complex that the cinema has created to this day [Fieschi 1968].

D. N.

3

4

Fig. 5: Production Shot: Set with Movable Skyscraper Mock-Ups © CEPEC/PANORAMIC.

Fig. 6: M. Hulot Searches for His Business Partner. *© CEPEC/ PANORAMIC.*

Fig. 7: Claudia Sees the Eiffel Tower. *© CEPEC/PANORAMIC.*

5

6

8

9

10

11

Blade Runner

U.S.A., The Ladd Company/Warner Bros., 1982

Director: Ridley Scott. *Script:* Hampton Fancher and David Peoples, based on the novel *Do Androids Dream of Electric Sheep?* by Philip K. Dick. *Sets:* Lawrence G. Paull (production designer), David Snyder (art director), Syd Mead ('visual futurist'). *Camera:* Jordan Cronenweth. *Cast:* Harrison Ford (Deckard), Rutger Hauer (Batty), Sean Young (Rachel), Edward James Olmos (Gaff), M. Emmet Walsh (Bryant), Daryl Hannah (Pris), William Sanderson (Sebastian), Brion James (Leon), Joe Turkel (Tyrell), Joanna Cassidy (Zhora), James Hong (Chew), Morgan Paull (Holden), Kevin Thompson (Bear).
Premiere: 25 June 1982, Los Angeles.

Literature: Philip K. Dick, *Do Androids Dream of Electric Sheep?* (New York: Random House, 1968); Richard Corliss, "The Pleasures of Texture," *Time* (12 July 1982), p. 68; Pauline Kael, "Baby, the Rain Must Fall," *New Yorker* 58, no. 3 (12 July 1982), pp. 82–85; Joanne Ostrow, "'Retrofitting' the Future," *Washington Post* (27 July 1981), p. C7; Herb Lightman and Richard Patterson, "*Blade Runner:* Production Design and Photography," *American Cinematographer* 63, no. 7 (July 1982), pp. 684–87, 716-21; Paul Sammon, "The Making of *Blade Runner,*" *Cinéfantastique* 12, nos. 5–6 (July–August 1982), pp. 20–47; Andrew Sarris, "Cold Wars and Cold Futures," *Village Voice* 27, no. 27 (July 1982), p. 47; Don Shay, "*Blade Runner:* 2020 Foresight," *Cinefex* 9 (July 1982), pp. 5–71; Marshall Deutelbaum, "Memory/Visual Design: The Remembered Sights of *Blade Runner,*" *Film/Literature Quarterly* 17, no. 1 (1989), pp. 66–71; Judith B. Kerman, ed., *Retrofitting* Blade Runner: *Issues in Ridley Scott's* Blade Runner *and Philip K. Dick's Do Androids Dream of Electric Sheep?* (Bowling Green: Bowling Green State University Popular Press, 1991); "Lawrence G. Paull," in Vincent LoBrutto, *By Design: Interviews with Film Production Designers* (Westport: Praeger, 1992), pp. 165–78.

Fig. 1: Hades Landscape. *Photo: Virgil Mirano, Los Angeles.*
© *1982, The Blade Runner Partnership.*

Fig. 2: Syd Mead, L.A. Cityscape: Preliminary, *1980. Gouache on board, 38 x 50.8 cm. Courtesy Syd Mead Inc., Los Angeles. Original Art Work created for Warner Bros. motion picture* Blade Runner. *© 1982.*

Fig. 3: Street Scene. Photo: Virgil Mirano, Los Angeles. © 1982, The Blade Runner Partnership.

In the manner of a futuristic *film noir*, we accompany the Blade Runner, Rick Deckard, on a mission he has accepted reluctantly. Deckard lives in the polluted, crime-ridden Los Angeles of 2019, which has long been abandoned by the wealthy middle class for a better life on other planets and seems to be inhabited mostly by outcasts and criminals under constant surveillance by armed police cars and helicopters. Deckard's mission is to track down four "replicants" — genetically engineered humanoids designed by the powerful Tyrell Corporation. Four examples of a highly developed model have returned to earth (leaving a trail of gruesome murders) to track down the head of the corporation in order to force him to prolong their four-year life-span. Deckard tracks down and kills three of them. The fourth replicant reaches the end of his life span at exactly the moment when he is about to kill Deckard after a long fight on the roof of a downtown office building. Deckard falls in love with Rachel, the ultra-lifelike prototype of a new replicant, who is not aware of her own artificiality. As they leave the city together in the final scene, we are left with an uneasy feeling that Deckard might be a replicant himself.

Blade Runner was re-edited a few years ago in a "director's cut" version in which Deckard can more easily be identified as a replicant and in which the upbeat ending and his *film noir-*style voice-over have been eliminated.

Echoing H.G. Wells's famous verdict about Fritz Lang's *Metropolis* — instead of being "a 100 years hence," he considered it a third of a century out of date — Ridley Scott wanted a "film set forty years hence, made in the style of forty years ago" (Ostrow 1981). This premise is not the only connection to *Metropolis*, to which *Blade Runner* owes much in terms of ideas for individual settings and the imagery of the city. Most importantly, it shows a city with history, with buildings that have been there for a long time and have survived beneath gargantuan modern high-rises. In *Metropolis*, these survivors were the cathedral, the house of the inventor, and the ancient catacombs. In the decaying Los Angeles of the future, we find the Yukon Hotel, Union Station (1931–39), the Bradbury Building (1893), and Frank Lloyd Wright's Ennis Brown House

2

3

(1923). The men who create androids — Rotwang in *Metropolis*, Sebastian in *Blade Runner* — are the characters most deeply rooted in history, the ones who live in the oldest buildings: a medieval hut in *Metropolis* and the Bradbury Building in *Blade Runner*. The architectural treatment of Deckard's apartment — inspired by and partially filmed at the Ennis Brown House — contains one of the clues to the nagging central question about his being a replicant. Wright's characteristic treatment of his ornamented concrete blocks was based on the imagery of Mayan architecture. In the film, two Mayan-inspired pyramids house the headquarters of the Tyrell Corporation, producers of the replicants. A key concept for the design of the city's architecture was that of "retrofitting" or "layering" — the continuous repair and adaptation to changing needs, which lead to the compelling imagery of buildings covered by webs of pipes, ducts, and technological debris.

The development of the design for Los Angeles's future manifestation is well documented. Far from being one person's vision, it was the product of a broad collaboration among the director Ridley Scott, the production designer Lawrence G. Paull, the visual futurist Syd Mead, and many others, including special effects supervisor Doug Trumbull and matte artist Matt Yuricich. In addition to evoking both past and future, the film's architectural concept is very much part of its time. Like many architects of his generation, Mead, for instance, had been developing ideas for huge megastructures since the 1960s. Inspired by an as yet unbroken faith in technological progress and unlimited resources, visions of monolithic cities for hundreds of thousands of people were believed to contain the essential ideas for future town planning. Ten years later, arguments for a soft, flexible approach to architecture allowing adaptation to changing needs would surface, as for instance in Peter Cook's visionary Trickling Towers (1978–79), in which initally slick megastructures change their appearance over time.

Blade Runner is usually categorized as a dystopian vision of a future L.A. And indeed, there is acid rain and constant darkness, and the city is inhabited mostly by criminals and outlaws. But underneath all of this,

one recognizes the director's love of life in a big city, of urban density with crowds of people, colorful newspaper stands, shining neon lights reflected in puddles on the sidewalk, exotic fast food on sale in the streets. Today, there are very few places in America where this genuine urban intensity can be experienced. One of them, no doubt, is downtown L.A.

> For the buildings we did, I brought in all the photographs from Milan, and we took photographs of arcades, columns, Classical things, and all the architecture. I brought in just about my entire architectural research library, and we went from Egyptian to Deco to Streamline Moderne to Classical, from Frank Lloyd Wright to Antonio Gaudi. We turned the photographs sideways, upside down, inside out, and backwards to stretch where we were going and came up with a street that looked like *Conan the Barbarian* in 2020. That's basically where we were headed, because it had to be richly carved. I didn't want right angles; I didn't want slick surfaces ["Lawrence G. Paull" 1992].

> He lived alone in this deteriorating, blind building of a thousand uninhabited apartments, which like all its counterparts, fell, day by day, into greater entropic ruin. Eventually everything within the building would merge, would be faceless and identical, mere pudding-like kipple piled to the ceiling of each apartment. And, after that, the uncared-for building itself would settle into shapelessness, buried under the ubiquity of the dust. By then, naturally, he himself would be dead, another interesting event to anticipate as he stood here in his stricken living room alone with the lungless, all-penetrating, masterful world silence [Dick 1968].

D. N.

4

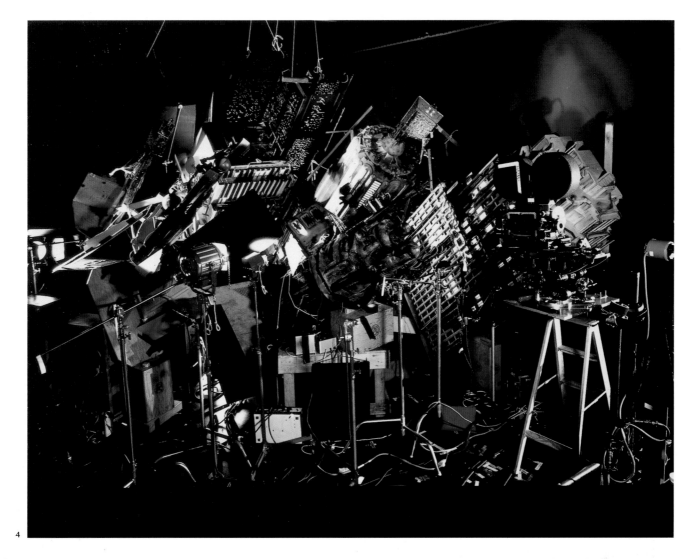

5

Fig. 6: Frank Lloyd Wright, Ennis Brown House, *Los Angeles, 1923. Photo: Julius Shulman, Hon. AIA. © Julius Shulman, Los Angeles.*

7

8

Fig. 7: Syd Mead, Set: Deckard's Kitchen, *1980. Gouache on board, 38 x 25 cm. Courtesy Syd Mead Inc., Los Angeles. Original Art Work created for Warner Bros. motion picture* Blade Runner. *© 1982.*

Fig. 8: Syd Mead, Street Set, 1980. Gouache on board, 38 x 25.3 cm. Courtesy Syd Mead Inc., Los Angeles.

Fig. 9: Syd Mead, Street set: Salons, *1980. Gouache on board, 38.1 x 25.3 cm. Courtesy Syd Mead Inc., Los Angeles. Original Art Work created for Warner Bros. motion picture* Blade Runner. *© 1982.*

Fig. 10: Syd Mead, Street set: Corner Bookshop, *1980. Gouache on board, 38.1 x 25.3 cm. Courtesy Syd Mead Inc., Los Angeles. Original Art Work created for Warner Bros. motion picture* Blade Runner. *© 1982.*

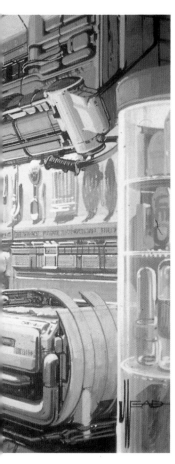

9

10

Fig. 11: An Advertising Blimp Seen Through the Glass Roof of the Bradbury Building. *Photo: Virgil Mirano, Los Angeles. © 1982, The Blade Runner Partnership.*

Fig. 12: George Herbert Wyman, The Bradbury Building, Los Angeles, 1893. Photo: Julius Shulman, Hon. AIA. © Julius Shulman, Los Angeles.

Fig. 13: Syd Mead, Set: Sebastian's Laboratory, *1980. Gouache on board, 38 x 25.3 cm. Courtesy Syd Mead Inc., Los Angeles. Original Art Work created for Warner Bros. motion picture* Blade Runner. *© 1982.*

11

12

Fig. 14: Peter Cook, Trickling Towers Project, 1978–79.

Fig. 15: Spinner Approaching the Headquarters of the Tyrell Corporation. *Photo: Virgil Mirano, Los Angeles. © 1982, The Blade Runner Partnership.*

Fig. 16: Mark Stetson, Insert Miniature of the Tyrell Skyscraper, *ca. 1980. Wood, metal, fiberglass, 134.62 x 163.83 x 142.24 cm. American Museum of the Moving Image, Gift of Mark Stetson. Photo: David Sundberg.*

14

15

Batman

U.S.A., Warner Bros., 1989

Director: Tim Burton. *Script:* Sam Hamm, Warren Skaaren, Charles McKeown, based on characters created by Bob Kane. *Sets:* Anton Furst (production designer), assisted by Nigel Phelps. *Cast:* Kim Basinger (Vicky Vale), Michael Keaton (Bruce Wayne/Batman), Jack Nicholson (The Joker), Jack Palance (Carl Grissom), Robert Wuhl (Alexander Knox).
Premiere: June 1989, Los Angeles.

Literature: John Marriott, *Batman: The Official Book of the Movie* (New York: Bantam Books, 1989), pp. 86–91; Benedict Nightingale, "Batman Prowls at Gotham Drawn from the Absurd," *New York Times* (18 June 1989), sect. H, pp. 1, 16; Adam Pirani, "Production: Batman," *Theatre Crafts* 23, no. 7 (August–September 1989), p. 21; Pilar Viladas, "Batman, Design for the Bad Guys," *Progressive Architecture* 70, no. 9 (September 1989), pp. 21–22; Clifford A. Pearson, "Urban Fright," *Architectural Record* 178, no. 1 (January 1990), pp. 206–07; Jody Duncan Shannon, "A Dark and Stormy Knight," *Cinefex* 41 (February 1990), pp. 4–33.

Fig. 1: The Skies of Gotham City. © *1989 Warner Bros. Inc.*

1

Fig. 2: The Axis Chemical Factory. © *1989 Warner Bros., Inc.*

Fifty years after *Batman*'s debut as a comic strip in 1939, Warner Bros. turned the theme into a major motion picture with a $27 million budget and a high-profile cast. Tim Burton, who had established a reputation for himself as an unusually creative visual stylist, was selected as director. The story was written by Sam Hamm, based on Bob Kane's original comic strip. Bruce Wayne, the enigmatic loner who as a child witnessed the murder of his parents, now fights evil in Gotham City in his disguise as a giant bat, supported by an impressive arsenal of sophisticated mountaineering and combat equipment. He falls in love with reporter Vicky Vale, whom he rescues in a final showdown from the hands of his adversary, the sinister and crazed crime boss "The Joker."

The film was produced at the Pinewood Studios outside London, which provided spacious soundstages and 95-acre outdoor backlots for the creation of an ambitiously complex city set: "The characters in the movie are so extreme that I felt it was important to set them in an arena that was specifically designed for them. . . . ' The thought of shooting *Batman* in some New York location just did not feel right to me," explained Tim Burton. Eventually, the 400-meter-long set became the largest and most expensive outdoor set built in Europe since the 1960 filming of *Cleopatra*. Created in the astonishingly short time of five months, it is also one of the most compelling urban visions in the history of filmmaking.

Furst was faced with the task of creating a gloomy, nightmarish city that was neither historically nor geographically identifiable, but that remained convincing as a somewhat familiar Western metropolis. He and Nigel Phelps produced a large number of conceptual sketches to be translated into models, large–scale sets, and matte paintings. Although the fast–paced, action–filled movie constantly distracts the viewer from contemplating the elaborate sets, Furst's drawings and interviews reveal how the city was designed around a number of carefully chosen parameters. At the core was the invention of a specific history for the city. When Batman begins his fight against crime, 200-year-old Gotham City has been in the hands of the mob for many decades:

The most important thing was that we find a feel for the city which was neither futuristic nor historical. We wanted it to be as timeless as possible, even though — since we were drawing from the original DC comic strip for inspiration — there was bound to be a certain '40s feeling to it. . . . [I]magining what might have happened to New York had there been no planning commission and had it been run by pure extortion and crime . . . we completely threw out any concept of zoning and construction laws that insure skyscrapers are built so that light will still fall on the streets below. Instead, we maximized space, bridged over streets, built the buildings cantilevering toward the streets rather than away from them . . . it was just a hell that had erupted through the pavement and kept on growing [ibid.].

Drawing on his rich historical knowledge, Furst created a breathtaking architectural panopticum for the city's details. He was clearly aware that his Gotham would be compared to its German predecessor:

Metropolis looks as if one person designed the whole town. But New York or any other real metropolis looks as if it is something that has been designed by thousands of architects over hundreds of years. So we went for a potpourri of different styles. . . . I chose styles which, when put together, would create its own kind of style — everything from the early brownstone buildings to modern brutalism, Gothic architecture to Italian futurism. We even tapped fascism for the city hall. For the Flugelheim Museum, I chose a modern Japanese architect named Shin Takamatsu who does this really brutal, locomotive type architecture — it has the look of nuts and bolts and castings and that sort of thing. So we put together this Dadaistic potpourri and we became quite comfortable with it. We began to formulate our own language of architecture [ibid.].

Other references include Konstantin Melnikov's workers' club in Moscow (1927), the precise turn-of-the-century details of Vienna's Otto Wagner, Milan's Torre Velasca (1956–58), and Norman Foster's structural expressionism. Said Furst: "I translated images of architecture, not architecture itself, into set designs." Gotham City's cathedral was carefully designed as another reference to *Metropolis* and as a visual anchor and counterpoint to the rest of the city.

Fig. 3: Antonio Gaudí, Sketch for the Sagrada Familia, ca. 1908.

Fig. 4: Anton Furst, Preproduction sketch: Gotham City Cathedral, 1989. © 1989 Warner Bros. Inc.

Fig. 5: Anton Furst, Preproduction sketch: Gotham City Skyline. © 1989 Warner Bros. Inc.

Fig. 6: Anton Furst, Preproduction sketch: Gotham City Main Street. Copyright © 1989 Warner Bros. Inc.

"We had these other broad-stroked, straight-lined structures," Furst said,

so when we came to the cathedral, I thought we should offset that with an organic building devoid of any straight lines. . . . I had always been fascinated by the work of Antonio Gaudí. There is a Gothic feeling to it, and yet it is not Gothic. It is very difficult to position in time, which made it perfect for the cathedral. I've also always liked the house in Hitchcock's *Psycho,* so I topped off the cathedral with the top of the Hitchcock house. . . . It really had to be a forbidding looking thing in my view — as if it had been closed down because God had left the city years ago [ibid.].

None of Furst's points of reference, it turns out, were historicist buildings, such as the Neoclassical banks and office buildings typical of American cities in the 1940s. Instead, he created an array of unornamented, structurally expressive, industrialized buildings, a dark résumé of a century of architectural modernism. In striking contrast, Batman himself lives in an historic country house. In fact, two of Great Britain's finest stately homes were used for the shooting of Batman's abode: Hatfield House (1607–12) and Knebworth Manor (ca. 1492). The architectural press noted the striking contrast between the range of rundown modern masterpieces in the crime-infested city and the historical Wayne Manor as the home of the hero, suspecting another populist attack against modernism. Do *Batman's* sets imply, worried *Progressive Architecture,* "that contemporary design isn't quite suitable for nice, normal folk?" (Viladas 1989).

Anton Furst received an Oscar for his production design in 1990.

D. N.

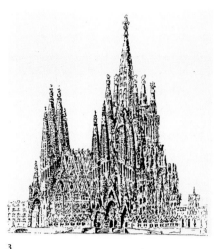

3

4

5

6

Fig. 7: *Production Shot:* Gotham City Main Square under Construction. © *Warner Bros. Inc.*

Fig. 8: *Anton Furst, Preproduction sketch*: In the Streets of Gotham City. © *1989 Warner Bros. Inc.*

Fig. 9: *Shin Takamatsu, "The Arch," A Dentist's Clinic, Tokyo: Elevation, 1981–83. Pencil on paper, 79 x 109.5 cm. Deutsches Architektur-Museum, Frankfurt am Main.*

7

8

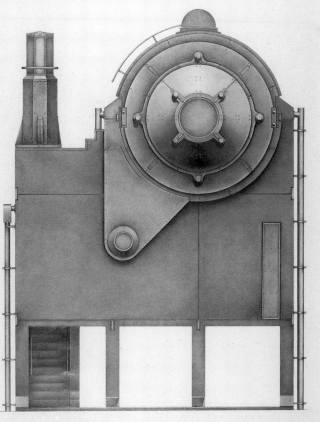

Fig. 10: The Skyline of Gotham City. © 1989 Warner Bros., Inc.

10

Dick Tracy

U.S.A., Walt Disney Co., 1990

Director: Warren Beatty. *Script:* Jim Cash and Jack Epps, Jr. and Bo Goldman and Warren Beatty, based on characters created by Chester Gould. *Sets:* Richard Sylbert (production designer). *Visual Effects:* Michael Lloyd and Harrison Ellenshaw. *Camera:* Vittorio Storaro. *Cast:* Warren Beatty (Dick Tracy), Madonna (Breathless Mahoney), Glenne Headly (Tess Trueheart), Charlie Korsmo (The Kid), Al Pacino (Big Boy Caprice), Seymour Cassel (Sam Catchem), James Keane (Pat Patton), Bill Forsythe (Flattop), Mandy Patinkin (88 Keys), R.G. Armstrong (Pruneface), Ed O'Ross (Itchy), Dustin Hoffman (Mumbles).
Premiere: 15 June 1990, Los Angeles.

Literature: Garyn G. Roberts, *Dick Tracy and American Culture: Morality and Mythology, Text and Context* (London: McFarland and Co., 1973); Mike Bonifer, *Dick Tracy: The Making of the Movie* (New York: Bantham, 1990); Glenn Campbell, "Crimestoppers Textbook," *Cinefex* 44 (1990), pp. 24–49; Vincent Canby, "A Cartoon Square Comes to Life In 'Dick Tracy,'" *New York Times* (15 June 1990), sect. C, p. 6; Richard Corliss, "Extra! Tracy is Tops: Warren Beatty Creates the Best Comic-Strip Movie Yet," *Time* (18 June 1990), pp. 74–76; Michael Quintanilla, "Slick Tracy," *Los Angeles Times* (20 June 1990), sect. E, p. 1.

Fig. 1: The Kid Escapes Tracy by Ducking in Front of the Train. © 1990 The Walt Disney Company.

1

Chester Gould's comic strip "Dick Tracy" first appeared in the *Chicago Tribune* in 1931, a contemporary of "Buck Rogers" (1929), "Superman" (1938), and "Batman" (1939). Tracy's story as retold by Warren Beatty revolves around the police detective's relationships with his girlfriend Tess Trueheart, a street urchin (The Kid), the seductive singer Breathless Mahoney, and his great adversary, gangster boss Big Boy Caprice. By the end of the film, Tracy, Tess, and the Kid are about to establish a family; Breathless Mahoney and Big Boy Caprice have met their fate. "The real star of the film is the look," claimed the *Los Angeles Times* (Quintanilla 1990). Indeed, the film (which earned Richard Sylbert his second Academy Award for art direction) engendered its own brand of stylized reality so successfully that it made it seem possible to step into a comic strip.

The film opens with a grandiose traveling shot from the window of Tracy's apartment, climbing the facade of his brownstone and moving swiftly over adjacent roofs to pan across the enormous skyline bathed in the golden light of the setting sun, revealing another, poorer part of the city, where we have our first encounter with the Kid. The city is thus established as a major player in the picture. Its visual concept was reportedly the single most debated concept during the production of the movie. Although Chicago might have been an obvious choice for the setting — Chester Gould had established a clear relationship with that city in the strip — the set hints more clearly at New York City. It has a distinctive 1930s and '40s feel to it, a period which Beatty considered quintessentially American: "I would say that prewar, just on the brink of war, there probably was a naïveté about America in that period, about good and evil, law and order. It's just before America took over. The last days of innocence. Just before our loss of innocence as a country" (Campbell 1990). On the other hand, the setting for a comic strip had to exist at a distance from reality. "I knew the past didn't hold the answer. It could not be realistic. We had to create a parallel world that you believed in, but were not familiar with," recalled Richard Sylbert. "There is nothing fancy in the picture — a room is either a rectangle or a square or a narrow passage. A ware-house is just that; a diner is just a diner, with no names. All the cars are just cars — no model names. It's absolutely stripped, and what happens is you see a world that's so simplified, it becomes sophisticated" (ibid.). Sylbert suggested that the color scheme be reduced to vibrant primary and a few secondary colors, recalling the simplified color-printing process of early comic strips. Accordingly, all the yellows, reds, and blues have the same hue and intensity.

The urban setting of *Dick Tracy* compresses the imagery from New York City's most celebrated and heroic period, the 1920s to the early '40s, into a grandiose range of backdrops, street vistas, and matte paintings. Buildings reminiscent of well-known set-back skyscrapers such as the Chrysler (1929) or Empire State (1931) buildings or the Waldorf Astoria Hotel (1931) tower above street after street of typical early twentieth-century brownstones and brick buildings with protruding cornices and watertanks on their flat roofs. Generic billboards that advertise "Delicious Franks" or "Superior Telephones" carefully imitate the advertising style of the time. This is the New York City we know from photographs by Paul Strand or Andreas Feininger, from paintings by Charles Sheeler and Edward Hopper, from films such as King Vidor's *The Crowd* (1928) or Jules Dassin's *Naked City* (1948). In some ways, of course, the film's "Tracytown" is different. It seems to be much bigger than Manhattan was in the '30s, its skyline extending endlessly. The city has, it seems, continued to grow without adopting the stylistic changes brought about by European modernism in the late 1940s. This romantic daydream is the appropriate counterpart to *Batman*'s urban nightmare of the previous year, which had presented a city where architectural modernism had grown wildly out of control.

The film's magical atmosphere could only have been achieved through an intense use of matte shots that merge background paintings with filmed sequences. "I like the idea that for the first time we did not have to try to hide the matte shots," said Harrison Ellenshaw, one of the head designers. "Usually, you give the audiences as much reality as you can, then sneak a matte shot in there and hope nobody notices it. In

Fig. 4: Hugh Ferriss, Empire State Building, *ca. 1930. Sepia photoprint on paper, 99.1 x 48.3 cm. Columbia University, Avery Architectural and Fine Arts Library, New York.*

Fig. 5: Andreas Feininger, The Brooklyn Bridge and Downtown Manhattan, *1949. Copyright Time Life Inc. 1988.*

Fig. 6: Harrison and Peter Ellenshaw, Leon Harris, Michael Lloyd, Paul Lasaine, David Mattingly, and Michele Moen, Matte Painting: Panorama of the City, *Detail. Acrylic on board, 122 x 244 cm. Courtesy of Buena Vista Visual Effects, Burbank, CA. All rights reserved.*

this movie the matte paintings are the reality" (ibid.). This traditional production method connects the film with early days of the medium and with the concurrent intense discussions about degrees of reality and the relationships among film, architecture, and painting. In addition, most scenes were filmed without camera movement, thus referring to the static scene-by-scene progress of the comic strip.

The well-documented production process is worth recalling here. With a large number of concept and design sketches, Richard Sylbert's art department had established — in bold strokes of comic-book colors — the general direction for the set design at the very beginning. Director of photography Vittorio Storaro developed an initial concept for light and color contrasts. The visual effects department at Disney's Buena Vista Studios took over at this point, led by Michael Lloyd, Harrison Ellen-

shaw, and Steve Rundell. Michele Moen and Paul Lasaine were selected as primary matte artists and produced 44 of the 55 matte shots in the film, among them the celebrated sequence in which the Kid leaps in front of an oncoming train and eludes the detective, a sequence that was achieved by a skillful combination of painted sets, live-action footage, and three-dimensional models.

The matte artists were soon joined by other draughtsmen, especially in the final phase of the project, when the large panorama for the opening traveling shot had to be painted. Among them was famed matte artist Peter Ellenshaw, who established the magical color scheme for the sky at sunset, the guideline for the rest of the panorama.

In the end, Warren Beatty liked what he saw. "God, this is so weird," he said. "I'd love to live there" (ibid.).

D. N.

Dick Tracy

Fig. 7, 8: *Six painters at work: Harrison and Peter Ellenshaw, Michael Lloyd, Paul Lasaine, David Mattingly, and Michele Moen. Courtesy of Buena Vista Visual Effects, Burbank. All rights reserved.*

Fig. 9: *The miniature set placed in the foreground of the matte painting. Built by Mark Stetson, Stetson Visual Services. Courtesy of Buena Vista Visual Effects, Burbank, CA. All rights reserved.*

Fig. 10: *Harrison and Peter Ellenshaw, Leon Harris, Michael Lloyd, Paul Lasaine, David Mattingly, and Michele Moen, Matte Painting:* Panorama of the City, *Detail. Acrylic on board, 122 x 244 cm. Courtesy of Buena Vista Visual Effects, Burbank, CA. All rights reserved.*

7

8

9

Fig. 11: Night Scene. © *1990 The Walt Disney Company.*

Fig. 12: Edward Hopper, The City, *1927. Oil on canvas, 70 x 90.4 cm. The University of Arizona Museum of Art, Tucson, Gift of C. Leonhard Pfeiffer.*

Fig. 13: The Bridge, a Car, the City and a Starry Night. © *1990 The Walt Disney Company.*

11

12

Film and Architecture:
Selected texts from the
Weimar Republic

Metropolis, *Erich Kettelhut, "Dawn". Oil and gouache on card-board, 39 x 54.5 cm. Stiftung Deutsche Kinemathek, Berlin.*

The Film Set: A Contribution to Artistic Direction

In one of his lecture evenings at Lessing University, Herbert Eulenberg felicitously coined the phrase "the black and white art of the film," an art to which many talented artists should devote themselves. The following short essay will demonstrate how this black and white art is aspired to and achieved in set design as well. Even in situations where artistic direction is normally valued, amazing indifference often prevails on precisely this point.

Usually, construction in the studio takes place as follows: a few days (usually only three or four) before the beginning of shooting, the set designer finds out what he is to build. He does not usually read the script first. Instead, the director tells him: "I need a bedroom, an anteroom, etc." Then, the set designer chooses furniture from rental firms, and with that and the resources available he improvises his set. Usually, he only makes quick sketches, showing the ground plan and merely presenting an outline for the director. Looking at pictures made under these circumstances, one can excuse them by saying: "How can anything good be accomplished when the set designer has to design twenty-five sets, procure the furniture, and organize and supervise construction in three or four days?!"

Unfortunately, sets in this country have a much too rigid pattern. One only ever sees small variations in the assemblage of available resources. Even the unbiased regular moviegoer will eventually recognize individual pieces of furniture which have been rented time and again, or architectural elements (arches, doors, etc.) that reappear constantly. He can often guess what firm owns the properties in question. Enough of this pattern ("a decoration" of rooms surrounded by any number of preferably crooked walls with ever new variations in the furniture arrangement), and let us have real art instead! Why not build rooms, corners, or even a single wall, which, thanks to its simple disposition, is genuine architectural art? It would even be easy to make every set as unique and beautiful as designs in a good book on interior decoration. In the same way that I look forward to the next picture as I turn each page here and yet cannot tear myself away from the one I'm looking at right now, each new film set should affect the moviegoer as an exemplary design. The sight of the living rooms

should immediately make the viewer think: "That is how I would like to furnish my room!" Of course, I would like any set to appear modest throughout. It should always remain a mere framework, not like the gilt plaster frame of current practice, but like refined woodwork that accentuates the picture by the simplest means. At this moment, I can picture the following set. I will describe it in order to show how simply one can work: a light, delicate wallpapered wall, a plain bench or backrest against it, on the bench a pot-bellied container with a large bunch of brightly colored flowers, and around the base of this container a folded brocade cloth, draped forward slightly over the bench. This is almost window dressing, but it is enough. The flat wall will enhance the action all the more.

Such a set, however, belongs to a very particular scene. It can and must not be misused for anything other than the intended scene. It is therefore absolutely impossible to work without a script, as many people do. I need to know the person in question and only then can say: "Such and such a setting is where he will move, such and such is how he will furnish his place!" In my opinion, the set should also suit the person. That is to say, the set should evolve from the plot. And for that you need atmosphere!

Atmosphere! Anyone working in the hectic setting of the film studio is familiar with this word today?! And yet, it is the prime prerequisite for truly good artistic work! It calls for the strictest abstraction, complete immersion in the material — above all, peace and quiet, and time! Once these conditions are met, very, very good work can result. Improvising in construction is quite nice, but only the method recommended above can bring about true art!

Now, we proceed to the question: How should the design be put on paper? With a ground plan by any chance? No, impossible. Only perspectives can be of any value. In fact, the design should be made to look exactly like what the moviegoer will see in the cinema later, with all the furnishings, including — above all — the light and shadow, perhaps also the distribution of groups of people. That is, not only the structure itself but also the lighting effects should be easy to recognize in the design. These lights and shadows are after all what give the picture atmosphere in the first place. It is wrong if the cameraman indicates during the shooting how the lights are to be arranged, because he has only one aim in mind. He wants his take to be as clear as possible. He wants as much light as possible, so that he cannot

be reproached for unrecognizable facial expressions afterwards. Naturally, I don't mean that light can't be very beautiful — but light is only effective when there is shadow as well! Terrible sins are still being committed in this respect. It is not yet understood how to work with good effects. I once had a corridor built along which a corpse was to be dragged. Due to the dim light shining in from two side passages, the murderer approached with the body in eerily alternating light and shadow. I didn't feel it was necessary to see the murderer's facial expression in detail already from the end of the corridor, and so saved it for when he stepped into the second circle of light just in front of the camera. Unfortunately, I was not present during the shooting. Behind each protruding pillar they had placed a man with a spotlight, thus of course completely obscuring the intended atmosphere. Unfortunately, it is still not understood that too much effect results in no effect at all.

I would even go so far as to give the question of light frequent priority over the question of furnishings. To my mind, it is not always necessary at all to perceive every detail of the decor down to the farthest corner. It is often quite immaterial whether a chair is standing next to a certain wall or a painting is on it. On the other hand, what often does matter is: Is the wall light or dark? And no cameraman should decide that, but only the designing artist. Only he should indicate the distribution of light and shade, because only he knows what atmosphere a room is to have. It probably goes without saying that it is his responsibility that a good take is photographically possible with certain lighting directives in the first place.

Originally published as: "Das Szenenbild," *Der Film*, no. 49 (7 December 1918).

No details of Kaufmann's life are known.

Bruno Taut

Artistic Film Program

The achievements of film, those that it may be expected to contribute to art, can basically be divided into three categories. By the nature of the subject, these three overlap and complement each other: for example, an instructive film imaginatively presented always affords artistic enjoyment; similarly, the film as an autonomous artistic creation is also instructive.

The three categories are as follows: (1) the generally stimulating film, which kindles the artistic imagination; (2) the instructive film, produced as an aid to the teaching of art, craft, or architecture; (3) the film as an autonomous work of art.

First Category
For this, films from the whole field of the natural sciences, most of which have already been shot, should be selected and manufactured, not for their scientific or purely practical interest, but for that in the artistic beauty of natural forms, in their growth, etc. and in the image itself.

Example: Crystal formations in ice, snow, minerals, etc. Growth of plants as seen in seeds, leaves, and whole trees. Zoological films, with particular emphasis on the beauty of animal form and motion. Use of time-lapse cinematography.

Second Category
Films of the making of works of art, and of good craftsmanship. The hands of the good craft worker are filmed in the act of making a beautiful piece.

Examples: The silversmith making a beautiful ring, the engraver at work, the pillow-lace maker, the stained-glass artist, painting and inserting glass in cames, etc. We watch the pieces taking shape, they are turned around, etc., and then alongside them a piece is shown that merely imitates the good artistic forms and is badly made in itself. The difference between genuine and imitation lace — between a good and a bad piece of work in ceramics, metalwork, or whatever — will become clearly apparent, leading the viewer to conclude that a good piece, in spite of its higher purchase price, is essentially cheaper than a bad piece (Werkbund work). The same principle may be applied to purely artistic work: woodcut, linocut, lithography, etc.

Architecture: Films of buildings and groups of buildings, shot by moving the camera around them, coming closer to show the detail, and finally entering. The student of architecture, like the layman, will thus acquire a lively notion of the true essence of architecture. He will free himself of the pictorial notions fostered hitherto by perspectival renderings and will learn to comprehend the building as a unified organism that grows inevitably out of the determinant factors of function, location, and the rest. The significance of details and fittings, right down to the furniture, is made evident within their total context.

Examples: A filmed sequence of a residential neighborhood: first a walk through the streets, then around the outsides of individual houses, and finally inside individual homes. Likewise factories at work, schools in use, railroad stations, churches, crematoria, theaters, etc. In the case of theaters, filming during performances, both in front and behind the scenes, would demonstrate the close relationship between the architecture of the building and the drama. Complemented by sectional drawings with animation. The same principle for whole cities: Danzig, Goslar, etc., first from the air, then driving around in an automobile, then individual buildings as above — in short, a sightseeing tour of the whole town. Also bad examples, such as tenement areas and squalid housing.

Dance and Gymnastics: Films of dance schools to show the teaching method; use of slow-motion technique to evaluate various methods. Comparative sequences of animals filmed in slow motion, as in the first group.

Third Category
Film as art.

(a) Dance with music, as product of school of dance and gymnastics. Extension into filmed mime. Important to exert an influence on the existing dramatic film, in which whole scenes are ruined by characters who are seen speaking and writing, because the word is a medium completely alien to film.

(b) Mime without figures. Fantasy scenery in motion. Architectural drama and the like (cf. my own architectural drama, *Der Weltbaumeister*). Connection with symphonic music.

(c) "The mobile image." Abstract painting transposed into film by showing an image in which the forms are constantly in motion. Made from drawings by artists, technically similar to the existing — mostly puerile — joke animations, as shown in the movie houses.

(d) The kaleidoscope. Camera points directly into the kaleidoscope tube. A projector adapted to show the kaleidoscope directly has the advantage of reproducing colors accurately, but it is expensive, and beyond a certain size of projected image (1.2 meters), it is blurred and unclear. The lack of color should be made up by skillful coloring; the same goes for (b) and (c). But the black and white image is also adequate in itself. When the tube is loaded by artists, the kaleidoscope can produce extraordinary artistic effects. (Glass house at Werkbund exhibition, Cologne 1914.)

Originally published as "Künstlerisches Filmprogramm," *Das hohe Ufer* 2 (1920), pp. 86-88.

Taut (1880–1938) was a central figure in the German architectural avant-garde before and after World War I. During the same period, he published a magazine entitled *Frühlicht* and established a correspondence group with other artists, the Gläserne Kette. Bruno Taut had intended to turn his above mentioned 'architectural drama' *Der Weltbaumeister* into a film, and contacted Walter Reimann, one of the architects of the *Caligari* film. Nothing came of this project, but it inspired other film scenarios from Taut's friends Wenzel Hablik and Hermann Finsterlin.

Heinrich de Fries

Spatial Design in Film
(excerpts)

At a time when most architects have been prevented from building for years and will be for a long time, it seems worthwhile to look at how space continues to be dealt with nonetheless. Due to the special nature of contemporary conditions, there is even a pressing and fervent need to find solutions. The extraordinary rise of the film industry created unique conditions under which, after a long, abnormal standstill, spatial design entered a phase of almost too rapid tropical growth. Seedlings are sprouting in the most unexpected areas, luxuriant foliage is unfurling, and in the strictly academic, boring garden of our dearly beloved art of building facades, blossoms of fanciful shape are opening. We almost dare to hope that some elements arising from this sudden, virtually unique, and almost unavoidable special development are of significant value beyond the needs of film for the rebirth of architecture currently in progress. For the time being, as far as the essence of architecture is concerned, only beginnings exist. All the more lively, however, is the problematic debate about the artistic conception of space and spatial design in film itself.

Before separate tendencies and individual results can be discussed, the special features of film architecture should be considered briefly. It should first be mentioned that film is a kind of stage, film stories being stories taken from real life and somehow intensified. Of the countless potential plots in question, the only ones relevant to our observations are those capable of transcending the limits of reality (even potential reality) with the help of an imagination freed from earthbound matters. An awareness of the fact that visibly displayed inner processes, unparalleled in the familiar reality of existence, also call for unreal space led to a corresponding remodeling of space on stage and in literature long ago. May we remind anyone lacking comparative examples of Strindberg's "Traumspiel." Above all, the significance of a sense of the indissoluble relationships between people, space, and fate in these works should be strongly emphasized. All films touched upon here — in fact, all films relevant to our considerations — are films about unreal existence, dream fantasies, fantastic events, placed in the distant past (*Golem*) or the distant future (*Algol*). Or else real-life events are so extraordinarily and potently concentrated that such frantic condensation makes them appear unbelievably intensified and unreal (*Von Morgens bis Mitternachts*). Or the human brain, robbed of certain inhibitions through some trauma or other, sees mental processes physically. This makes such a powerful visual impression that real existence pales by comparison, and fiction takes its place (*Caligari*). In all these plots, the human element has been wrenched out of its confines and is at the mercy of its own phantoms. And it is the most highly significant characteristic of film that it must manage almost completely without the spoken dialogue common on stage to make mental processes clear (the more it does so, the better it is). In film, these mental processes have to be transformed completely into visually understandable pictures. Pictures that are actually not pictures, because they encompass not being, but action. Pictures that have ceased capturing the moment on a surface for eternity, but that show a series of moments in space for a short time. Pictures that are no longer pictures, but space surrounding live action.

It is essential to emphasize strongly the differences between a picture and space; this is of the greatest importance for the problem of space. Granted, a motion picture is first of all a picture, showing the viewer some physical shapes or other on a two-dimensional surface, only from one side at a time. Each individual frame on a film reel is thus unquestionably a picture. But that a sequence of takes capturing action (and even showing a landscape) is space, is likewise unquestionable. Observation: The addition of live action (also of a mental nature) necessarily parallels the addition of the third dimension. A picture becomes space through the third dimension (even if it is only the illusion of the third dimension). The third dimension — that is, the dimension of spatial depth away from the picture surface — is the most decisive factor in the ideal aim for the synthesis of man and nature, of the activity of human existence and the surroundings — up to the stars — in which it takes place. A picture is a state, part of an action, in itself dead. Space is the whole course of the action, a sequence of states, hence a sequence of pictures, utterly alive. Architectural objects thus embody the process of a mental activity, repeating itself for every viewer. Structures are alive to the highest degree; the concept of the picture as a work of art is infinitely heightened and intensified in them. It is hard to foresee to what extent designing space will someday outstrip creating pictures as an art. After centuries of civilization, we are now standing on the threshold of a gate opening onto something tremendous. The end of painting as an independently evaluated art seems to be approaching. Its defeat by the far greater expressive power of space shaped by architecture seems possible. I mention this in passing, so that it will not be forgotten.

That mental space is somehow identical with physical space will also only be mentioned in passing. For both, it is the third dimension — i. e., depth — that is decisive. That will do.

The particular conditions of film have led in a very unusual way to highly remarkable developments in the perception of physical space. Doing without stage dialogue necessarily led to reinforcing action — in other words, to powerful gestures. The increasing preference of the audience, and not only of its unintellectual members, for physical appearances over the representation of psychological processes has also encouraged these same powerful gestures.

Briefly then: Film requires powerful gestures, intensified action. The ability to satisfy this demand is technically limited in some respects, since, for example, an individual frame is still a framed picture, and a certain framework is necessary even though there is greater freedom than on the stage. This framework naturally exists only two-dimensionally, in width and height. The depth of the picture, or its space, is unlimited by comparison, and to an infinitely greater degree than on the stage. Powerful action in film will therefore always take place in the third dimension and only attain its highest potential for effectiveness there.

The main impression of this effect lies in the third dimension's essential secret, in perspective. For example, when a person appears, he seems much more powerful when he enters from the depths of the picture toward the surface. Something small and obscure, via numerous intermediate stages, finally is clearly and precisely outlined. With the help of space, he develops from the typical to the individual. On the other hand, when a person has to escape, he could not express it more strongly than by moving from the picture surface into the distance. Corresponding to his inner intentions, he becomes increasingly smaller in perspective, less visible, unclear, until he disappears completely. That is, he is swallowed up by space. Thus, mental processes and the essence of space are extraordinarily linked.

All the means to reinforce the impression of depth in film space cannot be explained here. A practicing architect is not a lecturer; an article is not a lecture for set designers. The two major methods for working out perspective depth deserve brief mention. One is a strong emphasis on the process (spatial depth is a process, not a state) by which recession into the distance is indicated. The converging lines running from the picture surface into depth are thickly applied and emphasized. Perspective shortening of space is distorted for the strongest effect. Everything should be not only linear but also stereometrically worked out if possible. As inclining the space downward toward the far distance would make the perspective process disappear from the picture, it is usually made to rise into the distance in stages, by means of steps, slanted levels, freestanding structures, etc.

The second method does not show recession into depth fully, but only major steps in this progression. Delineation is not carried out, but highlights of the perspective are emphasized instead, without the line itself appearing. The former method underscores continuing action, the latter is more suitable for action toward the back or the front in fits and starts. This as an aside.

It should be noted that the set designer, who nowadays is usually a painter, knows little about these issues. There is nothing wrong if he can nevertheless master this much and more unconsciously. Surely, it is even advantageous for the impression of continuous space if its creator is free of these difficulties. But since space is starting to become the decisive issue of our time, it would be of considerable value to become clear about how the impression of space in film can be intensified to the greatest possible extent. Despite many a good individual achievement, everything is of course still in the earliest stages of development, for the very reason that architecture is still in such an embryonic stage. Moreover, a painter cannot after all capture space as profoundly as an architect. Of course, architects are not made; they are born. Nevertheless, the results achieved so far are of considerable value, in part exactly because they have been reached by outsiders to the field, who are unburdened by history, conventional training, and traditional patterns.

A number of illustrations are reproduced here, taken from the films mentioned above. They are intended to clarify what had necessarily to be said in a somewhat abstract way. What is shown in these illustrations is a limited, but perhaps characteristic selection of the attempts at spatial design in film. It is most remarkable that the leading companies of the film industry have so much insight and understanding concerning the intimate connection between the story and space that these companies have permitted and even sponsored a selection of somewhat eccentric space designs, as shown in the following illustrations. No doubt the importance of sensation in film plays a role in this. But it is remarkable that this sensation is no longer sought in the story alone, but also in the space, and that the intimate connection between space and life has finally been grasped. This is definitely a great step forward. That the overly powerful expressive force of space sometimes makes the story secondary is symptomatic, but this is a visionary flash of the inconceivable potential of the effect of space. In the midst of the final spasms of the past, we are on the verge of a beginning.

At the beginning of this article, I mentioned the progress that has been made through film regarding the problem of artistically designed space. It is extremely important at a time when the normal creative areas of architecture are closed to almost all architects. The uniqueness of this process surely permits us to ignore the economics and uses of structure for a while, allowing a higher appraisal of expressive form and a bitterly needed emphasis on creative production. Perhaps this strange interconnectedness of things will lead to inspiration and results that would never have been reached, or only too late, along the well–beaten track of architecture. All this can certainly not come to fruition in film. The whole connection with an extraordinarily intensified

dramatic plot already speaks against it, as do the conditions of the short pseudo-life of stage sets and, last, but not least, the exclusion of utility and of economic and technical fundamentals. So many of the inhibiting factors in the normal functions of architecture are removed in film. Lifting these restraints allows accelerated progress and the obviously very lively discussion regarding purely artistic questions of space. I think what is most valuable for the future in this is that space is an issue once again, that old patterns are breaking up, that the past — not the future — is an illusion. Awareness of the vitality of space is already growing, and comprehension of the third dimension is progressing. The surface of a painting as the topmost limit of expression in the visual arts of our time has been shattered. The artistic permeation of the world by spatial design is now only a matter of time.

Originally published as: "Raumgestaltung im Film," *Wasmuths Monatshefte für Baukunst*, nos. 1–2 (1920–21), pp. 63–82.

De Fries (1887–1938), an architect and writer, published widely on contemporary architecture in Germany and also brought out a monograph about Frank Lloyd Wright in 1926.

Ludwig Hilberseimer

Film Opportunities

Technical inventions only achieve decisive success when there is a certain need for them. Photography and — to a still greater extent — film prove this. Both fully satisfy the modern person's demand for a radical illustration of the reality of life. And in fact, they do so in a way no human being ever could. In his biography of Philipp Hackert, Goethe relates that the painter was commissioned by the Russian empress Catherine II to paint a series of battle scenes. One of them was to show, among other things, a ship blown into the air by a gunpowder explosion. It seemed impossible for the artist to produce a realistic image of the incident. This obstacle was therefore removed in grand style. Near Livorno, before a huge crowd of people, a frigate loaded with gunpowder was set on fire and immediately exploded into the air. An enormous sensation at the time, with which the world of film began. A lack of imagination required help from reality, which of course can be fantastic enough.

Film could have recorded in all its successive phases what was a grand event for that period and shown it for all the world to see. Instead, after all that production, only a harmless painting resulted. For all its effort to approximate reality, it only captured one miserable episode. The aim of painting, which ever since the Renaissance has been to master reality, has been realized by film in an unanticipated way. From the Renaissance point of view, it seems a miracle. Painting was thus liberated from the disastrous problem of reality and became able to return to its actual issues.

Looking at film superficially, it seems merely to be a means for reproduction. Its main purpose would then be to reproduce reality, precluding any creative opportunity. So far, of course, creativity has scarcely begun. Film has instead been regarded as a purely technical matter. Artistic possibilities have not even been considered. Or only, at best, in the worst possible "Romantic" sense, as the means to reproduce a fake world. Artificiality has been preferred to natural conditions, instead of external authenticity being valued all the more. Thus, film has created an entire fake civilization, one that is so admired that Berlin schoolchildren were led through the counterfeit city of an Egyptian feature film in order to get to know the "beauties" of Egyptian art. These spectaculars with their ostentation correspond perfectly to the false pathos of our time. Monuments in every style are built out of fakes, for immediate delivery. Especially in Germany, these films have attained unimaginable heights. Makart [the historicizing Austrian painter] still thrives here, along with the formal chaos of our loudest period, the stucco kitsch of the Kurfürstendamm, and the grotesque monumentality of Wilhelmine structures. Work in film is being done in the same way as for stage scenery; they inspire one another, making use of dishonest romanticizing. Film directors and architects are only now dusting off and exploiting the accomplishments of the Meiningers [a nineteenth-century traveling theater company] for film.

An especially low standard distinguishes so-called exotic films, despite the fact that film is particularly suited to communicate exotic life and its characteristic features and to open the eyes of many a European to our colored fellow men. Instead, directors feel very superior and display arrogant Europeanness in order to cover up their inability to understand. A disastrous ignorance, of which only Europeans are capable. Colored people, especially the Indians who are so popular, play the roles of barbarians in such films, whereas those who assign them this role have no conception of their own barbarity. These films rely on completely erroneous assumptions; they show absolutely no consideration for actual circumstances, manners, and customs; they owe their production purely to stupid sensationalism. No better are so-called historical films, which are especially distinguished by their lack of character. Yet, the historical film in particular could be eminently instructive and do valuable educational work. But using any means whatsoever to achieve intellectual aims is still a long way off (except when it comes to authoritarianism, which has always known how to use everything for its own ends, as it does with film now). Yet, film provides the opportunity for influencing large masses. Because just as every newspaper gets read, so every film gets seen.

Following the law of lethargy, one remains at the presumed point of departure: the theater. Just as old cars copied the shape of coaches, carefully ignoring their own potential, so the film clings to the theater, without understanding its own spirit, without imagining that film points to a new future.

It appears that films so far have relied on people's need for banality. They are a mixture of saccharine and technics. With the exception of an infinitely small number of examples, all films are confined to the level of pulp fiction. They do not even attain the level of a decent light novel. E.T.A. Hoffmann turns into a real "Ghost Hoffmann" in film, which — granted — he is in the minds of our educated people anyway. While the theater yielded certain art forms unique to it, film tries to shoot all of world literature. Only in an infinitesimal number of cases has anyone considered probing into the potential of film and in this way looking for a creative basis.

In some films, the achievements of individual actors are amazing. But they are reminiscences of the stage; they have little to do with the film as such. Actors' opportunities to have an impact in film are fundamentally different from those on stage. While the stage actor employs language and gesture as dramatic elements, the film actor has a much broader range of possibilities. Though he has to do without the spoken word, he has all the more means at his disposal that can be intensified to unimagined heights. These, of course, are just in the process of being discovered. The expressive possibilities of each art need to evolve from its material. With the slightest outward effort, it must express the strongest inner emotion. Ignoring its inherent laws, film has so far exhausted

itself in externals and has not even begun to recognize its basic elements.

When have the possibilities of varying motion by exaggerated fast or slow shooting, and of distortion by changes in proportion, by shortening and lengthening, ever been used as expressive elements? Or has anyone ever considered the expressive potential of reversing action (reverse shooting)? Some American films are beginning to work with these methods. Actions are intensified to the level of paradox by their rapid succession. Sometimes they attain a superb unreality, leading us into another world.

So far, only Charlie Chaplin has understood how to make use of the potential of film, especially its mechanical aspect. This makes him seem incredibly fantastic. His comedy is completely self-contained, neither intellectual nor unintellectual and completely unliterary, the essence of pantomine. He typifies the grotesqueness of daily life. By reducing the plot to a minimum, he achieves a maximum of effect. (In order to be fully receptive to it, an understanding is, of course, required which, particularly among the educated, is usually undeveloped.) Here is something new, something absolute. Through his imaginative creation, Chaplin was the first to raise film into the sphere of art.

Originally published as: "Filmmöglichkeiten," *Sozialistische Monatshefte* 59, no. 17 (July–December 1922), pp. 741–43.

Hilberseimer (1885–1967), a member of the most important German avant-garde groups, taught at the Bauhaus between 1929 and 1933 and, from 1938, at the Institute of Technology in Chicago. He became widely known for his austere urban visions of dense high-rise cities.

Kurt Richter

Contemporary Film Architecture

Film architecture developed as an accompaniment to the supreme photographic achievement of film. It was not needed earlier because backgrounds played too insignificant a part in the first films to receive much attention. Whoever has been following film from its beginnings knows the sort of thing built only 15 years ago, and what a minor role the set designer played, if one was consulted at all. Italian feature films then came to require monumental structures, which could really no longer be built by a film studio's master carpenter, nor could they be photographed from the reality of actual buildings. Eventually, feature films appeared in all countries, aiming especially for impressive architecture and providing the builder with the most satisfying challenges. At first, the public behaved like the audience in Tieck's "Gestiefelter Kater," applauding the rising curtain with shouts of "An encore for the scenery!" The larger the structure, the higher the building costs listed in the program, the more enthusiasm there was. Films were made at that time that showed nothing but architecture in some scenes. That must have flattered every set designer, but it was clear from the start that this state of affairs could not last. In the end, it could only harm the architect working for films, which is what finally happened in America. Anyone believing that their imitation of Indian architecture would launch a new era, or thinking that their exhibition of drawings and models was doing film a service, did not know the public. It wants above all to see people in films, and for them it would trade the most beautiful landscapes.

The public is capricious, but no one has ever figured out the rules governing its moods. The fact remains that it wants to see people, animals, or at least moving objects in films. Hence the success of Swedish films, from which even directors in countries where these films were not necessarily box office successes learned a lesson. Swedish architecture happens to be contemporary, or rather, Swedish style is. The Swedes seldom fail in decorative matters. A good set designer should have no greater ambition than to build a suitable framework for a scene. That sounds straightforward and self-evident, yet it absolutely is not. If nothing else, it regularly leads to battles with the director and leading actors, who usually want a framework for their dramatic achievements that presents them as if on a silver platter. The most important requirement, however, is an understanding between the set designer and the cameraman. What is the use of the most beautiful set if it does not come across photographically, or if the cameraman adds to his takes that theatrical tendency of illuminating only the main character while submerging the backgrounds in darkness? If cameramen reproach some set designers (and not without justification) for knowing little about photography, it must be countered that even more cameramen have not a clue about architecture. Hanns Kräly just informed me by letter that a kind of film chemistry is being developed in Hollywood to predict the photographic shades of the colors to be used for structures. Today's set designer does without everything that was considered the height of film art only two years ago. He does without all the detail of miniature painterly naturalism, adhering instead to a broad overall line. The controversial issue of "stylization" is another matter. It is not suited to all subject matter, and in its most extreme form it does not have the public's approval. Only a very intellectual public is capable of grasping the expressionistic play of line and the cube-shaped rhythms of architecture. *Caligari* was so successful in America because it was understood as a comedy; its imitations were flops here as well.

Any original architecture is an experiment that first awakens a certain mistrust among the public. The contemporary audience is so used to Expressionism that it means nothing unusual any more. But Expressionism is only one example in architecture after all, and by no means the final solution of modern art theories, which can be rejected or enthusiastically approved as required. Film conditions being what they are, Expressionism will not be capable of creating an architectural principle from within itself. It will always have to depend on influences from the other arts, because architecture is three-dimensional in reality, but can only be two-dimensional in film. Any innovation therefore remains an experiment.

In a period of economic decline, experiments are not possible. The set designer has to adapt to contemporary construction, which calls for simplification in everything. First of all, however, he must demand that the script not impose extra work. Only designs for scenes that will actually be shot should be expected of him. Unfortunately, it is still common to make him deliver work that may look fine in the context of an overambitious script, but that is then deleted at the beginning

of shooting. He can ask not to have to create designs that will not be constructed when they turn out to be too expensive, because in any serious organization an estimate for the scenes should be made in the first place. The set designer also rarely succeeds in recommending slight changes in interior decoration in order to transform one room into another. He can best achieve this with neutral wallpaper (there are some strange patterns that change their appearance depending on how the light hits them) or a plain coat of paint, which can be given a different appearance with the addition of molding at various levels or a change in wall decoration. In Hollywood, they know how to cut costs by building stairways, dance halls, offices, etc., solidly once and for all. Their prominent parts are interchangeable, allowing an apparently new structure to be made instantly for any film. In fact, it has already been shot often, but keeps getting a new look by means of slight changes. We are not at that stage yet. We insist on building every structure from scratch; unfortunately, even in the most established studios we lack everything that makes the Americans able to set up a simple set within 15 minutes. Of course, even in Germany it does not tend to be the set designer's fault when one scene is shot half a dozen times or more. Yet, these repeated takes are exactly what increases the costs of German films so enormously.

Originally published as: "Zeitgemässe Filmarchitektur," *Der Kinematograf* 17, no. 872 (4 November 1923), p. 8.

Richter (dates unknown) was a frequently employed German set designer in the early 1920s. He worked on almost all of Ernst Lubitsch's early films.

Hugo Häring

Building for Film

A question that could be of professional interest is: "Are there special architectural problems in film?" First of all, films are not made because of a spiritual need, but because business wants to make money with them. If this state of affairs could be changed, reversed, so to speak — have no fear, there is no danger of it happening — one could attach great importance to our question. Meanwhile — that is, for the present and the immediate future — getting involved in the problem of set design is not a priority. Nevertheless, we will try to establish the basics of the problem, not least because current issues of architectural design can be clarified in set design. In other words, giving primary importance to our spiritual need, we will try to understand the design problems in the reality of film.

Building for film is not real building, but building for a motion picture. The structures exist here in the motion picture, having been built to exist in substance, because this cannot be avoided if they are to exist in the motion picture. Thus, only what works in the motion picture matters. So one question is: "What *works* in the motion picture?" And another: "*What* works in the motion picture?"

Of course, this observation excludes reconstructions of historic and contemporary structures, designed for their imitative and veristic impression and for the specific demands of shooting for the purposes of illustration or rather as a backdrop. We are only concerned with what affects the impact of the motion picture by means of design. This problem cannot be contemplated from the point of view of architecture, but only from that of film. The self-transforming motion picture is a given fact, and the remarkable thing about it is the transformation. The film lives on this fact. Its focal point is action; therein lies its vitality and immediacy. What exists is not essential and hence important for film, but what happens is. A photograph can also show what exists; only the film reel can show what happens. Structural design in film must adjust itself accordingly. It must second what happens in the film. It should therefore bring about an intensification of the proceedings and events, as well as clarification, explanation. Can structures be formative? Absolutely. It is up to the creative intelligence to decide how in each case. But the fact that space can be shaped to correspond to the particular destiny and unique occurrence of an event is the most basic certainty of creative experience. Works of architecture are ambiguous; they incorporate the excitement of many hours, days, and years, the influences of mornings, noons, evenings, and nights, of happy hours and the hours of dread and fear; they live on in the power of a daring will and indicate bogs of shattered desire. Space in film need only be obvious, only be unique, only be for a single event, only exist for one minute of joyful radiance or for one moment of dread. A festive hall in a fairy-tale film, for example, does not need and must not have real walls, real parquetry, nor be bound to shapes and measurements stemming from construction requirements and restrictions in reality, should not have chandeliers with real candles made by some candlemaker. Nothing is more unrealistic here than realism. To want real spaces is all wrong. It is even more wrong to build all four walls all around. That leads to photographic reproduction, to the art of genre painting, departs from making a motion picture, leads to seeking motifs and struggling for the perfect moment. Because of this, the take on location is confused with the studio take, the latter measures its value by its competitiveness with the former. It attains the artistic level of a panopticon. This is not meant to belittle other merits of such films — only a few, though, are exceptions. It is merely intended to define the state of affairs, and to realize and declare that architectural design has nothing to do with it.

As far as the motion picture is concerned, the procedure is clear. It presumes a viewpoint from which the action can be recognized, captured, and shaped. The viewpoint is to be determined first, chosen with an eye to the form given to the action. Architectural design can then step in effectively. Space can be created to intensify drama, expand destiny, and surroundings can be made to participate in the action.

Let us not forget to recall the fantasies of Baroque architects here. The only seriously relevant film in this respect is *Caligari*.

But is such design for the sake of a certain expression, rather than design for the sake of ideas of a superior legality, still architectural design? In a practical sense and as far as film is concerned, such a question is irrelevant, but it is nonetheless important. It is often claimed that designing space in particular is the ultimate goal of architecture. We will leave that issue open for now, yet it is remarkable that in film only the expressive values of space are effective; hence only those effects matter for the design. Once the expressive values of space are made primary and constitute the absolute goal, we find ourselves opposed to the architectural spirit, if we consider as architectural whatever opposes anything dynamic, changing, instinctive, momentary, high-strung — the Dionysian — with the will to permanence, solidity, rest, rigidity, unchangeablity — the Apollonian. The world of the painter and sculptor is expressiveness (I would like to emphasize their opposition to architecture once again); the origin and aim of the architect are legality. More about this some other time.

The will to build therefore does not encounter any problems in film.

Originally published as: "Filmbauen," *Der Neubau: Halbmonatsschrift für Baukunst* 6 (10 June 1924), pp. 117–18.

Häring (1882–1958), an architect and theoretician, was a member of the major German avant-garde groups of the 1920s and, with Hans Scharoun, the most important representative of "organic" architecture.

Paul Leni

Architecture in Film

The attempt to introduce designs by German set designers to the public for artistic contemplation at the *Große Berliner Kunstausstellung* can be considered a success. Response among the public and in the press indicates that the set designer is no longer considered a craftsman's assistant in the studio, but an independently creative artist whose contribution is essential to lend a film its characteristic style. The aim and purpose of architecture in film are based on this attitude that the film should not be a mere photographic imitation of reality, but must have its own style.

I have always seen my work in film as putting a decorative framework around the proceedings the director had to stage, expressing the same atmosphere in my materials as that which inspired the director in his production. In order to create this kind of atmosphere, one must not restrict oneself to copying beautiful rooms that can be found in castles and homes. Instead, one should compose decor corresponding to the spiritual content of the scene, in the characteristic colors of the atmosphere, so to speak. Of course, the set designer is not free to prevail; he is determined and limited by the director, who will always be the master of the scene.

The kinds of takes, of pans, of movements show the set designer his way, as do the position of the lights, the location of the camera, the angle, and the purpose of the close-up. It is a question of talent to remain able to express artistic demands within such severe limitations.

Lighting technology gradually led to the building of typical urban scenes and landscape details in the studio or outdoors. If the set designer were to build photographic imitations, the film scene would have no face or personal touch. He should have the opportunity to emphasize the essential and characteristic features of a natural object and to work them out so that they impress style and color on the scene. Let me remind you of Joe May's *Tragödie der Liebe* [Tragedy of Love, 1923], in which we even shot takes like the one of the little station with the approaching train in the studio. The point was to give the impression of a small, wintry railway station on a frosty night. If we had shot the takes in some existing station, it would doubtless have been true to nature, but we would never have succeeded in creating the impression of loneliness, backwoods, winter night, frost, and poverty to the intense degree the studio structure permitted. Viewing angle, lighting technique, and decor were precisely attuned to each other there.

It is especially necessary to build characteristic natural objects for films playing in an unreal world to begin with. For my film *Das Wachsfigurenkabinett*, I tried to create architecture that was so stylized that the thought of reality would not arise in the first place. I built a fairground that dispenses with details and aims to create only the indescribable flow of lights, bodies in motion, shadows, lines, and curves. It is not reality that the camera perceives; it is the reality of experiencing, which is much deeper, much more effective, much more moving than what we see everyday with our own eyes. I also believe that film is able to communicate this heightened reality effectively.

Let me to remind you of the *Caligari* film, of the *Golem*, whose monumental image was created by Hans Poelzig. My point is to emphasize how far the set designer needs to get away from the everyday world we see before he can touch the true nerve center of the world.

I am faced with the major task of creating a decorative framework for the new film by Joe May, who is just beginning to shoot Georg Kaiser's comedy *Kolportage* [Pulp Fiction, 1924], as is well known. Castle halls, hotels, large and small rooms suggest themselves to the set designer as projects ready to hand. But an artist like Joe May expects something more and different. A few more or less tasteful rooms in the studio will not do. He demands rooms that themselves create, by their appearance alone, the atmosphere expressed in the acted scene.

We have undertaken long trips in order to avoid any discrepancy in detail arising between the indoor and outdoor takes and to determine how far the set designer can proceed independently without obscuring the character given to an outdoor take.

Obviously, the demands made on the set designer are not at all to build "beautiful rooms." He must reach beyond the surface to the heart of things. He must create atmosphere even when he has to assert his independence in the face of an object seen only with everyday eyes. And that is what makes him an artist — otherwise I would not know why the set designer is justified at all, and why he is not replaced by a talented carpenter's apprentice.

Originally published as: "Baukunst im Film," *Der Kinematograph*, no. 911 (4 August 1924).

Walter Reimann

Film Architecture — Film Architect?!

For the sake of order, it should be emphasized right away that these two terms developed and were retained out of thoughtless habit, in spite of the fact that they label a very important area of film work completely inappropriately.

Building film sets is in no way identical with the working methods and aims of an architect — in terms of its distinctiveness and destination, it belongs instead to the field of painting.

Creating buildings, rooms, and architecture that are practical and that form a self-contained unit is not the point when it comes to film. Instead, it is only about imitations, whose job it is to be a foil and backdrop for a portrayal of fate by actors.

The law governing the composition of a film set is that of a figurative painting, concentrating in this case on the actor. His acting and his movements within the area of the set are demarcation points, according to which the decor is structured. Form, line, and surfaces of the latter are deter-mined by the curves of motion and points of rest of the acting.

The stylistic interpretation, the line of a film, evolves from the direction of a triumvirate: the director, the cameraman, and the painter. But these three, despite of course having to be independent artists, are mere servants in their work on a film. Because they are capable of independent artistic inspiration, they are assigned to realize an idea for the approach to a film.

All of the arts that are usually independent unite, give up their independence for the sake of the whole, and create a film by working hand in hand. In the final analysis, everything to do with film is thus only a means to an end. Deliberate subordination to the whole, born of artistic conviction, is a quality and approach the artist working in film must possess. One could say that this ability, which can only develop from artistic seriousness and spiritual maturity, is the sole qualification for artistic work in film. Subservience to one's work, suppressing everything individual and personal in view of the whole — always somehow keeping an eye on the whole and never getting lost in detail — is indispensable for any artistic teamwork and also the most essential requisite for film. That is the first important thing to understand — it is the necessary discipline without which any work in the arts fails.

The artist wishing to demonstrate his genius by insisting on his opinion — and often stubbornly as well — is unsuited for cooperative artistic work, hence also unsuited for film.

No one in film should say: "I want it such and such a way" — not even the director, who unfortunately is often too high-handed! Only the events in the scene determine: "Such and such is how it has to be!"

The solution eventually chosen for each scene is found in meetings of the triumvirate mentioned above. It is the essence crystallized as the optimal outcome after examining the technical requirements, the direction, the photography and the lighting, and the set thoroughly.

Like an infinite, perilous sea, technical requirements abound in film. They are a threat to the inexperienced, who can make themselves and the whole film fail because of only one of them. For the experienced, however, they are bridges and catapults to new ideas and possibilities time and again.

Thus, film is a strange combination of artistic dedication to a preconceived idea, of knowing and mastering film technique in all areas, and of mutual accommodation.

What has been said here in the form of general observations applies specifi-cally to each area of film work in particular. Building sets requires not only the experience of building but also that of building for film; that includes recognizing and acknowledging the requirements of directing and lighting, such as adjusting the colors to the photographic effect and design of perspectival sets.

Everything up to this point has been about technical requirements, pure craftsmanship. We will now deal with the attainment of artistic expression alongside the absolute mastery of craftsmanship.

It is here that the function of art originates — art that cannot revel in abandon and freedom, but that is bound to organic and technical laws, achieving its highest goal in the strictest conformity to these laws.

Good craftsmanship is not yet art, but in this particular case it is the only bridge leading to art!

In film sets, a clever structure taking all technical requirements into consideration is not yet an artistic achievement. It can only become one once it underscores the dramatic content of the scene in form and atmosphere, taking it to the most powerful finale, and subordinates itself as a suitable backdrop to the acting of the players.

There is one technical requirement in particular that makes artistic work in film very difficult: only in the rarest cases is it possible to shoot the individual scenes of a script in the normal sequence of the dramatic action. The danger of loosing track and of obscuring the harmonious rise and fall of the dramatic sweep is considerable due to this difficulty, which has solely to do with the shooting technique.

Even in the briefest scene, the line, or thread, must be taken into account and the whole film kept in mind. Confusing or obscuring the general idea temporarily during shooting can have unpredictable consequences for a film.

Film can be compared to a tremendous mosaic, of which each little stone is produced individually and outside the sequence of subsequent artistic integrity. Each one of these little stones acquires its individual shape and color through separate treatment by the director, the cameraman, and the painter.

Work on the days of shooting signifies only the fabrication of individual little stones — their assemblage takes place during weeks of laborious work once the shooting machinery has been stilled.

Should one of these pieces be taken out occasionally for individual contemplation, it may appear dead and empty — possibly because it was specifically meant to be a transition, a mediator to an especially brilliant piece next to it. One can therefore never infer from one scene to a whole film — unless one has first carefully studied the whole thing, the script.

The designs for film scenes . . . are not to be seen as parts of a film, but as designs for parts of a film.

They are designs for the preparation of one of the many little mosaic stones needed for the complete mosaic of the film.

They are simply notes, possessing any eventual graphic beauty only as a private curiosity. Their artistic value is proportionate to their usability for the film they were made for. It may be possible to extrapolate the general idea of the film approximately from some of these leaves, from the atmosphere in their composition of the scene, from their distinctive approach to pictorial space, and from the relationship between light and dark tones. An unusual artistic approach may even be surmised. But only watching the completed film will make it possible to appreciate them properly along with the achievement of the set.

Showing set designs is just as awkward as occasionally watching during film takes. The eternally critical spirit, which likes to see an entirety, is usually disappointed, because it is reluctant to accept that it is only seeing part of the whole.

These individual parts are frequently so fascinating, so enveloped in a cloud of self-sufficiency, that they only too often provoke a spontaneous opinion. This is a wicked trap, unintentionally set by the strangeness of a new art form — it has already claimed many a victim and caused much annoyance. We professionals in the middle of a film often hear: "Well, why do you do that in such and such a way — that doesn't fit, or can't be right. . ." The calm, confident spirit replies with a shrug and the laconic comment: "Wait until the film is finished!" The nervous and insecure one starts to scold and then . . , but politeness wins out.

To curious and precipitate onlookers, I'd say: "Watch out . . . !"

This look behind the scenes in film is mainly intended to illustrate the artistic achievement of a very important and inadequately acknowledged branch of film, which is that of building sets.

It may be building — but of such strange things that they are hardly covered by the normal sense of that term *building*. The desired pictorial expression can often not be obtained by means of a familiar form. This is especially true when the physical reality of buildings or space is no longer wanted, but only their visions, shadows.

Here, it is necessary to translate normal things, to heighten their natural im- pression to an Impressionist or Expressionist appearance — to invest them, so to speak, with a very specific form required for the very particular psychology of one scene.

This does not mean the usually quite absurd stylization, or rather manneristic transformation, of external form into some abstract or "Expressionist" one, but rather the intensificaton to a dramatic expression, its pictorial form depending on the content of the scene alone. Atmosphere and expression get built. In a scene calling for an exhaustingly endless country road, for instance, the motif to be built is not the country road, but the exhaustion, the endlessness!

But everything that is built or made for the set has to be such that it can be captured by the camera lens — that is, the science of building film sets, which must be expanded and enriched by a perpetually fertile imagination!

The essence of a set is the dramatic sweep — that is, motion — herein lies the open secret of the "moving picture."

Nothing in film should be dead — even the constructed backdrop, the set, must be alive. Achieving this is the artistic mission of set design!

Originally published as: "Filmarchitektur — Filmarchitekt?!" *Gebrauchsgraphik*, no. 6 (1924–25), pp. 3–13.

Paul Leni

The Superfluous Set Designer

It all boils down to an unbelievable ambition to be surrounded by people. If the director keeps a man to fan him with a peacock's feather — fine, that's something useful. But a set designer?

I'm not talking about the fact that every job in the studio should be judged according to the rule that no matter what you do, it's wrong. After all, you can get used to that. And to the fact that all the ideas are always somebody else's, even when there's documentary evidence in your sketchbooks. It happens to be a fast-moving trade.

The life of the set designer follows a well-established pattern. At first, everyone is enthusiastic about his sketches. After a few days come the first requests. A week later, there isn't much left of the original sketches. In the end, the result is something completely different.

Once this structure is standing, the following can happen: The director has a sudden inspiration that changes everything. He draws the set the way he imagines it now — exactly the way it was in the first sketch. Hence loud discussions are sometimes unavoidable.

I take building very seriously, by nature. The set should not only conform spatially to the proceedings; it should not only be effective and characteristic; it should also have some of the atmosphere of what takes place in it. As far as that is concerned, the director is usually of the opinion that the set designer doesn't understand a thing and is only a nuisance.

This is how work in the studio begins. The set designer is there at an incredibly early and late hour and argues about every curtain, about every inkwell. He is the master of the house and responsible for everything. Gradually, the others arrive. The set designer becomes increasingly invisible — only his responsibility remains. He gets to hear that from everybody.

Of course, everything is all wrong; nobody expected it any other way. Presumably, it's the floodlights that have a destructive effect on some people's memories. First, they all have very precise wishes. These have hardly been just as precisely fulfilled when memory begins to waver. Finally, it turns out they have all said something else, and things get very noisy again.

What does one keep set designers for? They are expensive, spend money, and delay the work. Whatever turns out to be good afterwards is by the others anyway. And even when a completed film makes a few friendly words altogether unavoidable, there is sure to be a kind soul who will patronizingly slap one's shoulder: "Wonderfully built, master. But if I may say so myself — a real film also works in front of four bare walls." Paradoxically, this is usually followed by a job offer.

I have never ended a film without the most horrible vows that this was the last time I'd build. Only directing from now on. And the films I've directed show I am right. Or don't you agree that *Das Wachsfigurenkabinett* is excellent?

But I have unpleasant surprises in directing, too. My set designer bothers me. He is stubborn, delays the work, and is always interfering in matters of lighting.

Sometimes I would be glad to get rid of him. And if my set designer were not called Paul Leni — it would have happened long ago. But how could one answer for a suicide because of a set designer?

Originally published as: "Der überflüssige Architekt," *BZ am Mittag*, no. 138, 22 May 1925.

Siegfried Kracauer

Calico World

The Ufa City in Neubabelsberg

In the middle of the Grunewald is a fenced-in area that one can enter only after going through various checkpoints. It is a desert within an oasis. The natural things outside — trees made out of wood, lakes with water, villas that are inhabitable — have no place within its confines. But the world does reappear there — indeed, the entire macrocosm seems to be gathered in this new version of Noah's ark. But the things that rendezvous here do not belong to reality. They are copies and distortions that have been ripped out of time and jumbled together. They stand motionless, full of meaning from the front, while from the rear they are just empty nothingness. A bad dream about objects that has been forced into the corporeal realm.

We find ourselves in the film city of the UFA studios in Neubabelsberg, whose 350,000 square meters house a world made of papiermâché. Everything guaranteed unnatural and everything exactly like nature.

In order for the world to flicker by on film, it is first cut to pieces in the film city. Its interconnections are suspended, its dimensions change at will, and its mythological powers are turned into amusement. This world is like a child's toy that is put into a cardboard box. The dismantling of the world's contents is radical; and even if it is undertaken only for the sake of illusion, the illusion is by no means insignificant. The heroes of antiquity have already made their way into the schoolbooks.

The ruins of the universe are stored in warehouses for sets, representative samples of all periods, peoples, and styles. Near Japanese cherry trees, which shine through the corridors of dark scenery, arches the monstrous dragon from the *Nibelungen*, devoid of the diluvial terror it exudes on the screen. Next to the mockup of a commercial building, which needs only to be cranked by the camera in order to outdo any skyscraper, are layers of coffins which themselves have died because they do not contain any dead. When, in the midst of all this, one stumbles upon Empire furniture in its natural size, one is hard pressed to believe it is authentic. The old and the new, copies and originals, are piled up in a disorganized heap like bones in catacombs. Only the property man knows where everything is.

On the meadows and hills the inventory organizes itself into patterns. Architectural constructions jut upward as if meant to be inhabited. But they represent only the external aspects of the prototypes, much the way language maintains façades of words whose original meaning has vanished. A Frisian village church, which beckons to simple piety from afar, turns out upon closer inspection to be a hut on a painted slope. And the cathedral a few hundred meters further contains no church choirs, since its roof adorned with gargoyles sits separately off to the side, for filming purposes. Together with the façades of a pleasure resort and a billionaire's club, it is part of the film *Metropolis* (1925–1926), which Fritz Lang is making. On some nights elegant extras live it up between the spiritual [*geistlich*] and worldly imitations. The underground city with its grottoes and tunnels — in which the film's narrative houses the thousands of workers — is already gone, blown up, flooded. The water was not really as high as it appeared in the film, but the burning elevators actually did come crashing down in their full, original size. Meticulously filed cracks in the furnaces still testify to those elemental events. Near the center of the catastrophe are stretches of decaying wall — a fortress with bowers, ramparts, and moats. It stymies the archeologists in the well-known film *Die Chronik von Grieshus*.

When mounted soldiers occupied it recently, in the Middle Ages, the director brought in croaking frogs, from ponds, to keep the troops in athe right mood. When it comes to deception, the heart and soul appreciate authenticity. In the meantime the fortress has fallen apart; the materials of its construction are peeking through. It cannot deteriorate into a ruin, because ruins have to be made to order. Here all objects are only what they are supposed to represent at the moment: they know no development over time.

The masters of this world display a gratifying lack of any sense of history; their want of piety knows no restraint — they intervene every-where. They build cultures and then destroy them as they see fit. They sit in judgment over entire cities and let fire and brimstone rain down upon them if the film calls for it. For them, nothing is meant to last; the most grandiose creation is built with an eye to its demolition.

Destruction catches up with some things when they've scarcely had a chance to enjoy their place in the sun. The racetrack tribune in front of which sensational sports events took place has been toppled, and the Vienna woods that rustled in *Ein Walzertraum* have been cut down. Other things change unpredictably. The remains of modern houses have been integrated into an old-fashioned alley, an anachronism that does not seem to disturb anyone. Political interests play no role in such reorganizations, no matter how violent the latter may be. A Bolshevist guardroom turns into a peaceful Swedish train station, which is subsequently transformed into a riding school and today is used to store lamps. It is impossible to tell what it will become next. The laws of these metamorphoses are unfathomable. No matter what may happen to the objects, however, in the end their plaster of paris shines through and they are junked.

The regime of arbitrariness does not limit itself to the world as it is. The real world is only one of the many possibilities that can be moved back and forth; the game would remain incomplete if one were to accept reality as a finished product. That is why its objects are stretched and shortened, make-believe objects are sprinkled among the existing ones, and miraculous apparitions are created without hesitation. The magic acts of yesteryear were a faint prelude to *cinematic special effects*, which give short shrift to nature. For them, the cosmos is a little ball to be batted around at will.

At times, the things projected onto the screen take on such a quotidian appearance that they seem as if one could encounter them on the street. Their creation, however, was marked by abnormal circumstances. Lampposts whose steel and cement existence seems tangible are made of wood and are broken off halfway up; the fragment suffices for the section framed by the image. An impressive skyscraper does not tower nearly as dizzyingly as it does in its screen appearance: only the bottom half is actually constructed, while the upper section is generated from a small model using a mirror technique. In this way, such structures refute the colossi: while their feet are made of clay, their upper parts are an insubstantial illusion of an illusion, which is tacked on.

The evocative powers of special effects lend themselves particularly well to the domain of the supernatural. The upcoming blockbuster film version of *Faust* being directed by W. Murnau uses them extensively. In a hall previously employed by priates for their life of thievery, the planet Earth now expands *en miniature*. Faust will fly throught the air from one backdrop to another. A wooden roller coaster that curves down to the valley describes his aerial itinerary. The camera glides down the chute and, thanks to expert guidance, spews forth images of the journey. Fog made of water vapor produced by a steam engine envelops the range of appropriately sculpted mountain peaks from which Faust emerges. For the horrible crash of the foaming deluge, some water is sprayed through a side canyon. The wild urges subside when the wheat covering the fields and meadows beneath the jagged, pine-covered summits rustles in the wind of the propeller. Cloud upon cloud wafts eastward, masses of spun glass in dense succession. Upon Faust's landing, huts surrounded by greenery will most likely shimmer in the blazing, high-wattage glow of the evening sun. Things are also rather Faustian in the Tempelhof UFA studios, where Karl Grune is directing *Die Brüder Schellenberg*. Here apocalyptic riders sweep across the glass studio on horses suspended in midair from the ceiling by wires. Among them is a menacingly huge set of black wings with which Jannings, as the head devil, casts shadows over cities, while the archangel Michael soars on a pair of white wings.

Nature, in body and soul, has been put out to pasture. Its landscapes are surpassed by those that are freely conceived and whose painterly appeal is no longer subject to chance. Nature's suns likewise leave much to be desired. Since they do not function nearly as reliably as floodlights, they are simply locked out of the newest American film studios. Let them go on strike if they want to.

Still, some remnants of the natural are put into storage on the side. Exotic fauna, the by-product of a few film expeditions, thrive along with representatives of the local animal world on the margins of the studio grounds. Some of the creatures captured in Brazil were transferred to the zoological gardens, where they can be a purpose unto themselves and enrich science. Those that have been kept function like a specialty act that travels with its own impresario. Each type of animal has its act in the program. In a sculptured garden, gold and silver pheasants can illustrate the luxury of American billionaires; the rare black hawk evokes the thrill of the exotic; cats in close-up shots lounge in salons. The doves from Berger's beautiful Cinderella film are still flying around. The wild boar that appears in hunting films and a swarm of live crocodiles number among the prominent beasts. They play a major role in the film *Die drei Kuckucksuhren*, directed by Lothar Mendes. The baby crocodile is a prop that one can hold in one's hands, but even the fully grown monstrosities are not as dangerous as their lifeless counterparts, which the monkeys fear. Greenhouses complete the collection: their vegetation forms the appropriate background for scenes of jealousy in the tropics.

The occupants of the wildlife preserve are lovingly cared for by the zoologist of the expedition. He calls them by name, grooms them, and gives them acting lessons. Despite their inherent imperfections as creations of nature, they are the most spoiled objects of the enterprise. The fact that they leap or fly without being moved by a Mechanism elicits delight, and their ability to propagate without the help of obvious special effects seems miraculous. One would never have thought these primitive creatures capable of this, so much do they seem almost like cinematic illusions.

The world's elements are produced on the spot in immense laboratories. The process is rapid: the pieces are prepared individually and delivered to their locations, where they remain patiently until they are torn down. They are not organisms that can develop on their own. Woodworking shops, glassmaking shops, and sculpture studios provide what is necessary. There is nothing false about the materials: wood, metal, glass, clay. One could also make real things out of them, but as objects in front of the lens *[Objektiv]* the deceptive ones work just as well. After all, the lens is objective *[objectiv]*.

Certain preparatory measures are necessary in order to integrate things and people. If both remained in their traditional state, they would stand apart like rare museum pieces and their spectators. Light — whose source is the huge electric power plant providing the energy for the entire undertaking — melts them together. The actors are groomed in the makeup room. This is not a workroom like any other but a studio full of skilled artistry. The physiognomies formed here from the raw materials of the human face reveal their secrets only under the beams of the spotlights. The masters of their discipline preside over makeup tables filled with cosmetics of every shade. A chart shows the degree of luminosity that the colors attain when photographed; but when subsequently forced into the black-and-white scale, their color values vanish. This makes the preparatory stage all the more seductive — the degenerate garishness of the wigs in glass cases. Portrai-like masks hang on the walls, fireproof creations that are custom-made for the main actors of whatever film is currently being produced. In certain scenes, these make it unnecessary for the actor to appear in person: other actors transform themselves into the stars by wearing their masks. These disguised figures are stiff and move about like the dead. In the adjoining screeing room, one can test the effect of a make-up job on film.

Both films and people are enveloped by this self-sufficiency; every available resource is used to ensure that they flourish. The means of technical reproduction — such as color film stock — are checked and improved in an experimental laboratory. Comparable energies are expended to train a new generation, which will know how to use the various techniques. A real fire department is standing by to put out real fires, and doctors and medics are on call at all times. Luckily accidents, as popular as they are, seldom occur. During the shooting of *Metropolis*, hundreds of children had to rescue themselves from the flood — a horrible sight in the film. The actual event was so harmless that the offstage nurses were left with nothing to do. One of the primary hubs is the canteen, where people in full costume sit among white-collar workers, technicians, and chauffeurs, looking like leftovers from a carnival. They wait.

They wait endlessly for their scene. There are many such scenes, pieced together like the little stones of a mosaic. Instead of leaving the world in its fragmented state, one reconstitutes a word out of these pieces. The objects that have been liberated from the larger context are now reinserted into it, their isolation effaced and their grimace smoothed over. Out of graves not meant to be taken seriously, these objects wake to an illusion of life.

Life is constructed in a pointillist manner. It is a speckling of images that stem from numerous locations and initially remain unconnected. Their sequence does not follow the order of the represented events. A person's fate may already have been filmed even before the events leading up to it are determined; a reconciliation may be filmed earlier than the conflict it resolves. The meaning of the plot emerges only in the finished film; during the gestation, it remains unfathomable.

The cells must be formed one after the other. Here and there, pieces of inventory come together to shape a light-drenched environment where things human unfold. The movements suffused in light are pursued by the cranking boxes. These perch in every spot where people can possibly be ensconced: on the floor, on scaffolding — no point of view is safe from them. Sometimes they pursue their victims. The smallest fragment is born only following terrible labor pains; assistants and assistant assistants are involved, and, amid much gesticulation, it slips out.

The director is the foreman. It is also his difficult task to organize the visual material — which is as beautifully unorganized as life itself — into the unity that life owes to art. He locks himself and the strips of film into his private screening room and has them projected over and over. They are sifted, spliced, cut up, and labeled until finally from the hue chaos emerges a little whole: a social drama, a historical event, a woman's fate. Most of the time the result is good: glass clouds brew and then scatter. One believes in the fourth wall. Everything guaranteed nature.

Originally published as "Kalikowelt," Frankfurter Zeitung, 18 January 1926.

Kracauer (1889–1966), was a journalist, writer, and film theoretician. As a member of the staff of the *Frankfurter Zeitung,* he wrote more than a thousand commentaries and film reviews during the 1920s. An abundance of architectural metaphors and a strong interest in the impact of set design (he was trained as an architect) are evident in his theoretical writings on film. In 1947, he published *From Caligari to Hitler,* one of the most influential accounts of Weimar Film.

Walter Reimann

Film Architecture — Today and Tomorrow?

There are people in the world who call themselves film architects. Poor people, who lead a strange life among diverse film artists — no one knows how and no one knows where.

They are not quite part of the building world; they are not rooted to the stage, and therefore one never knows whether to take them seriously or not. Yet, these underestimated people, ignored even by the press, belong to the so-called heavy workers of film, because their services are in demand, because they are needed!

Poor film architect! Oscillating between two worlds, that of the busily rushing calculator (= producer) and that of the idolized personality cult (= director), you are a necessary evil, and hence you are passed over in silence.

And so the film architect is dead before his work has even been baptized. The things he has contributed to the success of a work are carefully bound up into the bouquet handed over to others as a tribute. He remains who he is in reality, the man of the background.

The "architect" is disappearing in any case and, along with him, the scenic existence of architecture. Plaster palaces and stucco rooms will make way for better judgment. Everyone will recognize that film is the art of illusion and that imagination and atmosphere are decisive in this domain rather than so-called "genuine-ness" and "naturalness" and their imitations.

In no way are film sets architecture! (Wherever they are architecture, due to a confounding of the issues, they are false, and an unartistic burden on the film.) The film, the art of "optical" illusion, needs utopia. It needs a set that is utopian space, simulating the atmosphere of a space for the imagination.

What matters is the following: The film set is real and tangibly constructed work, erected with materials and objects that are easy to handle — erected in reality — but the construction of this work has nothing to do with genuine naturalness. Instead, it is built for the eye of the camera and is determined by the camera's properties. Additional structural elements of the film set are light, shade, and color.

Real architecture works with established and specific structural laws based on practical requirements. On the other hand, film sets very often reject these laws "deliberately," exploiting instead the elements of surface, depth, and atmosphere. Herein lie meaningful differences that depend on the study of the essentials in a photographic image.

Whoever would like to produce dramatic atmosphere with the help of optical mechanisms — in other words, whoever has seized upon film as the expressive medium for his artistic intent — must submit to the conditions of the camera lens.

Yet, these conditions are only acknowledged in the rarest of cases today. The camera today is still in most cases a box with which to "photograph" a stage play set up and arranged in the studio or outdoors. Everything is prepared for the apparatus to record as clearly and quickly as possible. Hence, the optical process of the camera is not made use of as an expressive artistic means, appropriately capturing each object in its distinctiveness, but only for the purpose of photographic reproduction. The actual significance, the true nature of the camera, is not yet understood.

Because when we take the trouble to think about film today, if we examine it seriously, we will soon realize that it is a mixture of elements from the theater, literature, and illustrative painting. This is how film is conceived today, is acted, and how its decor, make–up, and costumes are mounted! A dramatic incident is composed, it is acted in a studio, and just because the whole thing gets photographed, it is called a film! The essence of film — much discussed, but about which most film people do not have a clue — is forgotten.

The style or language of a film is dictated by the camera. The animation and vitality of this language depend on the assemblage of the many small frames captured by the lens!

Future films thus need film people who can all see through the eye of the lens and who are versed in photo technology. They no longer need stage directors or practicing architects, or stage actors! But the trade and sales personnel must adjust to the new film as well. They should not regard the production and distribution of films as a mere trade, but should consider film as a specialization in the sense of the art trade, which requires love of the particular subject and absolute expertise.

(May America produce as much and as enormously as it wants to for the soul of its own people! The soul of the people there is not the same as ours! We need to keep ourselves in mind and the characteristics of our own people!)

Away with all the superfluous and expensive ballast then! Let us gather around the camera and its cameraman, and compose, act, paint, and shape the melody it sings! To do this, we need people with flexible minds, people whose passion for work sparkles in their eyes! We need actors capable of enthusiasm, not society belles and fashion plates. We need men who can sculpt with light and shade, who can bend and shape space, so that it corresponds to the rhythm of people and the sweep of literature! Above all, we need writers!

Writers with terrific inspiration, healthy and vital ideas — no sickly neurasthenics and erotic droolers! And instead of aristocratic, sensationalistic reading matter, writers should put cameras under their pillows!

For all of them together, there are two rules which will have to be strictly followed: the study of the camera and the study of the public!!

And these will teach that future films will no longer need gigantic studios or warehouses full of props. The mobile camera, the mirror image, the painted backdrop, veils, smoke, fireworks, curtains, and a few clothes — and among them people, real people, with amazing expressiveness, and light in all nuances!

And from this, the new film will be formed, which will actually be a film for the first time, and not a photographed spectacular!

Therefore, you "architects," sell your storehouses of ornaments and go to America with the profits — or else: become film people!

Originally published as: "Filmarchitektur — heute und morgen?" *Filmtechnik und Filmindustrie,* no. 4 (1926), pp. 64–65.

Set Designers' Biographies

Collage for a Berlin Businessman, *Láslò Moholy-Nagy*, 1929.

Edward Carrere
(b. 1906)

Alexandra Exter
(1882–1949)

Anton Furst
(1944–1991)

Edward Carrere was born in Mexico City and educated in private schools there and at the Polytechnic High School in Los Angeles. Carrere went to Warner Bros.' art department from R.K.O. in 1932 and worked as a set designer there until 1969. Among his first and most famous assignments was the creation of the sets for King Vidor's *The Fountainhead*, for which he produced an evocative array of designs for the drawing boards of the architect hero, Howard Roark, and his teacher Henry Hull. For Roark, Carrere managed to merge European modernism with designs by Frank Lloyd Wright, while for Hull, he created remarkable proto-Brutalist designs. In the following years, Carrere worked with some of the most celebrated of Hollywood's directors, including Raoul Walsh (*White Heat* [1949]), Michael Curtiz *(Young Man with a Horn* [1950]), and Alfred Hitchcock *(Dial M for Murder* [1954]). The story of jazz musician Bix Beiderbecke told in *Young Man with a Horn*, shot mostly on location in New York City, gave Carrere the opportunity to present the architecture of that city and its jazz clubs. His credits also include such historical dramas as *The Adventures of Don Juan* (Vincent Sherman; 1948), *Flame and Arrow* (Jacques Tourneur; 1950), and the Broadway musical *Camelot* (Joshua Logan; 1967), for which he received an Oscar together with John Truscott and John W. Brown. Among Carrere's final professional assignments was the art direction for Sam Peckinpah's famous western *The Wild Bunch* (1969),for which he recreated the mainstreet of a small Texas town in 1913 and its Mexican counterpart.

Literature: "Designs by Edward Carrere," *Society of Motion Picture Art Directors Bulletin* 1, no. 4 (April 1951), pp. 8–9; Donald Albrecht, *Designing Dreams: Modern Architecture in the Movies* (London and New York: Thames and Hudson, 1987) pp. 169–74; Helmut Weihsmann, *Gebaute Illusionen: Architektur im Film* (Vienna: Promedia, 1988), p. 242; Robert S. Sennett, *Setting the Scene: The Great Hollywood Art Directors* (New York: Harry N. Abrams, 1994), pp. 142–43.

D. N.

Exter was one of the key figures in the artistic exchange between Moscow and Paris in the first quarter of the twentieth century. Having studied painting at the Kiev Art School in Russia from 1906 to 1907, in 1908 she went to study at the Académie de la Grande Chaumière in Paris. There, she became friends with Léger, Picasso, Apollinaire, and Delaunay; her early cubist work clearly reveals these influences. In 1915, back in Moscow, Exter's abstract paintings indicated her enthusiastic support of Kazimir Malevich's Suprematism. In 1918, she established her own painting studio in Kiev and, together with her students, created agitprop art in support of the Revolution. Her most remarkable works in those years were the agit-trains, painted railroad carriages used to spread enthusiasm for the Revolution to the farthest parts of the Soviet Union. These trains usually included a cinema carriage for documentary screenings and were painted with either heroic scenes from the Revolution or Suprematist compositions.

Exter had begun to design stage sets at Alexander Y. Tairov's Moscow Chamber Theater in 1916, attempting to reflect in her rhythmic abstractions the structure of the narrative rather than naturalistic settings. Her celebrated stage sets for productions such as *Salome* (1917) or *Romeo and Juliet* (1921), with their emphasis on simplified architectural forms and open spaces on different levels connected by wide staircases, still reveal the influence of Cubism. A similar formal language was applied to her sets and costumes for the Martian scenes in *Aelita — Queen of Mars*. Exter emigrated to Paris in 1924 and accepted a teaching position at Léger's Académie d'Art Moderne, which she held until 1930. Traveling frequently between Moscow and Western Europe, she was represented in a number of important exhibitions, including the Salon des Indépendants (1912, 1924), the *Esposizione libera futurista internationale* (1914), the Venice Biennale (1924), and the *Exposition des arts décoratifs* in 1925. In 1927, she exhibited theatrical designs and marionettes at the gallery Der Sturm in Berlin.

Literature: Selim Omarovich Khan-Magomedov, *Pioneers of Soviet Architecture: The Search for New Solutions in the 1920s and 1930s* (New York: Rizzoli, 1983); *Art into Life: Russian Constructivism 1914–1932*, exh. cat. (Seattle: Henry Art Gallery, University of Washington, 1990), p. 263; Anthony Parton and M.N. Yablonskaya, *Women Artists of Russia's New Age, 1900–1935* (New York: Rizzoli, 1990), pp. 117–40.

D. N.

British art director Anthony Francis (Anton) Furst was trained as a theater designer at London's Royal College of Art under Hugh Casson. He worked briefly as an architect and cofounded Holoco, a film effects company in London's Shepperton Studios, which was involved in making *Buck Rogers in the 25th century* (Daniel Haller, 1979), *Moonraker* (Lewis Gilbert, 1979), and *Alien* (Ridley Scott, 1979). Furst's first job as a production designer was with Neil Jordan's *Company of Wolves* (1984), for which he designed the psychologically charged dream world of a pubescent girl. This was followed by Stanley Kubrick's *Full Metal Jacket* (1987), for which Furst restaged scenes of urban destruction during the Vietnam War in London backlots. The triumph of his career was the creation of compellingly sinister sets for Gotham City in Tim Burton's *Batman*, for which he won an Oscar. After being offered a large number of new productions, he decided to work on the set of Penny Marshall's *Awakenings* in 1990. Soon afterwards, he settled in Hollywood and started his own production company with Sony-owned Columbia Studios. At the same time, his first architectural commission, the design for the restaurant Planet Hollywood, was taking shape in New York. Furst committed suicide in November 1991.

The grandson of renowned British art historian Herbert Furst, Anton's work bristles with art historical references. For the dreams and nightmares in *Company of Wolves,* he was inspired by the etchings of Gustave Doré; for the bright rooms of a Brooklyn hospital in *Awakenings,* he turned to Dada references, René Magritte, and the photography of Diane Arbus and Irving Penn. For Gotham City in *Batman,* he used an array of well-known modern buildings as a starting point. Furst mentioned the exciting sets of Fellini's films as close to his own intentions and argued in interviews against, for example, quasi-documentary cinema verité in favor of what he called "pure cinema," the conscious exploitation of the medium's potential and the creation of a powerful visual language. "The philosophy is pretty much, 'The more you explain, the more you've got to explain.' If you get an integral reality of its own, any kind of reality you like, then you can start heightening that reality into all sorts of areas. Otherwise, why make a movie? Go out into the real world" (Dollar 1990).

Literature: Liz Nickson and Nick le Quesne, "Designer," *Life* 12 (Spring 1989), pp. 84–86; Benefict Nightingale, "Batman Prowls at Gotham Drawn from the Absurd," *New York Times,* 18 June 1989, sect. H, pp. 1, 16; Steve Dollar, "Furst Has Big Designs on the Movies," *Atlanta Journal/Atlanta Constitution,* 18 February 1990, pp. L1, L7; Hugh Hart, "Cityscapes," *Chicago Tribune,* 29 November 1990, sect. 5, p. 8; Johanna Schneller, "Closed Set," *GQ* 62 (June 1992), pp. 78, 82, 84, 86, 88; Betsy Sharkey, "Anton Furst: Lost Soul in the Dream Factory," *New York Times,* 16 February 1992, sect. 2, pp. 1, 18–19.

D. N.

Rochus Gliese

(1891–1978)

After studying at the Staatliche Kunstgewerbeschule in Berlin from 1909 to 1911, Gliese began to work for various Berlin theaters as a stage designer. His talent did not escape the notice of Paul Wegener, who hired him to stage an early film version of *Der Golem* (Henrik Galeen; 1914), for which Gliese created innovative sculptural structures. Relating from the start to the camera-oriented view, he was among the first to construct sets specifically for the optical conditions of the film camera, consistently including perspective foreshortening in his sets and relegating the popular backdrops of the period to storage. A long-lasting collaboration developed, during which Gliese visualized the fantastic subject matter of Wegener's Romantic literary sources in special effects sequences and combination shots. Sad giants, doubles, seducers, and people without shadows were brought to life in such productions as *Rübezahl's Hochzeit* (Rübezahl's Wedding; 1916), *Hans Trutz im Schlaraffenland* (Hans Trutz in the land of Cockaigne; 1917), or *Der Rattenfänger von Hameln* (The Pied Piper of Hameln; 1918). Occasionally, Gliese took over the directing in Wegener's films (*Apokalypse* [1918]; *Malaria* [1919]) or worked on his own productions, partially commissioned by the state picture and film board. Gliese's teamwork with Paul Wegener ended with *Der Golem, wie er in die Welt kam.*

Der brennende Acker (Burning Acres; 1921–22) was Gliese's first film for F.W. Murnau, for whose self-contained visual compositions he did congenial preliminary work in further film projects. For Murnau's comedy *Die Finanzen des Großherzogs* (the Grand Duke's finances; 1923), Gliese created the monumental structures, ruins, and palaces of a southern state named Minorca, flowing architecture in moving space made to be experienced from all angles by the camera. In 1927, Gliese followed Murnau to America as the set designer for *Sunrise,* completing his design sketches during the Atlantic crossing. Their realization, however, turned out to be extremely difficult. Murnau insisted on many extravagant details, and Gliese himself had to come to terms with the American studio system. But he claimed that he acquainted American set designers with the latest techniques from Europe:

> It made the people laugh even more . . . because I built my spaces in perspective. I could do this because Murnau consistently followed my recommendations for focusing . . . It amused the Americans enormously that the water glass was as large as a pail and a toothbrush almost like a broom because . . . they had never seen such a thing [Lamprecht 1956].

Gliese's work gained recognition, and Cecil B. DeMille contracted him for directing, screenwriting, and staging. After returning to Germany, he worked mainly for the stage in Essen and Berlin (1934–44) and, after the war, in Weimar (1945–46) and Berlin (1947–48).

Literature: Gerhard Lamprecht, "Interview with Rochus Gliese on 11. August 1956," tape and transcription, Archive Stiftung Deutsche Kinemathek, Berlin; Erika Gregor and Ulrich Gregor, eds., *Rochus Gliese* (Berlin: Freunde der Deutschen Kinemathek, 1968); Jörg Schöning, "Rochus Gliese — Filmarchitekt, Regisseur," in Hans-Michael Bock, ed., *CineGraph: Lexikon zum deutschsprachigen Film* (Munich: Edition Text+Kritik, 1984ff.), pp. D1–D4.

P. L.

Stephen Goosson

(1893–1973)

Goosson studied architecture at Syracuse University and had his own architectural office in Detroit between 1915 and 1919. Having started his career with period sets for *Oliver Twist* (Frank Lloyd;1922) and *The Hunchback of Notre Dame* (Wallace Worsley; 1923), both produced by Columbia Studios, Goosson had his first chance to apply his training in contemporary architecture in *Skyscraper* (Howard Higgins; 1928). The success of his designs secured him the job for *Just Imagine,* for which he convincingly created an imaginative skyline for New York City in 1980. He demonstrated his knowledge of the utopian potential of different strands of modern architecture when he designed the sets for *Lost Horizon,* for which he received an Academy Award for art direction, the first for Columbia Studios. Another highlight of his career is the famous mirror cabinet in the final sequence of Orson Welles's *The Lady from Shanghai* (1948).

Literature.: Helmut Weihsmann, *Gebaute Illusionen: Architektur im Film* (Vienna: Promedia, 1988), p. 248; Robert S. Sennett, *Setting the Scene: The Great Hollywood Art Directors* (New York: Harry N. Abrams, 1994), pp. 147–48.

D. N.

Robert Herlth

(1883–1962)

Herlth studied painting from 1912 to 1914 at the Hochschule für Bildende Künste in Berlin. During the war, he obtained work at the army theater in Vilnius with the help of Hermann Warm; Walter Röhrig and Walter Reimann were also working there. In 1920, again through Warm, Herlth began his career in film, assisting Warm in *Masken* (Masks). In Rudolf Meinert's *Das lachende Grauen* (Laughing Horror; 1920), Herlth worked with Röhrig for the first time. From then on, they were the most progressive team of set designers in German film, developing into "poets of set design" (Esser 1992). Herlth usually designed the sets — his surviving drawings are of high artistic quality — and his designs were realized by Röhrig. In Fritz Lang's *Der müde Tod* (Destiny; 1921), Warm had the principal responsibility for the sets, although the German sequence and parts of the Chinese one were by Herlth. While in Joe May's *Herrin der Welt* (Empress of the World; 1919), the exteriors of the scenes set in China represent an attempt at authenticity by Otto Hunte and Erich Kettelhut — actual junks were used for the "Chinese" disguise of Potsdam harbor, and the calligraphy was done by Chinese extras — Herlth's China in *Der müde Tod* was the product of imagination. "There can therefore be no backdrop as such," he observed, "but only one created for the project, whether it be realistic, romantic or surrealistic" (Herlth 1951, from Längsfeld 1965).

Der letzte Mann marked the beginning of Herlth's intense collaboration with F.W. Murnau. This was followed by *Tartüff* (F.W. Murnau; 1925) and *Faust* (F.W. Murnau; 1925–26). In 1929, Herlth and Röhrig exported "German designs" to Great Britain. For *The Informer* (Arthur Robinson; 1929), narrow, winding streets were built at the Elstree studios. They were so three-dimensional "that one would hardly think they were studio sets, if one had not stood before these decorations in London one-self" (Herlth 1929, from Längsfeld 1965 1929). In the sound era, Herlth often participated in Ufa operetta productions. At the end of his career, he received the Bundesfilmpreis for the production of the film version of Thomas Mann's novel *Buddenbrooks* (Alfred Weidemann; 1959).

Literature: Robert Herlth, "Das Malerische am Film," *Film-Kurier,* 1 February 1923; Robert Herlth, "Konturen von F.W. Murnau," *Film für Alle,* 18 April 1931; idem, "Filmarchitektur," in *Wasmuths Lexikon der Baukunst,* vol. 5., suppl. (Berlin: Wasmuth, 1937); Wolfgang Längsfeld, ed., *Filmarchitektur — Robert Herlth* (Munich: Deutsches Institut für Film und Fernsehen, 1965; Hans-Michael Bock, "Robert Herlth — Filmarchitekt," in Hans-Michael Bock, ed., *CineGraph: Lexikon zum deutschsprachigen Film* (Munich: Edition Text+Kritik, 1984ff.), pp. D1 – D7; Michael Esser, "Poeten der Filmarchitektur: Robert Herlth und Walter Röhrig," in Hans-Michael Bock and Michael Töteberg, eds., *Das Ufa Buch: Kunst und Krisen, Stars und Regisseure, Wirtschaft und Politik: Die international Geschichte von Deutschlands größtem Filmkonzern* (Frankfurt am Main: Zweitausendeins, 1992), pp. 118 – 23.

P. L.

Otto Hunte
(1881–1960)

After training at the Hamburg Kunstgewerbeschule, Hunte worked as a stage designer in Berlin from 1900 on. After World War I, when theater decoration was dormant for a time, he accepted engagements in film, intended to be temporary. Together with Hermann Warm, the head set designer of Decla–Bioscop productions, he worked on Fritz Lang's adventure series *Die Spinnen,* (The Spiders; 1920). It was on this production that Hunte developed the means to bridge temporal and geographical distances in an instant, turning temple ruins of the Yucatan into prefilm reality in the sandy marshes near Berlin. In Joe May's eight-part film *Herrin der Welt* (Empress of the World; 1919), Hunte worked in the same genre, except that the architectural elements were even larger, more exotic, and more monumental. The sacrificial temple precinct for the fifth part, *Ophir, die Stadt der Vergangenheit* (Ophir, City of the Past), had dimensions hitherto common only in American or Italian films.

Hunte established himself as a specialist in the creation of monumental structures, again demonstrating his expertise in May's two-part film *Das indische Grabmal* (The Indian Tomb; 1921). Subsequently, he was responsible, together with Erich Kettelhut and Karl Vollbrecht, for the art direction of Fritz Lang's great silent film epics. For *Die Nibelungen,* the three designers created sets as spectacular as those they fabricated for *Metropolis.* The masses choreographed by Lang found their dramatic complement in the static, monumentally designed architectural spaces. At the same time, ambitious representations of modernity blended with cave architecture, and Neue Sachlichkeit was contrasted with romantic medieval images. "Here the stage designer, the last legacy of theater to film, is hard at work," raved the young Luis Buñuel in 1927.

> He can only be guessed at in the worst moments of *Metropolis,* in the sets of the emphatically named "Eternal Gardens", in their overflowing kitsch of unparalleled bad taste . . . Hunte oppresses us with his spectacular vision of the city in the year 2000. It may be false, even old-fashioned if judged according to the latest theories about the city of the future. Yet seen from the artistic point of view, its moving power, its indescribable beauty, constantly amazing all over again, remain unequalled. It has such cleverly devised technology that even under careful scrutiny the design method cannot be detected.

Otto Hunte adapted himself to sound at once: "While one used to pay attention to visual effects alone, one now has to build so that optimal accoustic conditions are created" (Hunte 1930). He contributed prominently to the first successful German sound films, Wilhelm Thiele's *Die Drei von der Tankstelle* (The Three from the Gas Station; 1930) and Josef von Sternberg's *Der Blaue Engel* (The Blue Angel; 1930). During this period, his material became smoother and more modern. In later years, Hunte worked on history and propaganda films for Ufa and DEFA.

Literature: Luis Buñuel, "Metropolis," Gazeta Literaia, Madrid (1927–28); Otto Hunte, "Der Baumeister von 'Metropolis'," *Illustrierter Filmkurier,* 1927; idem, "Aus der Praxis des Filmarchitekten," in *Feuilletons und Vornotizen für Die Drei von der Tankstelle* (Berlin: Ufa-Publikationen, 1930); Francis Courtade and Pierre Cadars, *Geschichte des Films im Dritten Reich* (Munich: Hanser, 1975),p. 272; Alfred Krautz, *Germany,* vol. 4 of *International Directory of Cinematographers, Set- and Costume Designers in Film* (Munich: K.G Saur, 1984).

P. L.

Erich Kettelhut
(1893–1979)

Kettelhut was apprenticed as a stage-set painter, studied drawing and painting at the Kunstgewerbeschule in Berlin, and held various appointments at provincial theaters. In April 1919, Joe May appointed him assistant set designer for *Herrin der Welt* (Empress of the World). Kettelhut assisted Otto Hunte, who was responsible for the artistic and technical direction as well as the overall plan of the structures. Around Berlin, at Weißensee, Potsdam, and Woltersdorf, fantastic monumental buildings began to appear that were intended to transport the audience all over the world, to China, Africa, America, and the legendary Ophir. With this production, Kettelhut acquired the tools of the set designer's craft. Together with the cameraman Karl Puth, he experimented with different heights and angles for perspective vistas and developed an understanding for the way film can represent architecture.

In his next projects, it was Kettelhut's job to convert designs by Hunte into ground plans and elevations for the construction of sets. Joe May's *Das indische Grabmal* (The Indian Tomb; 1921), Fritz Lang's *Dr. Mabuse der Spieler* (Dr. Mabuse the Gambler; 1921–22), and *Die Nibelungen* were construction assignments this team completed in spectacular fashion. But Kettelhut's specialty was above all architectural models, as well as the special effects necessary to make his trick buildings appear as actual architecture on the screen. As on *Metropolis,* Kettelhut worked mainly with Günther Rittau, a cameraman with a great interest in special effects.

From then on, Kettelhut was in charge as the art director. For Walter Ruttmann's *Berlin, die Sinfonie der Großstadt* (Berlin, Symphony of a Great City; 1927), he organized the sheltered and disguised sites for the camera in order to capture street scenes directly, authentically, and without interruption. One camera, for example, was installed in an advertising kiosk in front of the Anhalter railroad station in order to record the morning and evening traffic at this busy Berlin intersection. The experience of *Berlin* also contributed to the success of *Asphalt.* In Neue Sachlichkeit style, documentary takes of daily life in Berlin were incorporated into the opening scenes of the film by means of multiple exposures. For the action in the film itself, Kettelhut built a 230-meter street in the studio, made completely according to the demands of camera operation, and constructed a movable crane to provide interesting details for the panning lens.

Thanks to his diversity, Kettelhut remained in demand as a set designer after the end of World War II. Shooting for *Die 1000 Augen des Dr. Mabuse* (The Thousand Eyes of Dr. Mabuse; 1960) brought him and Lang together once again. With Lang's last film, Kettelhut also left the cinema. A few projects for television concluded more than four decades of work in film.

Literature: Irene Parker, "Hier wird 'nur' gebaut," *Die Filmwoche*, no. 45 (1932), pp. 1455–58; Erich Kettelhut, "Erinnerungen," unpublished manuscript, ca. 1960, Archive Stiftung Deutsche Kinemathek, Berlin); Alfred Krautz, *Germany*, vol. 4 of *International Directory of Cinematographers, Set- and Costume Designers in Film* (Munich: K.G. Saur, 1984); Wolfgang Jacobsen and Jörg Schöning, "Erich Kettelhut — Filmarchitekt und die Liste seiner Filmbauten," *Cine-Graph* 5 (1 December 1985, pp. D1–D6); Peter Mänz, "Modernität als Handwerk," in Michael Töteberg and Klaus Kreimeier, eds., *Asphalty — Ufa Magazin*, no. 7 (Berlin: Deutsches Historisches Museum, 1992), pp. 8–12.

P. L.

César Klein
(1876–1954)

Trained as a house painter, Klein studied painting in Berlin and Düsseldorf. His early work was inspired by Cézanne and late Impressionism, but around 1915, his style shifted toward that of the German Expressionists. Together with Erich Mendelsohn and a few others, Klein was a founding member of the Novembergruppe in 1918; they were soon joined by Walter Gropius, Mies van der Rohe, Paul Klee, and Wassily Kandinsky. Klein was among those in the group who formulated dreams of mighty glass buildings as spiritual centers of cities and as points of reference for a future architecture. He was asked by Walter Gropius in 1919 to join the newly founded Bauhaus in Weimar. Instead, he accepted a teaching position at the federal arts and crafts school in Berlin. Like most other Expressionist artists, he was dismissed in 1937 by the National Socialists.

Klein had worked since the turn of the century as a painter, designer, and interior decorator. In 1913, for example, he had designed the marble floors for the Siemens administration building in Berlin and the interior of the Marmorhaus movie theater in Berlin (where *Caligari* was to have its premiere in 1920). His work on the sets of *Genuine* was not considered entirely convincing by the critics, due to his difficulties with the translation of color decoration into the new black and white medi-

um. As a result of this work, however, he gained several commissions as a set designer for theater productions in Berlin, Vienna, and Hamburg. His late work concentrated on the painting of mythological themes.

Literature: Herbert Ihering, "Porträt César Klein," in *Regisseure und Bühnenmaler* (Berlin: O. Goldschmidt-Gabrielli, 1921), pp. 87–88; Kurt Dingelstedt, "César Klein als Bühnenbildner," *Kunst in Schleswig-Holstein* (1953), pp. 142–53; Rudolf Pfefferkorn, *César Klein* (Berlin: Rembrandt-Verlag, 1962); Joachim Hauschild, "Cesar Klein: Maler, Entwurfszeichner und Bühnenausstatter," *Weltkunst* 57 (1987), pp. 15–18.

D. N.

Vincent Korda
(1896–1979)

Korda was probably the most important British set designer working during the period between the 1930s and '60s. Having emigrated from Hungary to study painting in Paris, he moved to London in 1932 with his brother Alexander, a director and producer, to work for London Films' Denham Studios. Alexander and Vincent Korda collaborated on a number of films in the following years. Vincent was hired by William Cameron Menzies for *Things to Come* and *Thief of Baghdad* (1940). His many films include historical movies, mysteries, and adventure films, such as *The Private Life of Henry VIII* (Alexander Korda; 1933), *The Rise of Catherine the Great* (Paul Czinner; 1934), and *Rembrandt* (Alexander Korda; 1936). In 1942, Vincent Korda worked with Ernst Lubitsch on *To Be or Not To Be* and in 1949 on Carol Reed's world-famous *The Third Man*.

Literature: Karol Kulik, *Alexander Korda: The Man Who Could Work Miracles* (New Rochelle: Arlington House, 1975); Michael Korda, *Charmed Lives* (New York: Random House, 1979); Helmut Weihsmann, *Gebaute Illusionen: Architektur im Film* (Vienna: Promedia, 1988), p. 253.

D. N.

Jacques Lagrange
(1917–1995)

The son of an architect, Jacques Lagrange studied painting and etching at the Ecole des Beaux Arts in Paris. His paintings, murals and tapestries were exhibited widely and bought by major museums in

France. He created a number of architecture-related installations, such as the large floor mosaics at the Nouvelle Faculté de Sciences de Paris between 1965–1970. He worked as artistic collaborator on Jacques Tati's films "Les Vacances de M. Hulot" (1952), including "Mon Oncle" and "Playtime". Lagrange contributed numerous gags as well as architectural, visual and technical details, including construction drawings for the sets.

Literature: Jacques Chancel, *L'homme qui se cachait derrière Jacques Tati*, Paris-Jour (16 December 1967), p.6.

Paul Leni
(1885–1929)

After training in drawing and graphic art, Leni worked from 1910 on as a stage designer in Stuttgart and Berlin, where he created advertising posters and designed the interior of a Berlin movie theater. In 1914, with Joe May's film *Ein Ausgestoßener* (The Outcast), he began his career in film. After a series of jobs designing costumes and decor, he started directing as well. His early directing credits include the fairy-tale film of *Dornröschen* (Sleeping Beauty; 1917) and the spectacular historical film *Die Verschwörung zu Genua* (The Genova Conspiracy; 1920). Leopold Jessner's gloomy drama *Hintertreppe* (Backstairs; 1921) owed its success to the extraordinary density of Leni's set designs. For Joe May's major production *Tragödie der Liebe* (Tragedy of Love; 1922), with Mia May and Emil Jannings, Leni hired Erich Kettelhut, who built the sets Leni designed.

In the spring of 1923, Leni opened the painters' cabaret called Die Gondel in Berlin. His friend and colleague Ernst Stern designed the colorful interiors, and Leni and the painter César Klein did the stage sets. Leni's drawings were exhibited at the *Grosse Berliner Kunstausstellung* in the same year and at the Mayor Gallery in London two years later. The shooting for *Das Wachsfigurenkabinett*, which Leni both directed and designed, began in the summer of 1923. In countless articles in the trade press, he expounded on the problems of set design and developed the concept of the set as the "arena of the soul":

Only the mental content in the image is artistic expression in film. The film set is the representation of an experience sweeping through a person. A street in Paris is not a street from Paris but the artistic mental expression of people experiencing "Paris" at the moment. Thus each individual action engenders an individual style and there can be no artistic trends for film sets as there are for painting as such [Jawitz 1924].

Leni was contracted to Universal Studios in Hollywood in 1926 and in quick succession directed the crime film *The Cat and the Canary* (1926), *The Man Who Laughs* after Victor Hugo (1927), and *The Last Warning* (1928). The latter was his first sound film, and German critics especially praised the brilliant dissolves and special effects in the depiction of Broadway.

Literature: Paul Leni, "Das Bild als Handlung, der Maler als Regisseur," *Kunst im Film*, no. 2 (1921), pp. 12–14; Eduard Jawitz, "Malerei, Architektur, Plastik und Kunstgewerbe im Film," *Film-Kurier*, no. 33 (7 February 1924); Paul Leni, "Baukunst im Film," *Der Kinematograph*, no. 911, 4 August 1924; idem, "Der überflüssige Architekt," *BZ am Mittag*, no. 138, 22 May 1925; Alfred Krautz, *Germany*, vol. 4 of *International Directory of Cinematographers, Set- and Costume Designers in Film* (Munich: K.G. Saur, 1984); Hans-Michael Bock, *Paul Leni: Grafik, Theater, Film*, exh. cat. (Frankfurt am Main: Deutsches Filmmuseum, 1986); *Das Wachsfigurenkabinett: Drehbuch von Henrik Galeen zu Paul Lenis Film von 1923*, with introductory essay by Thomas Koebner and material about the film by Hans-Michael Bock (Munich: Edition Text+Kritik, 1994).

D. N.

Robert Mallet-Stevens

(1886–1945)

Mallet-Stevens studied architecture at the École Spéciale d'Architecture from 1905 until 1910, became a member of the Salon d'Automne in Paris, and opened his own practice in 1920. The strongest architectural influence in his early years seems to have been the erection of the Palais Stoclet in Brussels by Josef Hoffmann; this building was commissioned by Mallet-Stevens's uncle, Adolf Stoclet. Hoffmann's influence was to remain significant throughout Mallet-Stevens's career. In 1922, inspired by the simplified cubic style chosen by Tony Garnier for his Cité Industrielle, Mallet-Stevens presented drawings for "Une Cité moderne" depicting cubic prototypes for typically urban buildings such as a town hall, law courts, and a film studio. In the following decade, he became one of the most successful modern architects in Paris. Often collaborating with such colleagues as Pierre Chareau or Frantz Jourdain, he designed commercial and residential architecture, offices, and public buildings, furniture, and set designs and wrote a number of books and articles. His

first built work, a villa for the comte de Noailles in Hyères (1924–33), became the famous set for one of Man Ray's short surrealistic films, *Les Mystères du château du Dé* (The Mysteries of the Château of Dé; 1928).

In 1926–27, Mallet-Stevens was given the opportunity to design an entire group of residential buildings stretching on either side of a cul-de-sac in Paris. These cubic blocks represent his most important work up to that time and constitute a veritable manifesto of modern architecture: "A smooth surface, sharp edges, clear curves, polished materials, right angles, light and shadow, order — this is the logical, geometric house of tomorrow" (Mallet-Stevens 1926). Stylistically, Mallet-Stevens's designs embraced several strands of current architecture, including tendencies represented by his contemporaries Le Corbusier, Malevich, van Doesburg, Wagner, Loos, and Wright. He never fully abandoned architectural ornament, however, and remained committed to his decoratively conceived cubic compositions.

Mallet-Stevens designed the sets for 16 different films between 1919 and 1929. Among them are Raymond Bernard's *Le Secret de Rosette Lambert* (The Secret of Rosette Lambert; 1920), *L'Inhumaine*, Marcel L'Herbier's *Le Vertige* (Vertigo; 1926), and a number of historical films. He also deserves credit for being among the first to formulate a theory of set design. Most important are his two articles "Le Cinéma et les arts: L'Architecture" (1925) and "Le Décor moderne au cinéma" (1928), in which he outlined his vision of a profound connection between setting, actor, and narrative:

> The set must present the character before he appears, must indicate his social position, his tastes, his habits, his lifestyle, his personality. . . The decoration, furnishings, and costumes have a role in cinema. . . However, aided by these heterogeneous elements, the sets, in the strict sense of the term, would remain without dramatic effect if another dimension did not intervene in the composition of the image, that of "space", for even when carefully conceived they are not sufficient to define the individual" [Mallet-Stevens, 1925].

Literature: Robert Mallet-Stevens, "Le Cinéma et les arts: L'Architecture," *Les Cahiers du mois*, nos. 16–17 (1925); idem, "Le Décor," in *L'Art cinématographique* (Paris: Librairie Felix Alcan, 1926); idem, *Le Décor moderne au cinéma* (Paris: Massin, 1928); Pierre Vago, *Robert Mallet-Stevens, l'architetto cubista* (Bari: Dedalo Libri, 1979); Hubert Jeanneau and Dominique Deshoulières, eds., *Robert Mallet-Stevens, architecte* (Brussels: Editions des Archives d'Architecture Moderne, 1980); Jean-François Pinchon, *Rob. Mallet-Stevens: Architecture, Furniture, Interior Design* (Cambridge, MA: MIT Press, 1990).

D. N.

Syd Mead

(b. 1933)

Syd Mead studied from 1956 to 1959 at the Art Center School in Los Angeles, California. Immediately after graduation, he was employed by the Ford Motor Company as a designer and illustrator. Commissions and publications for other companies soon followed. With his own company, Syd Mead Inc., he has for many years worked as an independent illustrator, conceptualist, and designer, crossing the boundaries between industrial design, architectural vision, science fiction, and set design. This diversity provides him with a rather unique position among movie designers. Mead's signature streamlined style has consistently drawn on models of early master designers, such as Walter Gropius, Raymond Loewy, and Norman Bel Geddes. All of his work is characterized by a strong belief in modernist notions of a future global culture and the eventual triumph of technological progress. His designs for streamlined, towering megastructures place him in the company of Paolo Soleri, Kenzo Tange, and Peter Cook.

The dystopia Mead envisioned for *Blade Runner* (together with production designer Laurence G. Paull and director Ridley Scott) shows a dark, overcrowded Los Angeles. However, such a sinister vision contrasts sharply with Mead's usually bright images of a pleasant future. It speaks for his talent as a designer that this vision was as convincing as his other conceptual designs. His work on other film sets, often drawing from architectural models, has included *Star Trek — The Motion Picture* (Robert Wise; 1979), *Tron* (Steven Lisberger; 1982), *2010: Odyssey Two* (Peter Hyams; 1984), and *Aliens* (James Cameron; 1986).

Although he continues to use his favorite media of felt pen and gouache, Mead has also, for a number of years, worked intensively with computer graphics and animation. His work has been published frequently, and he has documented his style and approach on videos, laser discs, and CDs.

Literature: Syd Mead, "Designing the Future," in Danny Peary, ed., *Omni's Screen Flights/Screen Fantasies: The Future According to Science Fiction Cinema* (Garden City: Doubleday, 1984), pp. 199–213; idem, *Oblagon* (Tokyo: Kodansha, 1985); idem, *Sentinel II* (Tokyo: Kodansha, 1987); idem, *Kronolog: The Art of Syd Mead* (Tokyo: Bandai, 1991); "Future Concepts: The World of Syd Mead," *Car Styling* 89, nos. 1–2 (1993) (special edition); David Armstrong, "Design Has a Friend in Mead," *San Francisco Examiner*, 31 July 1994; Matt Del Lorenzo, "Syd Mead," *Autoweek*, 9 January 1995.

D. N.

Ludwig Meidner
(1884–1966)

After apprenticing as a mason in Silesia, Meidner studied art in Wrocław and Paris and began working as an illustrator. In 1908, he moved to Berlin and continued his artistic career, drawing realistic urban views. In 1912, he turned to Expressionism, creating portraits and urban views influenced by Delaunay, the Futurists, and Modigliani, having formed a friendship with the latter in Paris. His manifesto "Anleitung zum Malen von Großstadtbildern," inspired by the Futurists, appeared in 1914 in a leading German art magazine. In this piece, he argued against the soft style used by the French Impressionists in their urban views in favor of a creative reaction to the experience of the city: "A street isn't made out of tonal values, but is a bombardment of whizzing rows of windows, of screeching lights between vehicles of all kinds and a thousand jumping spheres, scraps of human beings, advertising signs, and shapeless colors."

During World War I, Meidner's style changed. Under the influence of religious visions and as a reaction against the war, he began a series of biblical scenes. In his essay "Aschaffenburger Tagebuch" (1918), he advocated a return to naturalism and a fervent search for truth, naming Grünewald, Bosch, and Bruegel as models. In 1919, he became a member of the Arbeitsrat für Kunst and also became more politically active. At the same time, he renounced Expressionism. In 1923, he designed the sets for *Die Strasse*. His early Expressionist–Futurist drawings are an important point of reference for many early German street films. In the '20s, Meidner also began to write short stories regularly for Berlin newspapers. During the early years of the Nazi dictatorship, he worked as an art teacher in a Jewish school; several works of his were exhibited in the *Entartete Kunst* exhibition. In 1939, Meidner emigrated to England, returning to Germany in 1952 and enjoying increasing public interest in his work.

Literature: Ludwig Meidner, "Anleitung zum Malen von Grosstadtbildern," *Kunst und Künstler* 12 (1914), pp. 299 ff; idem, *Im Nacken das Sternenmeer* (Leipzig: Kurt Wolff, 1916); idem, *Eine autobiographische Plauderei* (Leipzig: Klinkhardt and Biermann, 1923); *Ludwig Meidner: An Expressionist Master*, exh. cat. (Ann Arbor: University of Michigan Museum of Art, 1978); Carol S. Eliel, *Apokalyptische Landschaften* (Munich: Prestel, 1990).

D. N.

Lászlò Moholy-Nagy
(1895–1946)

Born in Hungary, Moholy-Nagy began his career working as an artist and writer for a variety of foreign-language journals in Berlin. He became acquainted with members of the De Stijl group, especially Theo van Doesburg, and became a friend of the Russian Constructivist artist El Lissitzky. Walter Gropius invited Moholy-Nagy to join the Bauhaus in Weimar as a master and professor in 1923. He stayed until 1928, becoming director of the preparatory class and leading the metal workshop. Being multi-talented, he worked in the fields of typography, photography, painting, and sculpture. In 1930, he exhibited his famous kinetic sculpture *Space–Time–Modulator*. A related abstract film, *Lightplay: Black, White, and Grey,* was produced that year. After emigrating to England in 1936, Moholy-Nagy contributed a short segment to Vincent Korda's futuristic film *Things To Come* and produced a documentary, *Lobsters* (1936). In 1937, he followed Walter Gropius to the United States, where he founded the New Bauhaus in Chicago.

Literature: Lászlò Moholy-Nagy, *Malerei, Photographie, Film* (Munich: Langen, 1925); idem, *The New Vision* (1928), 4th rev. ed. (New York: Wittenborn, 1947); idem, "Probleme des Neuen Films," *Die Form* 7, no. 5 (15 May 1932); idem, *Vision in Motion* (Chicago: Paul Theobald and Co., 1947); Terence Senter, "Moholy-Nagy's English Photography," *Burlington Magazine* 123, no. 944 (November 1981), pp. 659–71.

D.N.

Lawrence G. Paull
(b. 1948)

Having trained as an architect and city planner at the University of Arizona, Paull joined the art department of 20th Century Fox as an apprentice. At Paramount Pictures, he assisted Walter Tyler and John DeCuir. He specialized in period design, recreating southern towns and locations typical of 1939 for *The Bingo Long Traveling All-Stars and Motor Kings* (John Badham; 1976), for which he drew on the style of Walker Evans's photographs. Paull also transformed the central square of a small town from 1985 to 1955 for *Back to the Future* (Robert Zemeckis; 1985), for which he received a BAFTA nomination. For his work on *Blade Runner*, he was nominated for an Academy Award for best art direction and won a British Academy of Film and Television Arts Award. Among his other films are *Romancing the Stone* (Robert Zemeckis; 1984), *Project X* (William Castle; 1987), *Harlem Nights* (Eddie Murphy; 1989), *Predator 2* (Stephen Hopkins; 1990), *City Slickers* (Ron Underwood; 1991), *Unlawful Entry* (Jonathan Kaplan; 1992), and, most recently, *Sgt. Bilko* (Jonathan Lynn; 1995). Paull bases his period pieces on painstaking research and frequently makes reference in his work to architectural history. Museum designs by Richard Meier and Michael Graves were taken into consideration for *Project X;* for *Blade Runner,* Paull suggested that such L.A. landmarks as the Bradbury Building (1893) or Frank Lloyd Wright's Ennis Brown House (1923) be included. The extraordinary impact of the sets for certain films is apparent to Paull himself: "There are films where the sets are one of the stars. It happened in *Dick Tracy,* and it certainly happened in *Blade Runner"* (LoBrutto 1992).

Literature: "Lawrence G. Paull," in Vincent LoBrutto, *By Design: Interviews with Film Production Designers* (Westport: Praeger, 1992), pp. 165–78; *Cinematographers, Production Designers, Costume Designers and Film Editors Guide*, 4th ed. (Los Angeles: Lone Eagle Publishing Co., 1993).

D. N.

Hans Poelzig
(1869–1936)

After studying architecture at the Technische Universität in Berlin-Charlottenburg and working briefly as a government architect in the Prussian ministry of public works, Poelzig in 1900 became a professor of architecture at the Kunstgewerbeschule in Wrocław. From 1903 to 1916, he was the director of this institution, and from 1916 to 1920, he served as city architect of Dresden. For a decade beginning in 1923, Poelzig held a professorship at the university. First and foremost an architect, he nevertheless effortlessly crossed the boundaries between professions. Thus, he wrote articles, left a substantial painterly oeuvre, and designed stage and film sets. The distinctive style of his preliminary drawings profited from these interdisciplinary activities. Without determining details at too early a stage, they capture the spatial, decorative, and emotional essentials of a building.

Poelzig's approximately 50 completed structures and numerous projects are characterized by personal expressiveness affected neither by rigid doctrines nor by dominant fashions. His best-known buildings are the water tower in Poznan and the chemical factory in Luban (1911), his famous renovation of the Berlin Schauspielhaus (1919), and the Haus des Rundfunks (radio building) in Berlin (1929–30). He was a champion of the concerns of his profession, which he represented as president of the Deutscher Werkbund, member of the board of the Bund Deutscher Architekten, and member of the Prussian Academy. In his articles, designs, and structures, he took a passionate and original stand in many major debates among the architects of the Weimar Republic, including such issues as the nature of future urban architecture or the relationship between ornament and structure. Besides working for the film *Der Golem*, he participated in two other film projects: Paul Wegener's *Lebende Buddhas* (Living Buddahs; 1923–25), for which he designed Tibetan architectural backdrops, and Arthur von Gerlach's *Zur Chronik von Grieshuus* (The Grieshuus Chronicle; 1925), based on Theodor Storm's gloomy novella about envy and class arrogance. Here, Poelzig's ideas for the massive castle of Grieshuus, worn by the marks of time, and the squat local church and cowering houses were absorbed into the sets built by Robert Herlth and Walter Röhrig.

Literature: Theodeor Heuss, *Hans Poelzig: Lebensbild eines deutschen Baumeisters* (Tübingen: Rainer Wunderlich, 1939); *Hans Poelzig: Der dramatische Raum: Malerei, Theater, Film*, exh. cat. (Krefeld: Museum Haus Lange, 1986); Julius Posener, *Hans Poelzig: Reflections on His Life and Work* (New York and Cambridge: Architectural History Foundation and MIT Press, 1992).

D. N.

Walter Reimann

(1887–1936)

Having trained as a stage-set painter and taken evening art courses at the Kunstschule in Berlin, Reimann apprenticed at the Hamburg Schauspielhaus. After World War I, he was employed by the army theater in Vilnius, where he met the stage designers Hermann Warm, Robert Herlth, and Walter Röhrig. Warm found Reimann a job painting stage sets and perspective backdrops for the Decla production *Die Pest in Florenz* (The Plague in Florence; 1919), one of the many extravagant historical films produced very cheaply in the early Weimar Republic.

The idea of setting *Das Cabinet des Dr. Caligari* in painted fantastic architecture was Reimann's first major contribution to the history of German film. *Algol*, made shortly afterwards, was the first film for which Reimann had sole responsibility as art director. His subsequent set designs are like a journey through the history of styles: the Italian Trecento (Paul Wegener's *Herzog Ferrantes Ende* [The End of Duke Ferrante; 1921]) and Risorgimento (Arthur von Gerlach's *Vanina* [1922]), as well as revolutionary Paris (Paul Ludwig Stein's *Es leuchtet meine Liebe* [My Love is Shining; 1922]). Reimann also worked as a stage designer, in 1922 designing one of the famous Shakespeare productions by Leopold Jessner, *Macbeth*, at the Staatliches Schauspielhaus in Berlin. Reimann's "dream inspired" stage design was praised by the critics. Considered a specialist on the intersection of stage and film, he expressed his views fervently in a succession of articles about this relationship.

After numerous routine jobs for different producers, Reimann was called to Hollywood by Ernst Lubitsch to design *Eternal Love* (1928), for which he built a Swiss Alpine village in the California desert. Reimann came to terms with his American experiences in a series of articles about the differences between German and American studio and production techniques, published in the journal *Filmtechnik*. He was also active in the beginnings of sound film, working briefly in London. In the early '30s, his employment situation deteriorated dramatically. After repeated desperate requests for work with Ufa, he obtained a contract in 1936 to design sets for various insignificant short films.

Literature: Walter Reimann, "Einiges über die Bedeutung des Films und der Filmindustrie," *Neue Züricher Zeitung* 144, no. 1663 (1 December 1923); idem, "Filmarchitektur — Filmarchitekt!?," *Gebrauchsgrafik*, no. 6 (1924–25), pp. 3-3 (see pp. 185–86 of the present volume); idem, "Filmtexte," *Filmtechnik*, no. 6 (1925), p. 107; A. Kossowsky, "Die Filmarchitekten II: Walter Reimann," *Film–Kurier* 26 (30 January 1926); Walter Reimann, "Filmarchitektur — heute und morgen?" *Filmtechnik und Filmindustrie*, no. 4 (1926), pp. 64–65 (see p. 189 of the present volume); idem, "Filmbauten und Raumkunst," in *Das große Bilderbuch des Films* (Berlin: Film Kurier, 1926); idem, "Amerikanische Modelltechnik," *Filmtechnik*, no. 8 (1929); idem, "Die Arbeit des Art-Directors," *Filmtechnik*, no. 5 (1929), p. 85; idem, "Ateliers in Hollywood," *Filmtechnik*, no. 4 (1929), p. 65; idem, "Kalifornischer Außenbau," *Filmtechnik*, no. 6 (1929), p. 103; Alfred Krautz, *Germany*, vol. 4 of *International Directory of Cinematographers, Set- and Costume Designers in Film* (Munich: K.G. Saur, 1984).

P. L.

Walter Röhrig

(1863–1945)

Röhrig studied painting in Berlin and Zurich and then worked as a set painter in Zurich. In 1918, he returned to Berlin and became involved in film production. Together with Hermann Warm and Robert Herlth, he worked on *Das Cabinet des Dr. Caligari*. Röhrig also worked with Warm on Fritz Lang's famous film parable *Der müde Tod* (Destiny; 1921). Together with Herlth, Röhrig contributed to a series of outstanding German silent films in the 1920s, including *Der letzte Mann, Tartüff* (Friedrich Wilhelm Murnau; 1925), and *Faust* (F.W. Murnau; 1926).

In 1925, with the architect Hans Poelzig, Röhrig worked on the impressive sets for Arthur von Gerlach's film *Zur Chronik von Grieshuus* (The Grieshuus Chronicle; 1925). Nothing is known about the distribution of responsibilities in this collaboration; only the drawings for it by Röhrig have been preserved (Stiftung Deutsche Kinemathek, Berlin). It appears that Röhrig solved the technical problems rather than the conceptual ones. Yet, his sketches indicate that he had a talent for delineating atmosphere and was able to visualize not only spatial relationships but also lighting. Unaffected by the political changes after 1933, Herlth and Röhrig continued to work on a series of propaganda and historical films up until Röhrig's death right after the war. These include R. Berger's *Walzerkrieg* (War of the Waltzes; 1933), Gustav Ucicky's *Flüchtlinge* (Refugees; 1933), and R. Schünzel's *Amphitryon* (1935).

Literature: Alfred Krautz, *Germany*, vol. 4 of *International Directory of Cinematographers, Set- and Costume Designers in Film* (Munich: K.G. Saur, 1984), pp. 314–16; Günther Dalke and Günter Karl, eds., *Deutsche Spielfilme von den Anfängen bis 1933* (Berlin: Henschel, 1988), p. 368; Michael Esser, "Poeten der Filmarchitektur, Robert Herlth und Walter Röhrig," in Hans–Michael Bock and Michael Töteberg, eds., *Das Ufa Buch: Kunst und Krisen, Stars und Regisseure, Wirtschaft und Politik: Die international Geschichte von Deutschlands größtem Filmkonzern* (Frankfurt am Main: Zweitausendeins, 1992), pp. 118–23.

D. N.

Richard Sylbert

(b. 1928)

Few production designers have had careers as lengthy, diverse, and distinguished as Richard Sylbert. After studying art in Philadelphia, he worked as a set painter for television productions. Among his most significant early influences, he has mentioned his work for William Cameron Menzies and Elia Kazan (*Baby Doll* [1952]). During the following years, Sylbert worked on a large number of now famous film classics, such as *Who's Afraid of Virginia Woolf* (Mike Nichols; 1966), *The Graduate* (Mike Nichols; 1967), *Rosemary's Baby* (Roman Polanski; 1968), *Chinatown* (Roman Polanski; 1974), *Shampoo* (Hal Ashby; 1975), *Reds* (Warren Beatty; 1981), *Cotton Club* (Francis Ford Coppola, 1984), *Bonfire of the Vanities* (Brian de Palma; 1990), and *Dick Tracy*. Sylbert was nominated for six Academy Awards and won two Oscars for art direction for *Who's Afraid of Virginia Woolf* and *Dick Tracy*. He received an honorary doctorate of fine arts from the American Film Insitute in 1992.

What characterizes Sylbert's style is his search for a particular visual language that creates optical coherence for a film, based on a set of specific iconographic references, repetitive patterns, and a clearly defined palette. His work for *Chinatown* is often quoted as providing this type of subliminal visual undercurrent. In this story about a private detective who uncovers corruption surrounding water rights in California during a drought, the faded colors and off-white buildings make the heat in Chinatown tangible, and the frequent use of frosted glass creates associations with water. In *Dick Tracy*, Sylbert was responsible for the idea of creating the stylized world of a comic strip by working with a limited set of colors and reducing the decor, costumes, cars, and architecture to their transhistorical essentials. Although he is among the most outspoken and visible of Hollywood's production designers, he nevertheless emphasizes the set design's task to support the actors: "Acting is the only real architecture in a movie; that's what you are protecting all the time. You are making sure that nothing, absolutely nothing is interfering with the scene" (Lo Brutto, 1992).

Literature: "Richard Sylbert," *Film Comment* (January–February 1982), p. 44; "From Gorky Park to Chinatown, Paul and Dick Sylbert, Twin Film Designers, Divide and Conquer," *People Weekly* 21 (30 January 1984), pp. 73–74; Richard Sylbert, "Dialogue on Film," *American Film* 15 (December 1989), pp. 22–26; Christopher Michaud, "Richard Sylbert Works His Magic by Design," *New York Times*, 23 September 1990, sect. 2, pp. 1, 18; "Richard Sylbert," in Vincent LoBrutto, *By Design: Interviews with Film Production Designers* (Westport: Praeger, 1992), pp. 49–62; Doug Stuart, "Once They Pay $7, Moviegoers Want a Believable World," *Smithsonian* 23 (May 1992), pp. 100–111; Peter Biskind, "The Joy of Sets," *Premiere* (December 1993); Gerhard Midding, "Richard Sylbert, Production Design als Metapher," *Cinema* 40 (1994), p. 75–86.

D. N.

Jacques Tati
(1908–1982)

French film director Jacques Tati is known for having produced, designed, and starred in his own films. Instead of entering his parents' successful framing business, Tati began a professional career as a mime. From 1932 on, he turned some of his most successful numbers into short films and in 1949 began producing feature films with *Jour de Fête* (Mr. Hulot's Holiday). Among the five feature films he produced, *Mon Oncle* and *Playtime* stand out as being particularly centered on architectural themes. Tati worked closely with the architect and painter Jacques LaGrange on these two films and oversaw all the set designs, since the forms and details of the architecture in the films are their most essential components and provide the basis for innumerable gags: "Tati's films are not so much stories or character studies as they are explorations of the systems and structures that make up society: architecture, transportation, the home, time-saving appliances and the vacation, for example" (Maddock 1977). Tati's comedies — from his second major production, *Les Vacances* (Vacation; 1952) on, feature himself as M. Hulot and increasingly challenge established notions of filmic structure and narrative. His famous long shots and deep-focus photography often encompass several activities simultaneously, demanding the audience's attention and presenting the viewer with a certain freedom to focus on different subjects.

Literature: Penelope Gilliatt, "The Current Cinema: Jacques Tati," *New Yorker* (28 August 1971), pp. 58–61; Brent Maddock, *The Films of Jacques Tati* (Metuchen: Scarecrow Press, Inc., 1977); Lucy Fischer, *Jacques Tati: A Guide to References and Resources* (Boston: G.K. Hall and Co., 1983); Michel Chion, *Jacques Tati* (Paris: Cahiers du Cinéma, 1987); Jean-André Fieschi and Jean Narboni, "Le Champ large," *Cahiers du cinéma*, no. 199 (March 1988), pp. 6–22.

D. N.

Edgar George Ulmer
(1904–1972)

Born in Vienna, Ulmer was already helping out in film and theater productions as a schoolboy. According to his own recollections, in 1919 he also worked with Paul Wegener, Hans Poelzig, and Rochus Gliese on *Der Golem, wie er in die Welt kam*. Ulmer apparently also contributed to Fritz Lang's

Die Nibelungen and *Metropolis,* as well as to F.W. Murnau's *Sunrise* and *Der letzte Mann*. It is documented that he directed *Menschen am Sonntag* (People on a Sunday; 1929) together with Robert Siodmak. This movie in the tradition of German street films was influenced, according to Ulmer, by Dziga Vertov's *Chelovek s kinoapparatom* (Man with the Movie Camera; 1929). Independently produced by Ulmer, *Menschen am Sonntag* introduced him to Billy Wilder, who wrote the screenplay, and Eugen Schüfftan, the cameraman, and his assistant at the time, Fred Zinnemann.

Through his work for Murnau, Ulmer went to the United States, settling permanently in Hollywood by the end of the 1920s. He worked as a production assistant for a variety of films and was in charge of technical matters for Murnau's last film, *Tabu* (1931). He then produced a large number of so called B-movies, made in a short time with little money. Despite the limitations of these films, he succeeded in creating images of astounding visual power. They included *Damaged Lives* (1933), a film about sexually transmitted diseases for the Canadian Department of Health, and *The Black Cat*, which brought together the stars Bela Lugosi and Boris Karloff. Especially notable among the approximately 40 films directed by Ulmer are *Ruthless* (1948), *Detour* (1945), and *Naked Dawn* (1957), which inspired François Truffaut's *Jules et Jim* (1961). As Peter Bogdanovich put it,

> Nobody ever made good films faster or for less money than Edgar Ulmer. What he could do with nothing — occasionally in the script department as well — remains an object lesson for directors who complain about tight budget and schedules. That Ulmer could also communicate a strong visual style and personality with the meager means so often available to him is close to miraculous [Bogdanovich 1975].

Literature: Luc Moullet, "Edgar G. Ulmer," *Cahiers du cinéma* 25, nos. 150–51 (December 1963–January 1964); John Belton, "Edgar G. Ulmer," in *Hollywood Professionals* (London, New York: Tantivy Press; A. S. Barnes, 1974), pp. 173ff; Myron Meisel, "Edgar G. Ulmer: The Primacy of the Visual;" Peter Bogdanovich, "Interview with Edgar G. Ulmer," in Todd McCarthy and Charles Flynn, ed., *Kings of the Bs* (New York: E. P. Dutton and Co., 1975), pp. 147-152; 377–409 (a longer version of the Bogdanovich interview appeared in *Film Culture*, nos. 58–60 [1974], pp. 189–206); John Belton, *Cinema Stylists* (Metuchen and London: Scarecrow Press 1983), pp. 146–56; Paul Mandell, "Edgar Ulmer and the Black Cat," *American Cinematographer* (October 1984), pp. 34–47; "Le Chat noir," *L'Avant scène du cinéma* 338 (March 1985), pp. 20–51.

D. N.

Hermann Warm

(1889–1976)

In addition to his training as a stage-set painter in Berlin, Warm attended the Kunstgewerbeschule. Following his apprenticeship, he traveled to Düsseldorf and Frankfurt. In 1913, Jules Greenbaum's production company, Deutsche Vitascop, contracted Warm as a set painter. In his first film, Walter Schmidthässler's *Der Spion* (The Spy; 1913), he was already innovative, constructing a revolving wall behind which the spies suddenly disappeared. He succeeded in persuading Greenbaum that painted backdrops should be replaced by three-dimensional structures and suggested making the screenplay available to the set designer, so that appropriate design sketches could be created before the beginning of production. Warm designed models and replaced black and white backgrounds with colored sets, their half-tones heightening the photographic effect of the architecture enormously. In this way, he was one of the first stage designers to develop the independent professional profile of the set designer.

Until Warm was drafted in 1915, he worked mainly for the leading directors Max Mack and Harry Piel. From 1916 on, he worked for the army theater in Vilnius as a stage designer, calling on Walter Reimann and Walter Röhrig to join his team. In 1919, they all worked on Otto Rippert's *Die Pest in Florenz* (The Plague in Florence; 1919). With *Das Cabinet des Dr. Caligari*, the team of Warm, Reimann, and Röhrig created a new cinematographic style. Warm, by now permanently employed by Decla–Bioscop as an art director, proved to be a congenial designer on many productions, never imposing his personal style. He managed to work easily and at a high artistic level with directors as different as Fritz Lang and Friedrich Wilhelm Murnau. For Lang, he was the art director for *Die Spinnen* (The Spiders; 1920). In *Der müde Tod* (Destiny; 1921), he designed the Renaissance and Oriental episodes, as well as the Chinese imperial palace. For Murnau's *Phantom* (1922), he created traumatic sites between reality and hallucination, while in Carl Theodor Dreyer's *La Passion de Jeanne d'Arc* (The Passion of Joan of Arc; 1927–28), he translated the director's pictorial ideas into architecture. Warm worked on over 80 films from 1919 on, until his emigration in 1941 to Switzerland. Many are routine works for the film market; most of them no longer exist. In 1947, he returned to Germany, but only worked occasionally as a set designer.

Literature: Hermann Warm, "Aussenbau," *Filmtechnik,* no. 3 (1930); Gerhard Lamprecht, "Interview with Hermann Warm," 8 August 1954, Archive Stiftung Deutsche Kinemathek, Berlin; Wolfgang Längsfeld, "Der Mann der Caligari baute: Ein Gespräch mit dem Filmarchitekten Hermann Warm," *Der Film,* no. 7 (1965); Hermann Warm, "Die Dekorationen des Caligarifilms," *Baubeschreibungen und technische Erläuterungen,* unpublished manuscript, 1968, Archive Stiftung Deutsche Kinemathek, Berlin; Alfred Krautz, *Germany,* vol. 4 of *International Directory of Cinematographers, Set- and Costume Designers in Film* (Munich: K.G. Saur, 1984).

P. L.

Abel, Richard. *French Film Theory and Criticism: A History/Anthology*. 2 vols. Princeton: Princeton University Press, 1988.

Adkinson, R.V., ed. *The Cabinet of Dr. Caligari: A Film by Robert Wiene, Carl Mayer and Hans Janowitz*. London: Lorimer, 1972.

Albrecht, Donald. "Architecture and Film: Utopia Descending." *Modulus* 18 (1987). Pp. 121–34.

—. *Designing Dreams: Modern Architecture in the Movies*. London and New York: Thames and Hudson, 1987. Rev. German ed.: *Architektur im Film: Die Moderne als große Illusion*. Ed. Ralph Eue. Basel; Boston; Berlin: Birkhäuser, 1989.

Andrew, Dudley. *Concepts in Film Theory*. London: Oxford University Press, 1984.

Andrew, J. Dudley. *Film in the Aura of Art*. Princeton: Princeton University Press, 1984.

—. *The Major Film Theories*. London: Oxford University Press, 1976.

"Architektur im Film." *Cinema*, no. 4 (1981).

Arnheim, Rudolf. *Film As Art*. Berkeley: University of California Press, 1957.

L'Art et le 7e art: Collections de la Cinémathèque Française. Exh. cat. Paris: L'Hôtel de la Monnaie, 1995.

Ausstattung. Cinema, no. 40 (1994). Special issue.

Barlow, John D. *German Expressionist Film*. Boston: Twaine, 1982.

Barsacq, Léon. *Le Décor de film: 1895–1969*. Paris: Henri Veyrier, 1970.

Bartetzko, Dieter. *Illusionen in Stein: Stimmungsarchitektur im deutschen Faschismus*. Hamburg: Rowohlt, 1985.

Bay, Howard. *Stage Design*. New York: Drama Book Specialists, 1974.

Belton, John. *Cinema Stylists*. Metuchen and London: Scarecrow Press, 1983.

Benson, Timothy, ed., *Expressionist Utopias*. Exh. cat. Los Angeles County Museum of Art, 1993.

Berg-Ganschow, Uta. *Berlin: Aussen und Innen: Materialien zu einer Retrospektive*. Berlin: Stiftung Deutsche Kinemathek, 1984.

—, and Wolfgang Jacobsen. "Schauwerte: Architektur im Film: Materialien zu einem Symposium der Stiftung Deutsche Kinemathek." *Film: Zeitschrift des Evangelischen Pressedienstes* 4 (1987). Pp. 16–29.

—, eds. *Film...Stadt...Kino...Berlin*. Berlin: Argon, 1987.

Berger, Jürgen, ed. *Production Design: Ken Adam – Meisterwerke der Filmarchitektur*. Exh. cat. Munich: Deutsches Museum, 1994.

Berriatúa, Luciano. *Los Proverbios chinos de F.W. Murnau*. Madrid: Instituto de la Cinematografía, 1990.

Bock, Hans-Michael. *Paul Leni: Grafik, Theater, Film*. Exh. cat. Frankfurt am Main: Deutsches Filmmuseum, 1986.

—, ed. *CineGraph: Lexikon zum deutschsprachigen Film*. Munich: Edition Text+Kritik, 1984ff.

Bock, Hans-Michael, and Michael Töteberg, eds. *Das Ufa Buch: Kunst und Krisen, Stars und Regisseure, Wirtschaft und Politik: Die international Geschichte von Deutschlands größtem Filmkonzern*. Frankfurt am Main: Zweitausendeins, 1992.

Bonifer, Mike. *Dick Tracy: The Making of the Movie*. New York: Bantam, 1990.

Brennicke, Ilona, and Joe Hembus. *Klassiker des deutschen Stummfilms, 1910–1930*. Munich: Goldmann, 1983.

Brosnan, John. *Future Tense: The Cinema of Science Fiction*. New York: St. Martin's Press, 1978.

Budd, Mike, ed. *The Cabinet of Dr. Caligari: Texts, Contexts, Histories*. New Brunswick and London: Rutgers University Press, 1990.

Caligari und Caligarismus. Berlin: Stiftung Deutsche Kinemathek, 1970.

Cappabianca, Alessandro, and Michele Mancini. *Ombre urbane: Set e città dal cinema muto agli anni '80*. Rome: Edizioni Kappa, 1981.

Carrick, Edward. *Art and Design in the British Film: A Pictorial Directory of British Art Directors and Their Work*. 1948. Reprint, New York: Arno Press, 1972.

—. "Moving Picture Sets: A Medium for the Architect." *Architectural Record* 67 (1930).

Chion, Michel. *Jacques Tati*. Paris: Cahiers du Cinéma, 1987.

Cinema and Architecture. Iris 12 (1991). Special issue.

Cinemarchitecture. Design Book Review, no. 24 (Spring 1992). Special issue.

Cinematographers, Production Designers, Costume Designers and Film Editors Guide. 4th ed. Los Angeles: Lone Eagle Publishing Co., 1993.

Cinés-cités. Exh. cat. Paris: La Villette/La Grande Halle, 1987.

Cook, David A. *A History of Narrative Film*. New York: W.W. Norton, 1981.

Corliss, Mary, and Carlos Clarens. *Designed for Film*. Exh. cat. New York: Museum of Modern Art, 1978.

Cossart, Axel von. *Kino – Theater des Expressionismus: Das literarische Resümee einer Besonderheit*. Essen: Blaue Eule, 1985.

Courtade, Francis. *Cinéma expressioniste*. Paris: H. Veyrier, 1984.

—, and Pierre Cadars. *Geschichte des Films im Dritten Reich*. Munich: Hanser, 1975.

Dalke, Günther, and Günter Karl, eds. *Deutsche Spielfilme von den Anfängen bis 1933*. Berlin: Henschel, 1988.

"Le Décor de film." *Cinématographe*, no. 22 (December 1976).

Drawings into Film: Director's Drawings. Exh. cat. New York: Pace Gallery, 1993.

Eisner, Lotte. *Fritz Lang*. London: Secker and Warburg, 1976.

—. *The Haunted Screen*. Berkeley: University of California Press, 1973.

—. *Murnau*. Berkeley: University of California Press, 1973.

—. *Vingt ans de cinema allemand 1913–1933*. Exh. cat. Paris: Centre National d'Art et de Culture Georges Pompidou, 1978.

Esser, Michael. "Spaces in Motion: Remarks on Set Design in the German Silent Film." In *Berlin, 1900–1933: Architecture and Design*. Exh. cat. New York: Cooper-Hewitt Museum, 1987.

Färber, Helmut. *Baukunst und Film: Aus der Geschichte des Sehens*. Munich: privately printed, 1977.

Film und Architektur. Bauwelt 9, no. 85 (25 February 1994). Special issue.

Finch, Christopher. *Special Effects: Creating Movie Magic*. New York: Abbeville Press, 1984.

Fries, Heinrich de. "Raumgestaltung im Film." *Wasmuths Monatsheft für Baukunst*, nos. 1–2 (1920–21). Pp. 63–75.

Gandert, Gero. *Der Film der Weimarer Republik 1929*. Berlin and New York: Walter de Gruyter, 1993.

Geduld, Harry M. *Authors on Film*. Bloomington and London: Indiana University Press, 1972.

Gehler, Fred, and Ulrich Kasten. *Fritz Lang, Die Stimme von Metropolis*. Berlin: Henschel Verlag, 1990.

Greisenegger, Wolfgang. "Überlegungen zur Geschichte der Filmarchitektur." *Filmkunst* 96 (December 1982). Pp. 1–7.

Hans Poelzig: Der dramatische Raum: Malerei, Theater, Film. Exh. cat. Krefeld: Museum Haus Lange, 1986.

Harbou, Thea von. *Metropolis*. 1927. Reprint, Boston: Gregg Press, 1975.

Heisner, Beverly. *Hollywood Art: Art Direction in the Days of the Great Studios*. Jefferson, NC, and London: McFarland and Company, 1990.

Henderson, Brian. "Notes on Set Design and Cinema." *Film Quarterly* 17, no. 1 (Fall 1988). Pp. 17–28.

Henry, Michel. *Le Cinéma expressioniste allemand: Un Langage métaphorique*. Paris: Editions du Signe, 1971.

Images et imaginaires d'architecture: dessin, peintre, photographie, arts graphiques, théâtre, cinéma en Europe aux XIXe et XXe siècle. Exh. cat. Paris: Centre National d'Art et de Culture Georges Pompidou, 1984.

Jacobs, Lewis, ed. *Introduction to the Art of the Movies*. New York: Noonday Press, 1960.

Jacobsen, Wolfgang, ed. *Babelsberg: Ein Filmstudio 1912–1992*. Berlin: Argon, 1992.

—, Hans Helmut Prinzler, and Werner Sudendorf, eds. *Kino*Movie*Cinema*. Exh. cat. Berlin: Martin Gropius Bau, 1995.

Jordanova, Ludmilla. *Sexual Visions: Images of Gender in Science and Medicine between the Eighteenth and Twentieth Centuries*. Madison: University of Wisconsin Press, 1989.

Kaes, Anton. *Kino Debatte: Texte zum Verhältnis von Literatur und Film 1909–1929*. Munich: Deutscher Taschenbuch Verlag, 1978.

Kasten, Jürgen. *Der expressionistische Film: Abgefilmtes Theater oder avantgardistisches Erzählkino?* Münster: MaKs Publikations, 1990.

Kaul, Walter. *Schöpferische Filmarchitektur*. Berlin: Stiftung Deutsche Kinemathek, 1971.

Keiner, Reinhold. *Thea von Harbou und der deutsche Film bis 1933*. Hildesheim: Georg Olms Verlag, 1984.

Kerman, Judith B., ed. *Retrofitting Blade Runner: Issues in Ridley Scott's Blade Runner and Philip K. Dick's Do Androids Dream of Electric Sheep?* Bowling Green: Bowling Green State University Popular Press, 1991.

Kettelhut, Erich. "Erinnerungen". Unpublished manuscript, ca. 1960. Stiftung Deutsche Kinemathek, Berlin.

Kracauer, Siegfried. *From Caligari to Hitler: A Psychological History of the German Film*. Princeton: Princeton University Press, 1974.

—. "Kalikowelt." In *Ornament der Masse*. Frankfurt am Main: Suhrkamp, 1963.

—. *Theory of Film: The Redemption of Physical Reality*. London: Oxford University Press, 1960.

Krautz, Alfred, ed. *International Directory of Cinematographers, Set- and Costume Designers in Film*. 13 vols. Munich: K.G.Saur, 1981ff.

Kreimeier, Klaus, ed. *Die Metaphysik des Decors: Raum, Architektur und Licht im klassischen deutschen Stummfilm*. Marburg: Schüren, 1994.

Kurtz, Rudolf. *Expressionismus und Film*. Berlin: Verlag der Lichtbildbühne, 1926.

Längsfeld, Wolfgang, ed. *Filmarchitektur – Robert Herlth*. Munich: Deutsches Institut für Film und Fernsehen, 1965.

Lindsay, Vachel, *The Art of the Moving Picture*. In Dennis Camp. *The Prose of Vachel Lindsay Complete and with Lindsay's Drawings*. Vol. 1. Peoria: Spoon River Poetry Press, 1988. Pp. 211–337.

LoBrutto, Vincent. *By Design: Interviews with Film Production Designers*. Westport: Praeger, 1992.

Maddock, Brent. *The Films of Jacques Tati*. Metuchen: Scarecrow Press, Inc., 1977.

Magill, Frank N., ed. *Magill's Survey of the Cinema.* Englewood Cliffs: Salem Press, 1981.

Mandelbaum, Howard, and Eric Meyers. *Screen Deco: A Celebration of High Style in Hollywood.* New York: St. Martin's Press, 1985.

Mansfield, Howard. *Cosmopolis: Yesterday's Cities of the Future.* New York: Center for Urban Policy Research, 1990.

Marriott, John. *Batman: The Official Book of the Movie.* New York: Bantam Books, 1989.

Maryska, Christian. *Road to Yesterday: Entwürfe Amerikanischer Filmarchitekten 1924–1930.* Vienna: Böhlau Verlag, 1992.

Mast, Gerald, and Marshall Cohen, eds. *Film Theory and Criticism: Introductory Readings.* 3rd ed. New York: Oxford University Press, 1985.

McCarthy, Todd, and Charles Flynn, ed. *Kings of the Bs.* New York: E. P. Dutton and Co., 1975.

Mendelsohn, Erich. *Amerika: Bilderbuch eines Architekten.* 1926. Reprint, with commentary by Herbert Molderings, Wiesbaden: Vieweg Verlag, 1991.

Metropolis: Un film de Fritz Lang. Paris: Cinémathèque Française, 1985.

Moholy-Nagy, Lászlò. *Malerei, Photographie, Film.* Munich: Langen, 1925.

—. *Vision in Motion.* Chicago: Paul Theobald and Co., 1947.

Münsterberg, Hugo. *Film: A Psychological Study.* 1916. Reprint, New York: Dover, 1969.

Neumann, Dietrich. *Die Wolkenkratzer kommen: Deutsche Hochhäuser der Zwanziger Jahre.* Wiesbaden: Vieweg Verlag 1995.

Peary, Danny, ed. *Omni's Screen Flights/Screen Fantasies: The Future According to Science Fiction Cinema.* Garden City: Doubleday, 1984.

Peters, Benoît, Jacques Faton, and Philippe de Pierpont, eds. *Storyboard: Le Cinéma dessiné.* Exh. cat. Paris: Palais de Tokyo, 1992.

Pinchon, Jean-François. *Rob. Mallet-Stevens: Architecture, Furniture, Interior Design.* Cambridge, MA: MIT Press, 1990.

Pohl, Frederick, and Frederick Pohl IV. *Science Fiction Studies in Film.* New York: Ace Books, 1981.

Posener, Julius. *Hans Poelzig: Reflections on His Life and Work.* New York and Cambridge, MA: Architectural History Foundation and MIT Press, 1992.

Prawer, Siegbert Solomon. *Caligari's Children: The Film as Tale of Terror.* New York: Da Capo Press, 1988.

Puaux, Françoise, ed. *Architecture, décor et cinéma. CinémAction,* no. 75 (1995). Special issue.

Rand, Ayn. *The Fountainhead.* New York: Bobbs-Merrill Co., 1943.

Roberts, Garyn G. *Dick Tracy and American Culture: Morality and Mythology, Text and Context.* London: McFarland and Co., 1973.

Rohmer, Eric. *The Taste for Beauty.* Trans. Carol Volk. Cambridge: Cambridge University Press, 1989.

Rotha, Paul. *The Film till Now: A Survey of World Cinema.* New York: Funk and Wagnalls, 1949.

Saint, Andrew. *The Image of the Architect.* New Haven: Yale University Press, 1983.

Salt, Barry. *Film Style and Technology: History and Analysis.* London: Starword, 1983.

Scheffauer, Herman G. "The Vivifying of Space." 1920. In Jacobs, Lewis, ed. *Introduction to the Art of the Movies.* New York: Noonday Press, 1960.

Schönemann, Heide. *Fritz Lang: Filmbilder, Vorbilder.* Berlin: Verlag Edition Hentrich, 1992.

Sennett, Robert S. *Setting the Scene: The Great Hollywood Art Directors.* New York: Harry N. Abrams, 1994.

Sklar, Robert. *Film: An International History of the Medium.* New York: Harry N. Abrams, 1993.

Sterling, Anna Kate. *Cinematographers on the Art and Craft of Cinematography.* Metuchen: Scarecrow Press, Inc., 1987.

Sutcliffe, Anthony, ed. *Metropolis 1890–1940.* Chicago and London: University of Chicago Press, 1984.

Tafuri, Manfredo. *The Sphere and the Labyrinth.* Cambridge, MA: MIT Press, 1990.

Timms, Edward, and David Kelley. *Unreal City: Urban Experience in Modern European Literature and Art.* New York: St. Martin's Press, 1985.

Toy, Maggie, ed. *Architecture and Film. Architectural Design Profile* 112, 1994.

Usai, Paolo Cherchi, and Lorenzo Codelli, eds. *Before Caligari: German Cinema 1895–1920.* Pordenone: Le Giornate del Cinemata Muto, 1990.

Verdone, Mario. *Szena e costume nel cinema.* Rome: Bulzoni Editore, 1986.

Vidler, Anthony. *assemblage* 21 (1993). Pp. 45–59.

Visions urbains: Villes de l'Europe à l'écran. Exh. cat. Paris: Centre National d'Art et de Culture Georges Pompidou, 1994.

Das Wachsfigurenkabinett: Drehbuch von Henrik Galeen zu Paul Lenis Film von 1923. With an introductory essay by Thomas Koebner and material about the film by Hans-Michael Bock. Munich: Edition Text+Kritik, 1994.

Webb, Michael. "The City in Film." *Design Quarterly* 136 (1987), pp. 3–32.

—. *Hollywood: Legend and Reality.* Boston: Little, Brown and Co., 1986.

Weihsmann, Helmut. *Cinetecture: Film, Architektur, Moderne.* With an essay by Vrääth Öhner and Marc Ries. Vienna: PVS Verleger, 1995

—. *Gebaute Illusionen: Architektur im Film.* Vienna: Promedia, 1988.

Williams, Rosalind. *Notes on the Underground.* Cambridge, MA: MIT Press, 1992.

Willis, Carol. "Zoning and Zeitgeist: The Skyscraper City in the 1920s." *Journal of the Society of Architectural Historians* 45 (March 1986). Pp. 47–59.

Youngblood, Denise. *Movies for the Masses: Popular Cinema and Soviet Society in the 1920s.* New York: Cambridge University Press, 1992.

Zmegac, Viktor. "Exkurs über den Film im Umkreis des Expressionismus." *Sprache im Technischen Zeitalter,* no. 35 (July–September 1970). Pp. 243–57.

Film Credits

Sources of Illustrations

Academy of Motion Pictures Arts and Sciences, Los Angeles: 106:6, 122:1, 125:3, 125:4; Akademie der Künste, Berlin: 35:11; American Museum of the Moving Image, Queens, New York: 46:7, 46:8, 159:16; British Film Institute, London: 33:3, 85:1, 85:2, 86:3, 86:4, 87:5, 87:6, 87:7; 120:5, 140:1; Michael Brown, Boston: 63:1; Kevin Brownlow, London: 106:3, 106:4; Buena Vista Studios, Walt Disney Co.: 170:1, 175:6, 176:7, 176:8, 176:9, 176:10, 178:12; Bundesarchiv/Filmarchiv, Berlin: 90:6; Cinémathèque Française, Musée du Cinéma, Paris: 90:5, 102:18; Columbia University, Avery Architectural and Fine Arts Library, New York: 114:2, 174:4; Deutsches Filmmuseum, Frankfurt: 55:9, 74:1, 79:8, 98:5; Deutsches Architektur-Museum, Frankfurt: 64:8, 68:4, 167:9; Mme Jacynthe Moreau Lalande, Paris: 138:7; Los Angeles County Museum of Art, The Robert Gore Rifkind Center for German Expressionist Studies: 28:7; Syd Mead, Los Angeles: 44:2, 44:3, 47:9, 150:2, 154:7, 154:8, 154:9, 154:10, 157:13; Virgil Mirano, Los Angeles: 148:1, 150:3, 153:4, 153:5, 156:11, 158:15; The Museum of Modern Art, Film Stills Archive, New York: 81:1, 88:1, 89:4, 93:5, 107:8, 115:4, 115:5, 129:5; Dietrich Neumann, Providence: 90:7, 91:9; Österreichisches Theatermuseum, Vienna: 105:2; Ohlinger Collection, New York: 39:1, 39:2, 39:3, 40:4, 40:5, 41:8, 44:1, 93:3, 113:1, 114:3, 117:2, 117:3, 117:4, 119:1, 120:3, 121:6, 121:7, 127:1, 131:8, 133:12; Barry Salt, London: 26:1, 26:2; Julius Shulman, Los Angeles: 154:6, 156:12; Stiftung Deutsche Kinemathek Berlin: 13:1, 15:4, 15:5, 16:6, 18:7, 27:5, 30:8, 30:9, 31:10, 31:11, 34:4, 34:5, 34:6, 34:7, 36:12, 36:13, 37:15, 37:17, 38:18, 39:8, 50:1, 51:2, 54:6, 54:7, 54:8, 56:11, 59:1, 60:2, 61:5, 61:6, 69:7, 73:1, 73:2, 73:3, 74:2, 74:3, 75:4, 77:5, 78:6, 78:7, 79:9, 79:10, 83:5, 83:6, 83:7, 89:2, 91:10, 94:1, 97:2, 97:3, 97:4, 98:8, 99:9, 99:10, 99:11, 99:13, 103:19, 103:20, 106:5; 107:7, 108:1, 108:2, 110:4, 110:5, 111:6, 111:7, 120:4, 134:1, 137:2, 137:3, 138:6, 139:8, 139:9; Sprengel Museum Hannover: 26:3; Richard Sylbert, Los Angeles: 40:6, 40:7, 172:2, 172:3; Mme. Sophie Tatischeff, Paris: 143:3, 143:4, 144:5, 144:6, 145:7, 146:8, 146:9, 146:10, 146:11; Theaterwissenschaftliches Institut der Universität Köln: 60:3, 60:4; Time-Life Co.: 174:5; Gerhard Ullmann, Munich: 33:2, 63:2, 63:3, 63:4, 63:5, 64:9; University of Arizona Museum of Art, Tucson: 178:11; University of Southern California, Doheny Memorial Library, Special Collections, Los Angeles: 53:3, 53:4, 53:5; University of Southern California, Warner Brothers Collection: 42:9, 43:10, 132:9, 133:11; Warner Bros. Studios, Archive, Los Angeles: 165:6; Frank Lloyd Wright Foundation, Arizona: 132:10; Private Collection, Los Angeles: 45:4, 45:5, 45:6; *Architectural Record*, Dec. 1939: 124:2; August 1933: 130:6, January 1990: 166:8; 165:5; *L'Avant Scène Cinema* 338 (March 1985): 116:1; *Bauamt und Gemeindebau* 3 (1921): 102:16; John Brosnan, *Future Tense: The Cinema of Science Fiction* (New York: St. Martin's Press, 1978): 37:16; *Cinefex* 41 (February 1990): 160:1, 163:2, 166:7, 168:10; Léon Barsacq, *Le Décor de film 1895-1969* (Paris: Henri Veyrier, 1970): 89:3, 91:8, 120:2; *The Chicago Tribune Competition* (Chicago, 1923): 128:2, 128:3; Beatriz Colomina, ed., *Sexuality and Space* (Princeton: Princeton University Press, 1992): 23:11, 138:5; *Domus*, no. 688 (November 1987): 67:1, 68:3; *Der dramatische Raum: Hans Poelzig Malerei Theater Film*, exh.cat. (Krefeld: Krefelder Kunstmuseen 1986): 68:2, 69:6; Lotte Eisner, *The Haunted Screen* (Berkeley: University of California Press, 1973): 100:12; *Filmkurier* 263 (3 November 1929): 110:3; Norma Evenson, Paris: *A Century of Change* (New Haven and London: Yale University Press): 142:2; Roberto Gargiani, *Auguste Perret, 1874–1954, Teoria e opere*, (Milano: Electa 1993): 82:3; *Gebrauchsgraphik*, no. 6 (1924–25): 64:7; Johann Friedrich Geist, *Passage: Ein Bautyp des 19. Jahrhunderts* (Munich: Prestel, 1984): 19:10; Hubert Jeanneau and Dominique Deshoulières (Eds.), *Robert Mallet-Stevens, Architecte* (Brussels: Editions des Archives d'Architecture Moderne, 1980): 82:2, 83:4, 138:4; Selim Omarovich Khan-Magomedov, *Pioneers of Soviet Architecture: The Search for New Solutions in the 1920s and 1930s* (New York: Rizzoli, 1983): 93:1, 93:2, 93:4; *Kinematograph*, no. 933 (4 January 25): 33:1; Heinrich Klotz, ed., *Vision der Moderne: Das Prinzip Konstruktion* (Prestel Verlag, Munich: 1986): 158:14; Le Corbusier, *Vers une architecture* (Paris, 1923): 22:14; Vittorio Magnago-Lampugnani, ed., *Antonio Sant'Elia, Gezeichnete Architektur* (Munich: Prestel, 1992): 35:9; *Von Morgens bis Mitternachts* (Munich: Filmmuseum, 1993): 71:3; John Marriott, *Batman: The Official Book of the Movie* (New York: Bantam Books, 1989): 164:4; Erich Mendelsohn, *Amerika, Bilderbuch eines Architekten* [1926], reprint with a commentary by Herbert Molderings (Wiesbaden: Vieweg Verlag, 1991): 34:4; Winfried Nerdinger, *Walter Gropius* (Berlin: Gebr. Mann, 1985): 36:14; Gustav Adolf Platz, *Die Baukunst der neuesten Zeit* (1927): 102:15; Edward Timms and David Kelley, eds., *Unreal City: Urban Experience in Modern European Literature and Art* (New York: St. Martin's Press, 1985): 28:6; *Scientific American* 109, no. 4 (26 July 1913): 35:10; *Stadtbaukunst alter und Neuer Zeit* 5. 1924: 102:14; Christian W. Thomsen, *Visionary Architecture: From Babylon to Virtual Reality*, (Munich: Prestel, 1994): 22:15, 24:18, 98:7; *Wasmuths Monatshefte für Baukunst*, no. 1–2 (1920–21): 14:2, 15:3, 27:4, 64:6, 65:10, 65:11, 69:5, 70:1, 71:2, 71:4; Frank Lloyd Wright, *A Testament* (New York: Bramhall House, 1957): 130:2; Bruno Zevi, *Erich Mendelsohn* (Zürich: Artemis, 1983): 104:1.